HELLBOY™

WAKE THE
DEVIL

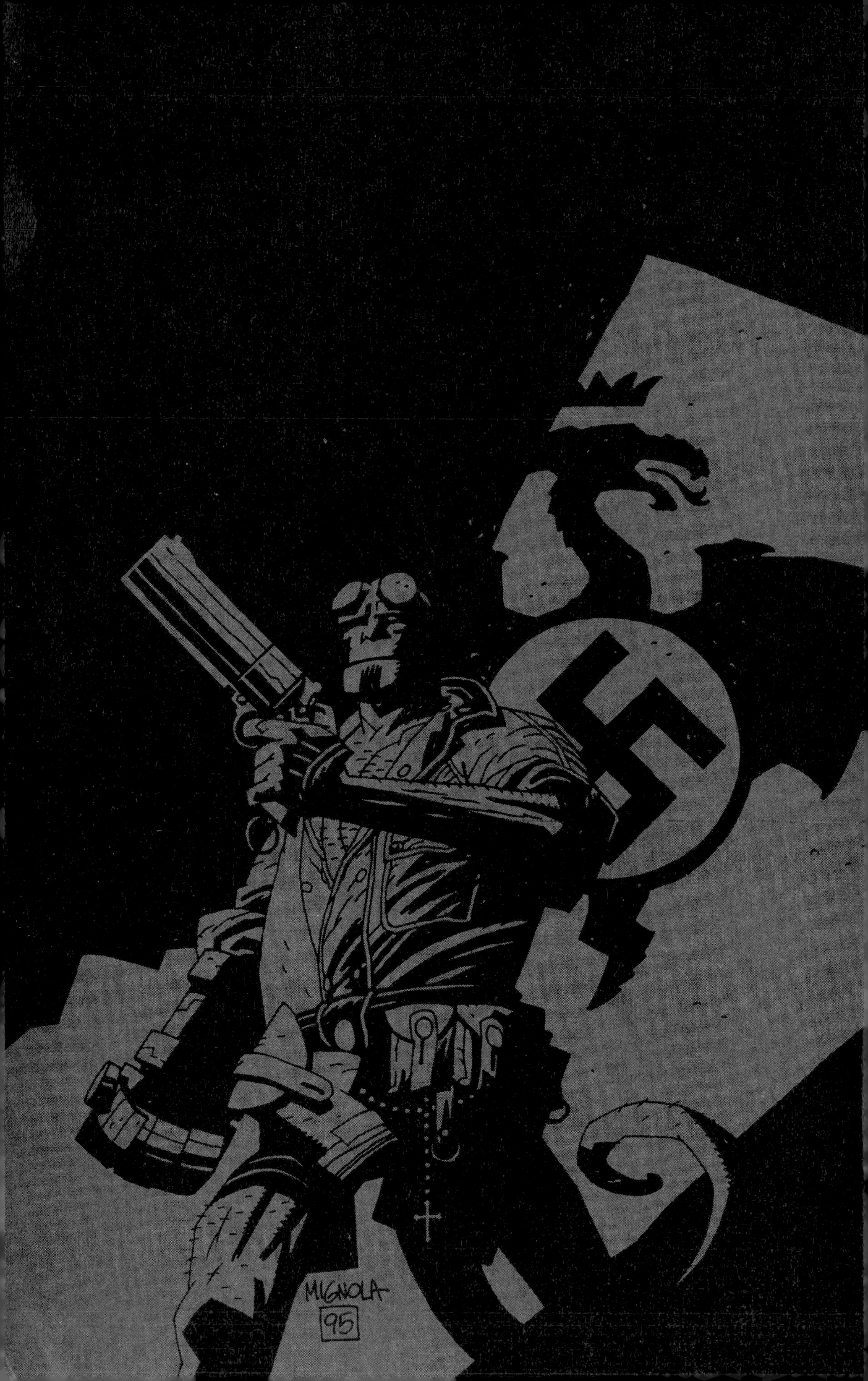
MIGNOLA
95

HELLBOY

WAKE THE DEVIL

by
MIKE MIGNOLA

Colored by
JAMES SINCLAIR

Lettered by
PAT BROSSEAU

✠

Introduction by
ALAN MOORE

Edited by
SCOTT ALLIE

Hellboy logo designed by
KEVIN NOWLAN

Color separations by
DAVE STEWART

Collection designed by
MIKE MIGNOLA & CARY GRAZZINI

Published by
MIKE RICHARDSON

DARK HORSE COMICS®

Mike Richardson ✠ *publisher*

Neil Hankerson ✠ *executive vice president*

David Scroggy ✠ *vice president of publishing*

Lou Bank ✠ *vice president of sales & marketing*

Andy Karabatsos ✠ *vice president of finance*

Mark Anderson ✠ *general counsel*

Meloney C. Chadwick ✠ *director of editorial adm.*

Randy Stradley ✠ *creative director*

Cindy Marks ✠ *director of production & design*

Mark Cox ✠ *art director*

Sean Tierney ✠ *computer graphics director*

Michael Martens ✠ *director of sales & marketing*

Tod Borleske ✠ *director of licensing*

Dale LaFountain ✠ *director of m.i.s.*

Kim Haines ✠ *director of human resources*

Published by Dark Horse Comics
10956 SE Main Street
Milwaukie, OR 97222

First edition: May 1997
ISBN: 1-56971-226-3

This book is collected from issues 1-5 of the Dark Horse comic-book miniseries *Hellboy: Wake the Devil.*

1 3 5 7 9 10 8 6 4 2

PRINTED IN CANADA

INTRODUCTION

by ALAN MOORE

THE HISTORY OF COMIC-BOOK CULTURE, MUCH LIKE THE HISTORY OF ANY CULTURE, is something between a treadmill and a conveyer belt: we dutifully trudge along, and the belt carries us with it into one new territory after another. There are dazzlingly bright periods setting black squalls, and long stretches of grey, dreary fog interspersed seemingly at random. The sole condition of our transport is that we cannot halt the belt, and we cannot get off. We move from Golden Age to Silver Age to Silicone Age, and nowhere do we have the opportunity to say, "We like it here. Let's stop." History isn't like that. History is movement, and if you're not riding with it then in all probability you're beneath its wheels.

Lately, however, there seems to be some new scent in the air: a sense of new and different possibilities, new ways for us to interact with History. At this remote end of the twentieth century, while we're further from our past than we have ever been before, there is another way of viewing things in which the past has never been so close. We know much more now of the path that lies behind us, and in greater detail, than we've ever previously known. Our new technology of information makes this knowledge instantly accessible to anybody who can figure-skate across a mouse pad. In a way, we understand more of the past and have a greater access to it than the folk who actually lived there.

In this new perspective, there would seem to be new opportunities for liberating both our culture and ourselves from Time's relentless treadmill. We may not be able to jump off, but we're no longer trapped so thoroughly in our own present movement, with the past a dead, unreachable expanse behind us. From our new and elevated point of view our History becomes a living landscape which our minds are still at liberty to visit, to draw sustenance and inspiration from. In a sense, we can now farm the vast accumulated harvest of the years or centuries behind. Across the cultural spectrum, we see individuals waking up to the potentials and advantages that this affords.

It's happened in popular music, where we no longer see the linear progression of distinct trends that we saw in the fifties, the sixties, the seventies, and so on. Instead, the current music field is a mosaic of styles drawn from points in the past or even points in the imagined future, with no single nineties style predominating. It's happened in the sciences, where mathematicians, for example, find valuable insights into modern theoretical conundrums by examining the long-outmoded Late Victorian passion for the geometric study of rope knots. It's happened in our arts and one could probably make a convincing argument that it has happened in our politics. Without doubt, it has happened in the comics field: the most cursory glance 'round at the most interesting books, whether we're talking about Seth's *Palookaville* or Chris Ware's *Acme Novelty Library* or

Michael Allred's *Madman*, will reveal that in even the most contemporary of modern comic books, our previous heritage looms large, and is in many ways the most important signifier. Which brings me to Mike Mignola's *Hellboy*.

Hellboy is a gem, one of considerable size and a surprising lustre. While it is obviously a gem that has been mined from that immeasurably rich seam first excavated by the late Jack Kirby, it is in the skillful cutting and the setting of the stone that we can see Mignola's sharp contemporary sensibilities at work. To label *Hellboy* as a "retro" work would be to drastically misunderstand it: This is a clear and modern voice, not merely some ventriloquial seance-echo from beyond the grave. Mignola, from the evidence contained herein, has accurately understood Jack Kirby as a living force that did not perish with the mortal body. As with any notable creator, the sheer electricity inside the work lives on, is a resource that later artists would be foolish to ignore just because times have changed and trends have fluctuated. Did we stop working in iron and stone the moment that formica was discovered? No. We understood those substances to be still-vital forms of mineral wealth that we could build our future from, if only we'd the wit and the imagination.

Mike Mignola has these qualities in great abundance. *Hellboy*'s slab-black shadows crackle with the glee and enthusiasm of an artist almost drunk with the sheer pleasure of just putting down these lines on paper, of bringing to life these wonderfully flame-lit and titanic situations. Images, ideas, and thinly disguised icons from the rich four-color treasure house of comics history are given a fresh lick of paint and are suddenly revealed as every bit as powerful and evocative upon some primal ten-year-old-child level as when we last saw them. This, perhaps, is *Hellboy*'s greatest and least-obvious accomplishment: the trick, the skill entailed in this delightful necromantic conjuring of things gone by is not, as might be thought, in crafting work as good as the work that inspired it really was, but in the more demanding task of crafting work as good as everyone *remembers* the original as being. This means that the work must be as fresh and as innovative as the work that preceded it seemed at the time. It's not enough to merely reproduce the past. Instead we have to blend it artfully with how we see things now and with our visions for the future if we are to mix a brew as rich, transporting, and bewitching as the potions we remember from the vanished years.

Hellboy is such a potion, strong and effervescent, served up in a foaming beaker from an archetypal Mad Scientist's dungeon or laboratory. The collection in your hands distills all that is best about the comic book into a dark, intoxicating ruby wine. Sit down and knock it back in one, then wait for your reading experience to undergo a mystifying and alarming transformation. *Hellboy* is a passport to a corner of funnybook heaven you may never want to leave. Enter and enjoy.

For Dracula and all those
other vampires I have loved.

CHAPTER ONE

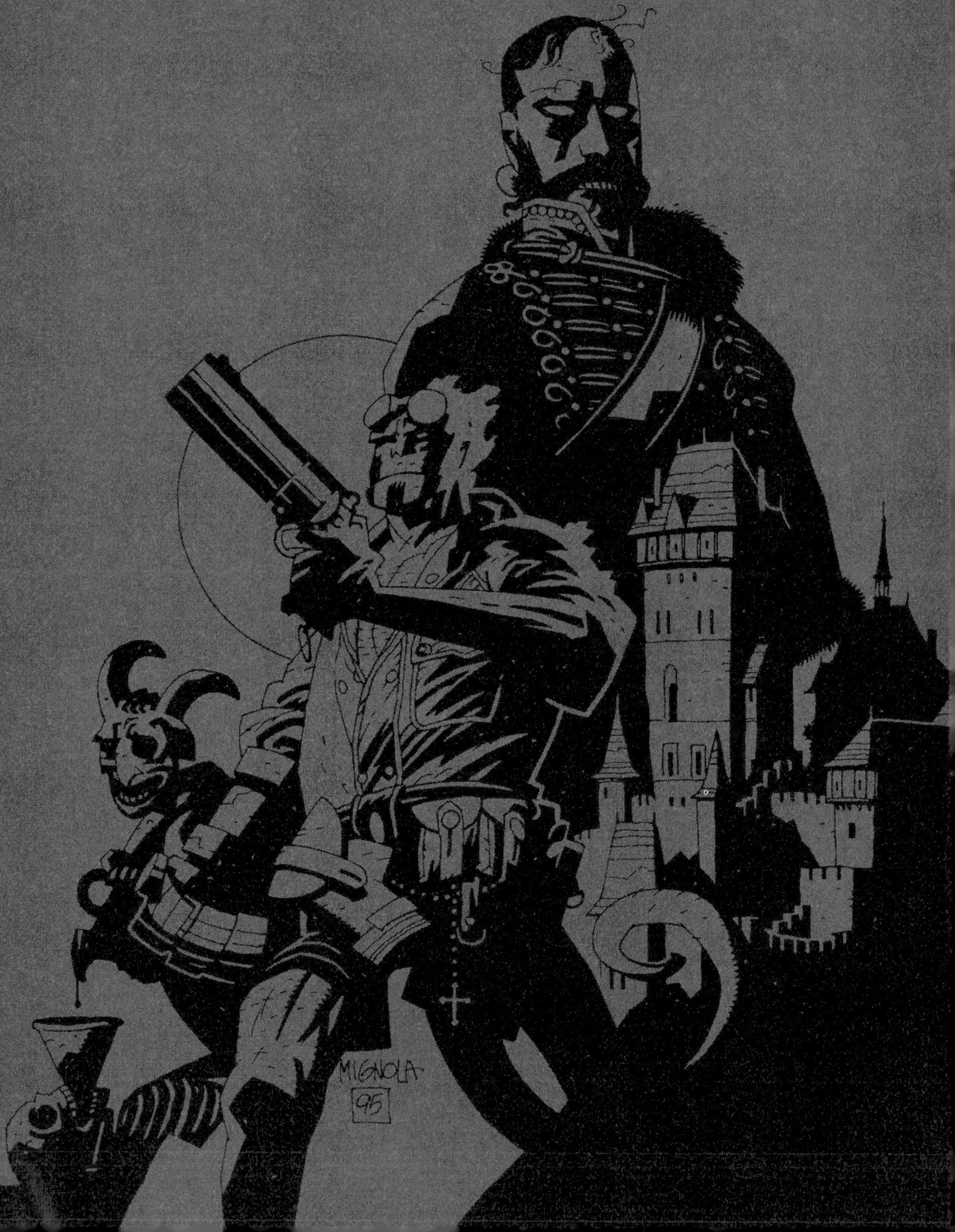
MIGNOLA
95

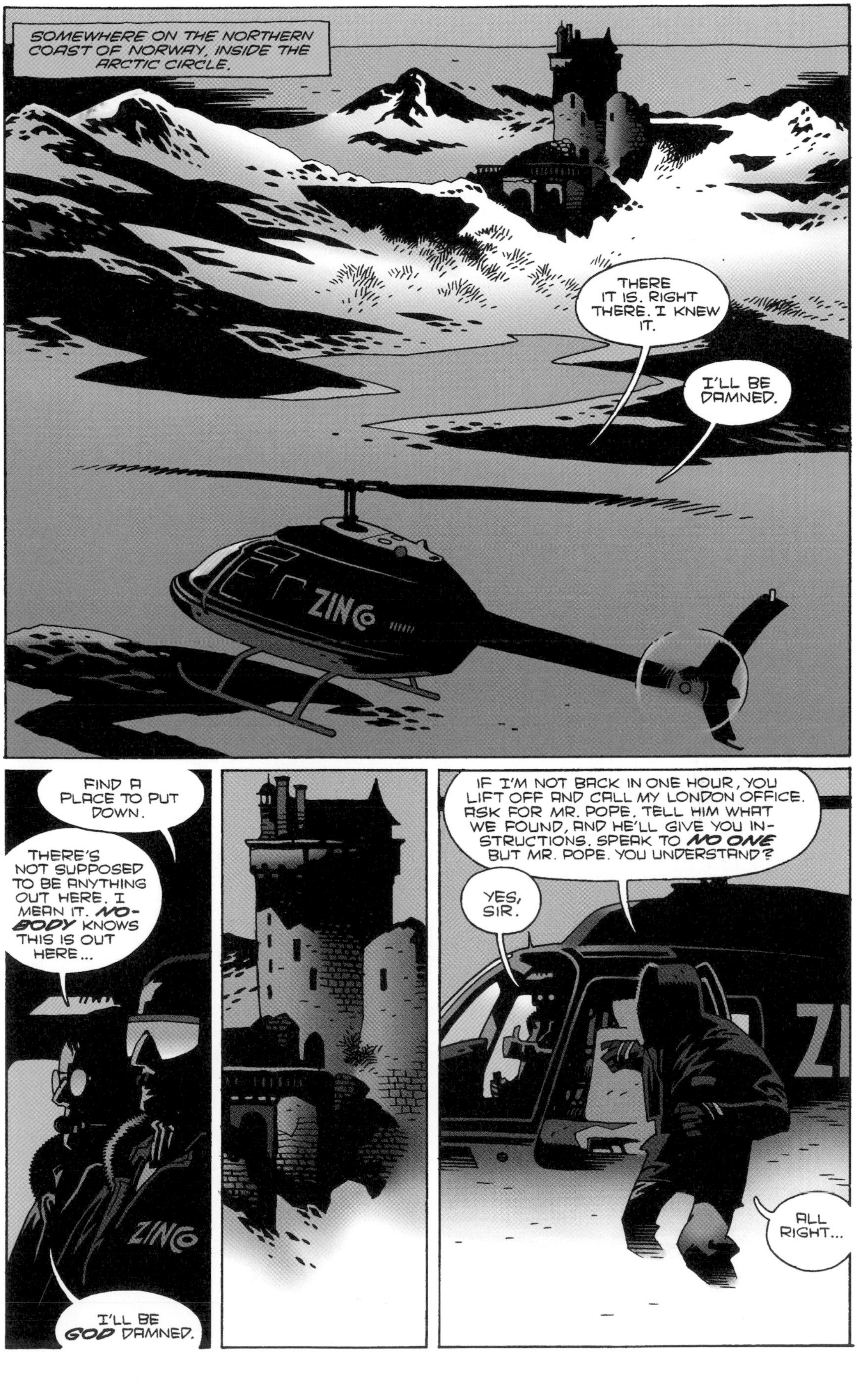
SOMEWHERE ON THE NORTHERN COAST OF NORWAY, INSIDE THE ARCTIC CIRCLE.
THERE IT IS. RIGHT THERE. I KNEW IT.
I'LL BE DAMNED.
FIND A PLACE TO PUT DOWN.
THERE'S NOT SUPPOSED TO BE ANYTHING OUT HERE. I MEAN IT. NO-BODY KNOWS THIS IS OUT HERE...
I'LL BE GOD DAMNED.
IF I'M NOT BACK IN ONE HOUR, YOU LIFT OFF AND CALL MY LONDON OFFICE. ASK FOR MR. POPE. TELL HIM WHAT WE FOUND, AND HE'LL GIVE YOU IN-STRUCTIONS. SPEAK TO NO ONE BUT MR. POPE. YOU UNDERSTAND?
YES, SIR.
ALL RIGHT...

IT'S
TRUE.

ZINCO

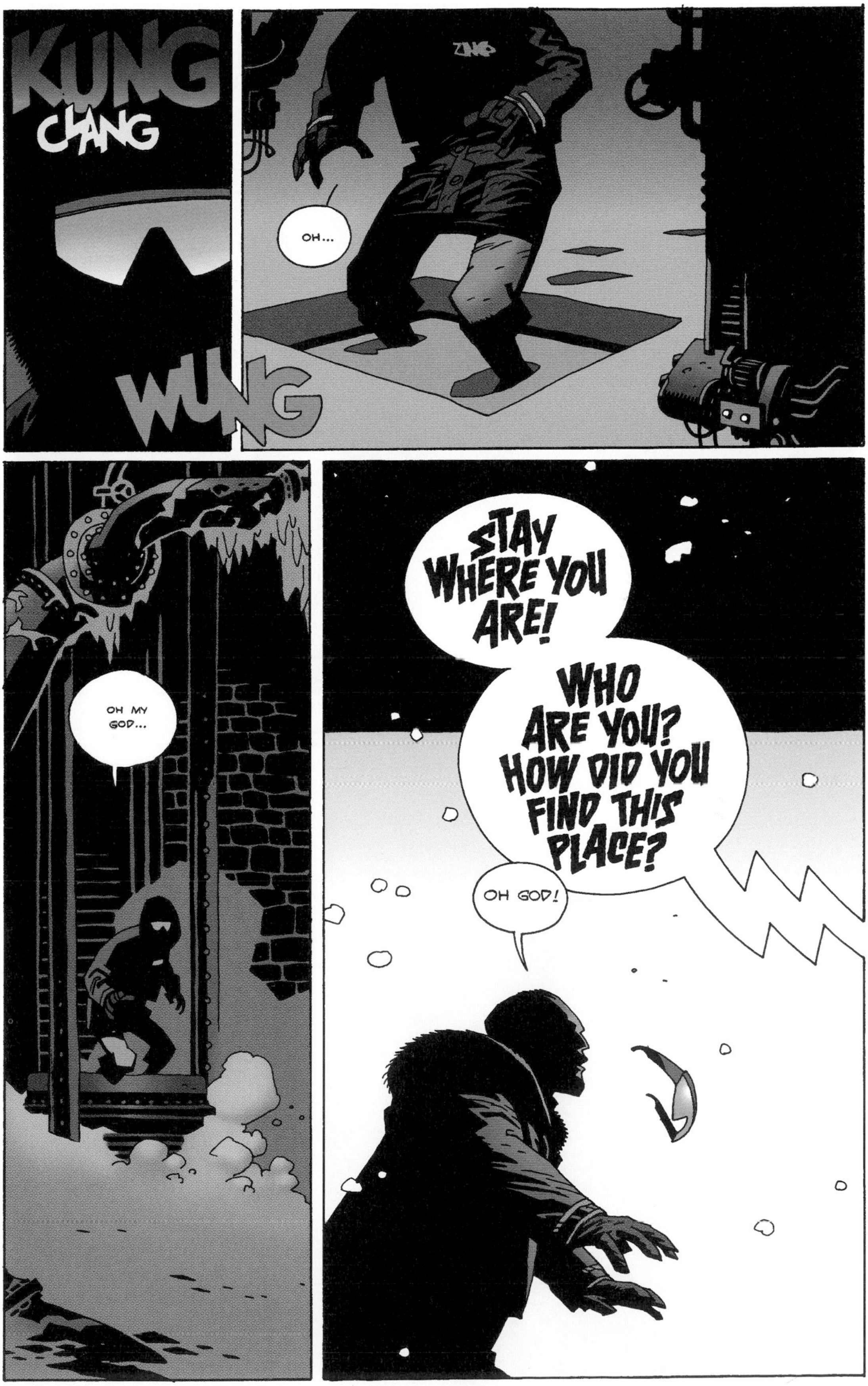
KUNG
CHANG
WUNG
OH...
OH MY GOD...
STAY WHERE YOU ARE!
WHO ARE YOU? HOW DID YOU FIND THIS PLACE?
OH GOD!

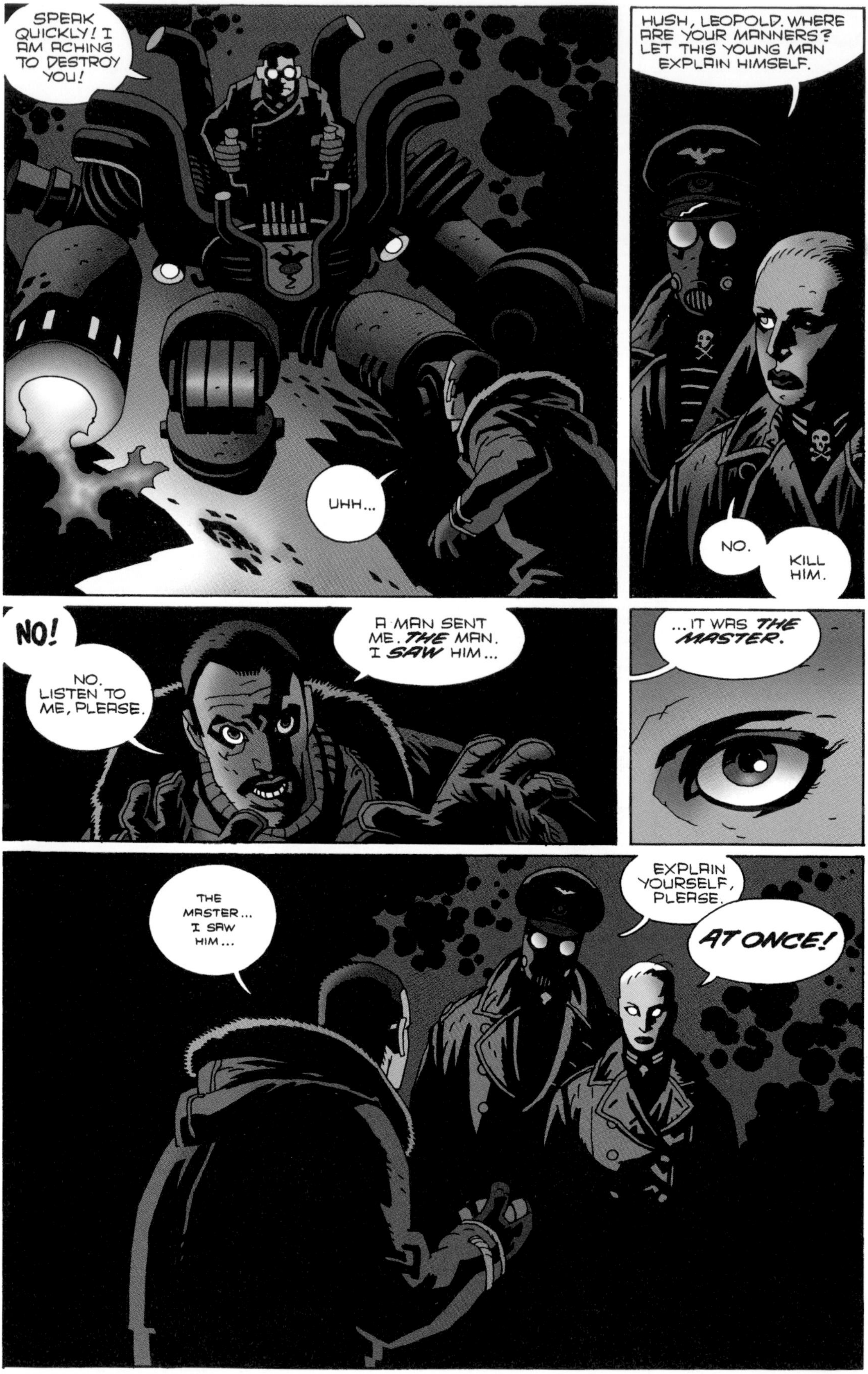
SPEAK QUICKLY! I AM ACHING TO DESTROY YOU!
UHH...
HUSH, LEOPOLD. WHERE ARE YOUR MANNERS? LET THIS YOUNG MAN EXPLAIN HIMSELF.
NO.
KILL HIM.
NO!
NO. LISTEN TO ME, PLEASE.
A MAN SENT ME. THE MAN. I SAW HIM...
...IT WAS THE MASTER.
THE MASTER... I SAW HIM...
EXPLAIN YOURSELF, PLEASE.
AT ONCE!

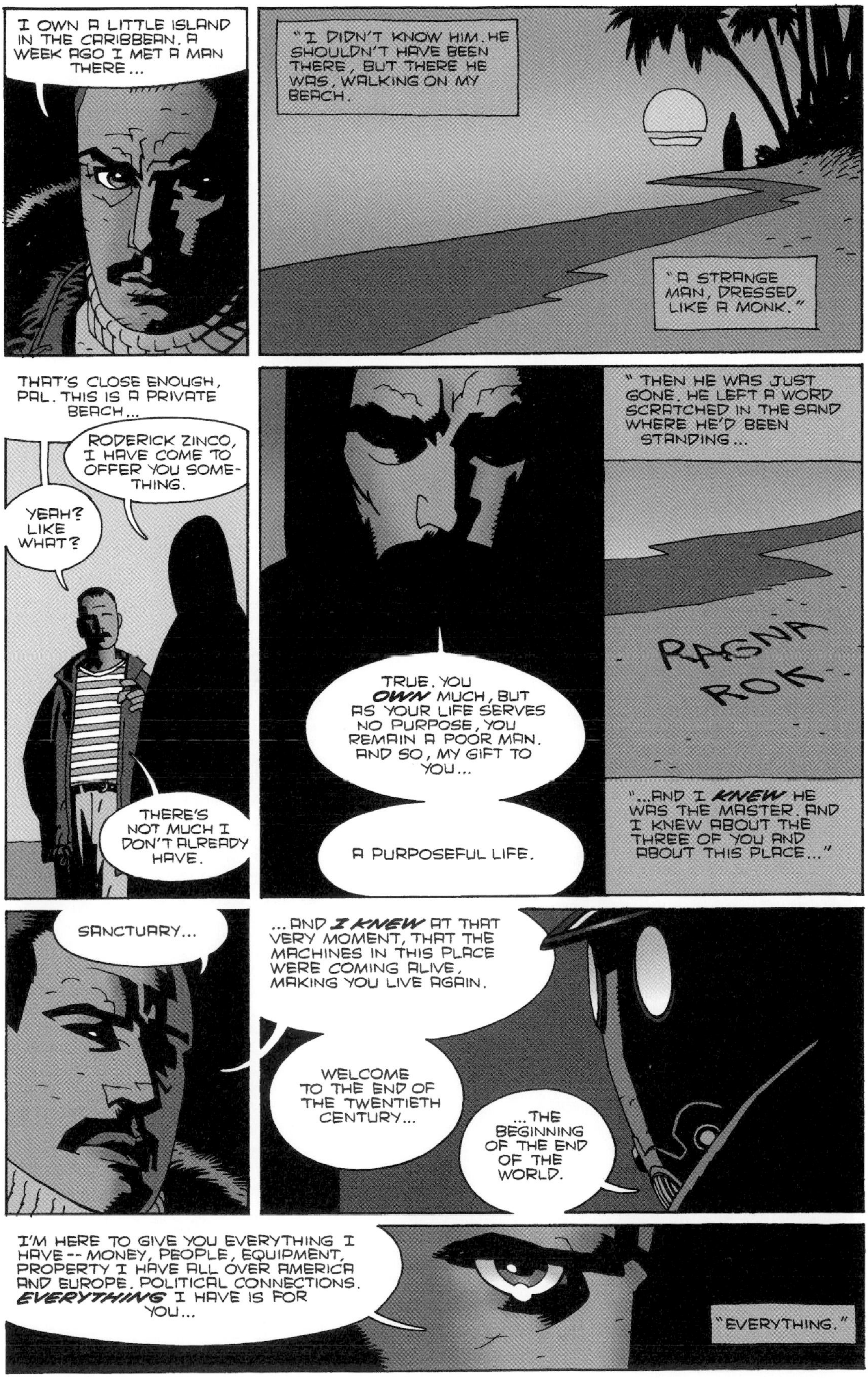

I OWN A LITTLE ISLAND IN THE CARIBBEAN. A WEEK AGO I MET A MAN THERE...
"I DIDN'T KNOW HIM. HE SHOULDN'T HAVE BEEN THERE, BUT THERE HE WAS, WALKING ON MY BEACH.
"A STRANGE MAN, DRESSED LIKE A MONK."
THAT'S CLOSE ENOUGH, PAL. THIS IS A PRIVATE BEACH...
RODERICK ZINCO, I HAVE COME TO OFFER YOU SOMETHING.
YEAH? LIKE WHAT?
THERE'S NOT MUCH I DON'T ALREADY HAVE.
TRUE. YOU OWN MUCH, BUT AS YOUR LIFE SERVES NO PURPOSE, YOU REMAIN A POOR MAN. AND SO, MY GIFT TO YOU...
A PURPOSEFUL LIFE.
" THEN HE WAS JUST GONE. HE LEFT A WORD SCRATCHED IN THE SAND WHERE HE'D BEEN STANDING...
RAGNA ROK
"...AND I KNEW HE WAS THE MASTER. AND I KNEW ABOUT THE THREE OF YOU AND ABOUT THIS PLACE..."
SANCTUARY...
...AND I KNEW AT THAT VERY MOMENT, THAT THE MACHINES IN THIS PLACE WERE COMING ALIVE, MAKING YOU LIVE AGAIN.
WELCOME TO THE END OF THE TWENTIETH CENTURY...
...THE BEGINNING OF THE END OF THE WORLD.
I'M HERE TO GIVE YOU EVERYTHING I HAVE -- MONEY, PEOPLE, EQUIPMENT, PROPERTY I HAVE ALL OVER AMERICA AND EUROPE. POLITICAL CONNECTIONS. EVERYTHING I HAVE IS FOR YOU...
"EVERYTHING."

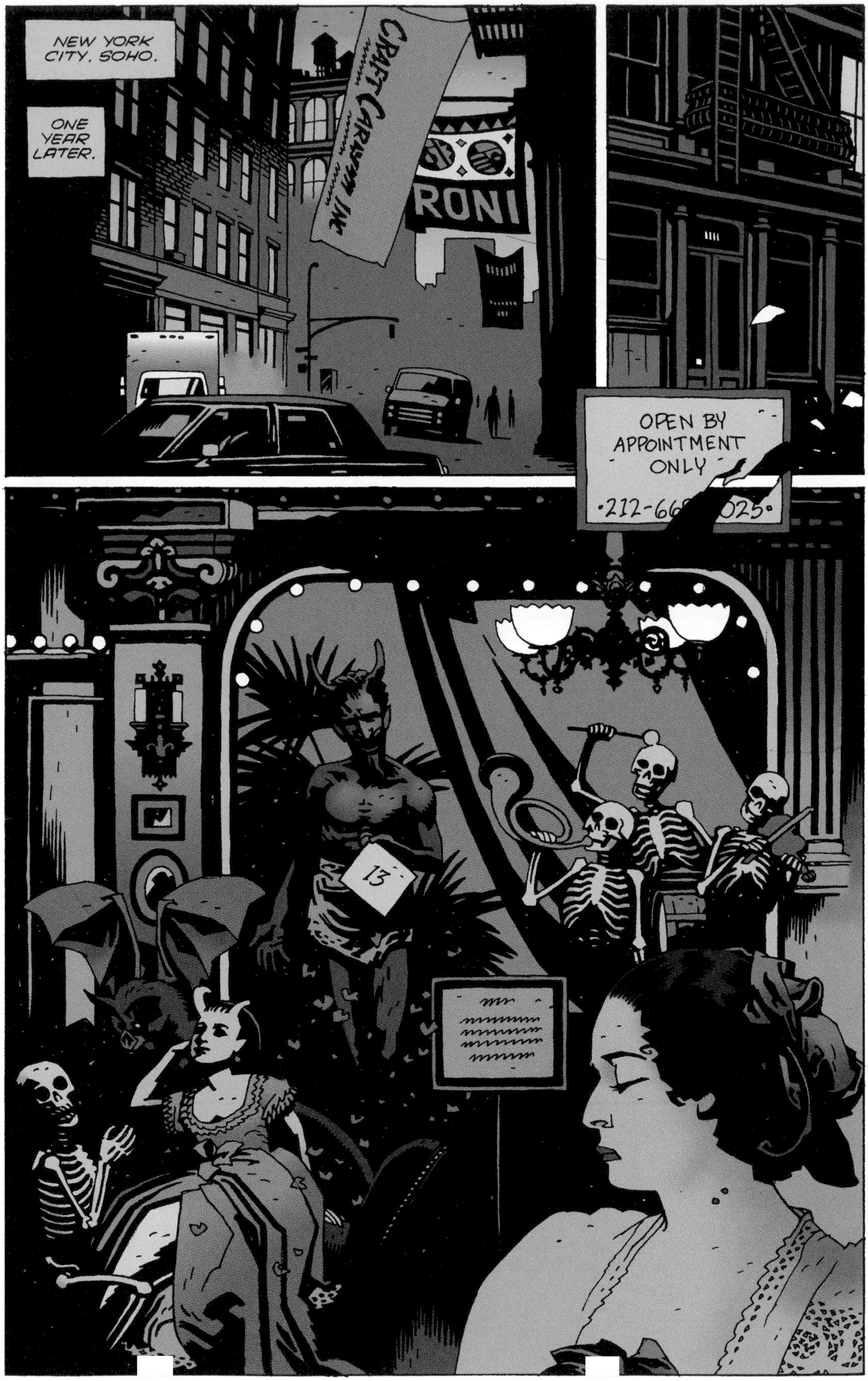

NEW YORK CITY, SOHO.
ONE YEAR LATER.
RONI
OPEN BY APPOINTMENT ONLY
13

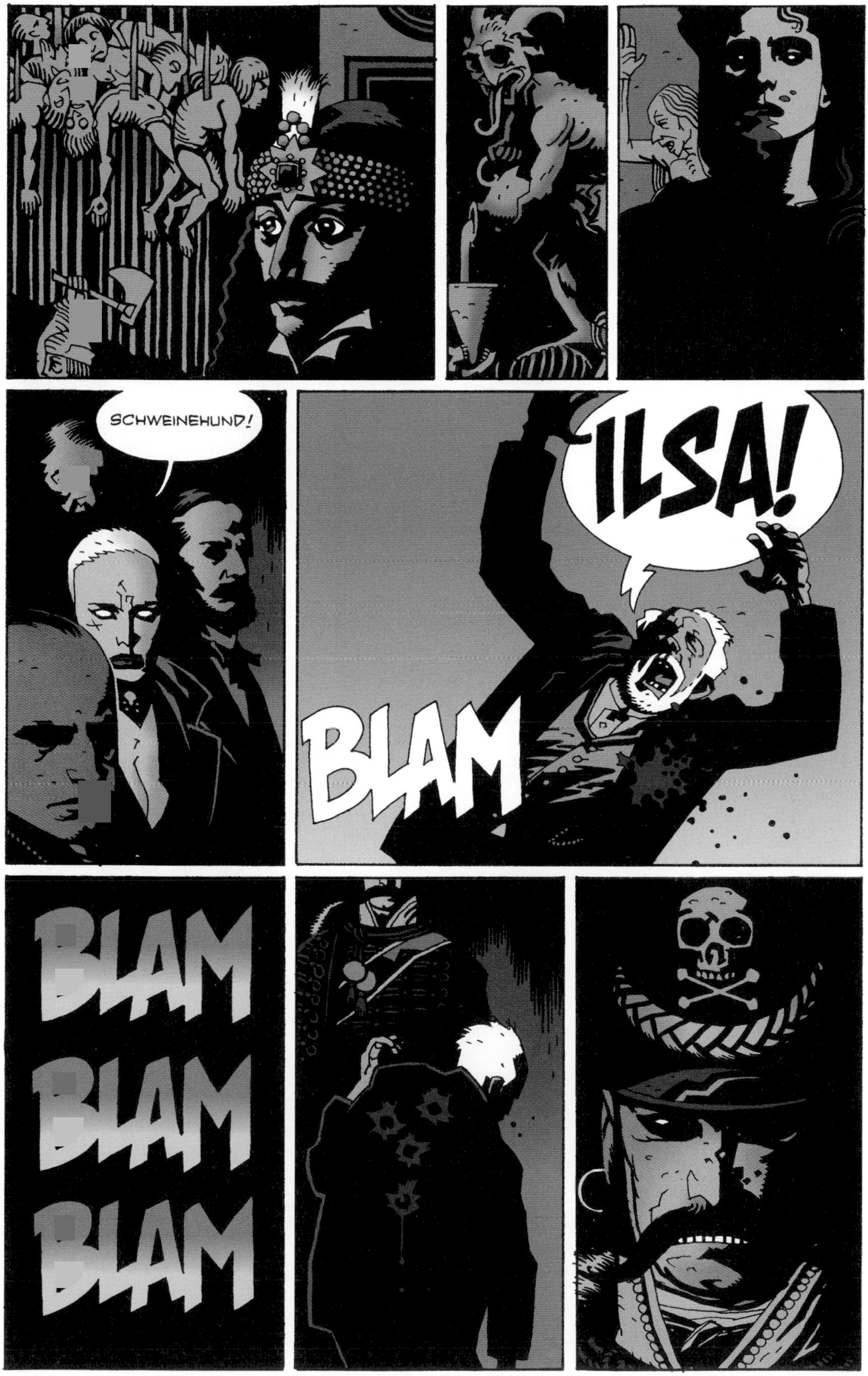
SCHWEINEHUND!
ILSA!
BLAM
BLAM
BLAM
BLAM

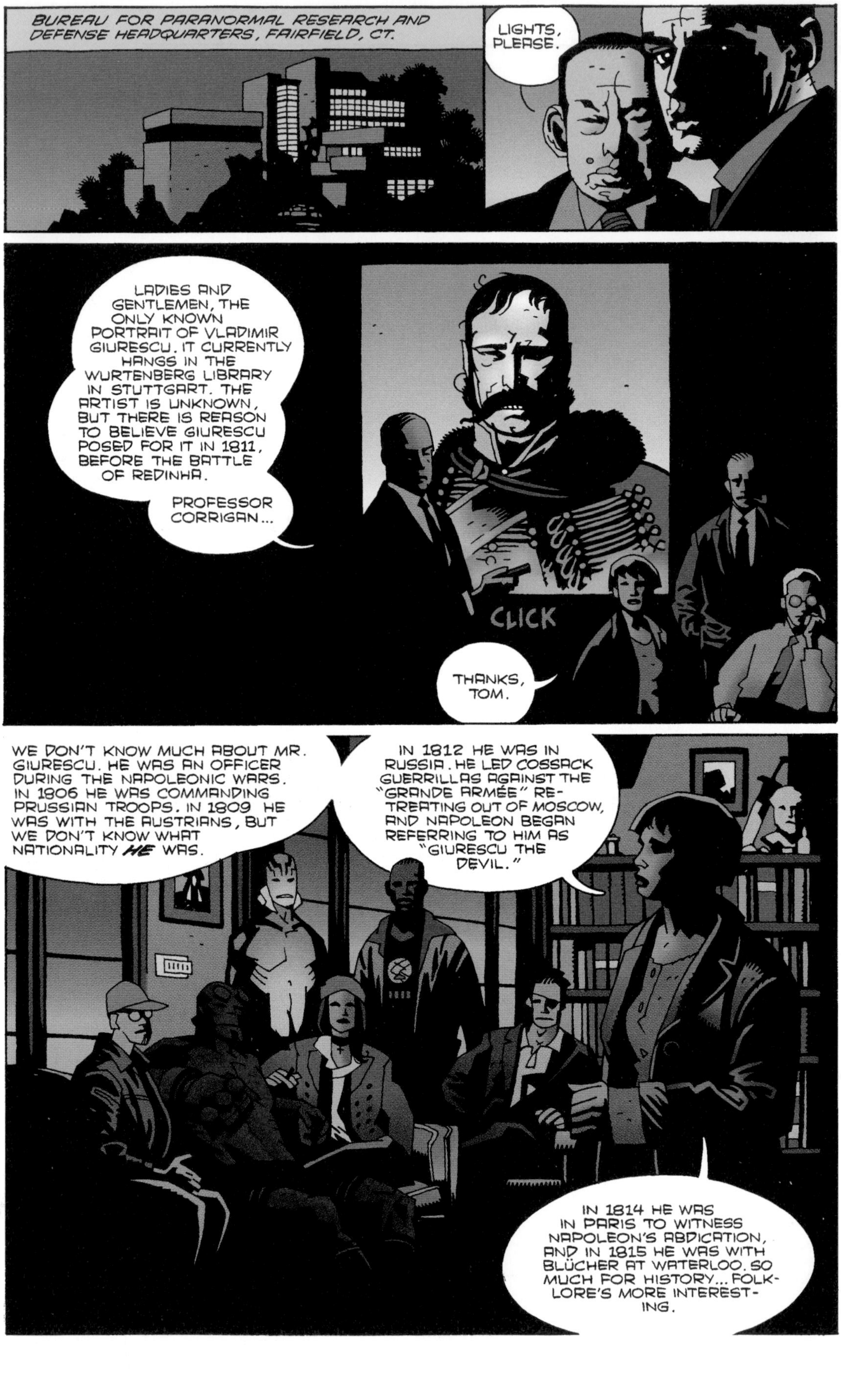
BUREAU FOR PARANORMAL RESEARCH AND DEFENSE HEADQUARTERS, FAIRFIELD, CT.
LIGHTS, PLEASE.
LADIES AND GENTLEMEN, THE ONLY KNOWN PORTRAIT OF VLADIMIR GIURESCU. IT CURRENTLY HANGS IN THE WURTENBERG LIBRARY IN STUTTGART. THE ARTIST IS UNKNOWN, BUT THERE IS REASON TO BELIEVE GIURESCU POSED FOR IT IN 1811, BEFORE THE BATTLE OF REDINHA.
PROFESSOR CORRIGAN...
CLICK
THANKS, TOM.
WE DON'T KNOW MUCH ABOUT MR. GIURESCU. HE WAS AN OFFICER DURING THE NAPOLEONIC WARS. IN 1806 HE WAS COMMANDING PRUSSIAN TROOPS. IN 1809 HE WAS WITH THE AUSTRIANS, BUT WE DON'T KNOW WHAT NATIONALITY *HE* WAS.
IN 1812 HE WAS IN RUSSIA. HE LED COSSACK GUERRILLAS AGAINST THE "GRANDE ARMÉE" RE-TREATING OUT OF MOSCOW, AND NAPOLEON BEGAN REFERRING TO HIM AS "GIURESCU THE DEVIL."
IN 1814 HE WAS IN PARIS TO WITNESS NAPOLEON'S ABDICATION, AND IN 1815 HE WAS WITH BLÜCHER AT WATERLOO. SO MUCH FOR HISTORY... FOLK-LORE'S MORE INTEREST-ING.

AT THE SIEGE OF HALBERSTADT, GIURESCU IS HORRIBLY WOUNDED. CAMP DOCTORS SAY HE'LL BE DEAD IN AN HOUR, BUT HIS SERVANTS INSIST ON CARRYING HIM HOME. TWO WEEKS LATER, HE REJOINS HIS TROOPS, "FULLY RESTORED TO YOUTH AND VIGOR."

THIS HAPPENS SIX OR SEVEN TIMES DURING THE WAR. EACH TIME HE'S BACK, GOOD AS NEW, IN A COUPLE OF WEEKS.

THE STORY GOES AROUND THAT THERE IS A SPECIAL ROOM IN CASTLE GIURESCU WHERE HIS BODY IS LAID OUT. HERE, THE LIGHT OF THE FULL MOON CAN SHINE DOWN ON HIM, AND *THIS* IS WHAT HEALS HIM.

SKIP AHEAD TO AUGUST 8, 1882. SIR EDWARD GREY* WRITES TO QUEEN VICTORIA, WARNING THAT A VISITING NOBLEMAN NAMED *GIURESCU* IS ACTUALLY A SUPERNATURAL BEING, PLOTTING TO "ESTABLISH A SECRET, EVIL EMPIRE" IN ENGLAND. AUGUST 19TH, HE WRITES THAT GIURESCU HAS FLED THE COUNTRY AND REFERS TO HIM, FOR THE FIRST TIME EVER, AS A *VAMPIRE.*

1944. HEINRICH HIMMLER PROPOSED PROJECT *"VAMPIR STURM."* A NAZI DELEGATION WAS SENT TO CASTLE GIURESCU TO RECRUIT GIURESCU TO THE WAR EFFORT.

HEAD OF THAT DELEGATION: *ILSA HAUPSTEIN.*

DECEMBER 3, 1944, HITLER AND GIURESCU MET AT WEWELSBURG. THE NEXT DAY, ORDERS WERE ISSUED FOR THE *ARREST* OF GIURESCU AND HIS "FAMILY."

CLICK

GUESS IT WAS A BAD MEETING.

COPIES OF GESTAPO RECORDS SHOWING THE ARRIVAL OF V. GIURESCU AND SIX OTHER "SPECIAL PRISONERS" AT DACHAU ON DECEMBER 16TH. ALSO A WORK ORDER, SIGNED BY HITLER, CALLING FOR THE EXTERMINATION OF THE GIURESCU "FAMILY."

IN 1956, THREE FORMER DACHAU GUARDS TESTIFIED THAT THEY WERE PRESENT AT THE EXECUTION OF SEVEN "SPECIAL PRISONERS" IN DECEMBER OF '44. ALL SEVEN -- A MAN AND SIX WOMEN -- WERE LYING IN DIRT-FILLED BOXES. THEY WERE IMPALED AND DECAPITATED, THEN BURNED. THE ASHES WERE SENT TO HITLER.

THE END OF VLADIMIR GIURESCU? MAYBE NOT...

* FAMOUS NINETEENTH-CENTURY PARANORMAL INVESTIGATOR

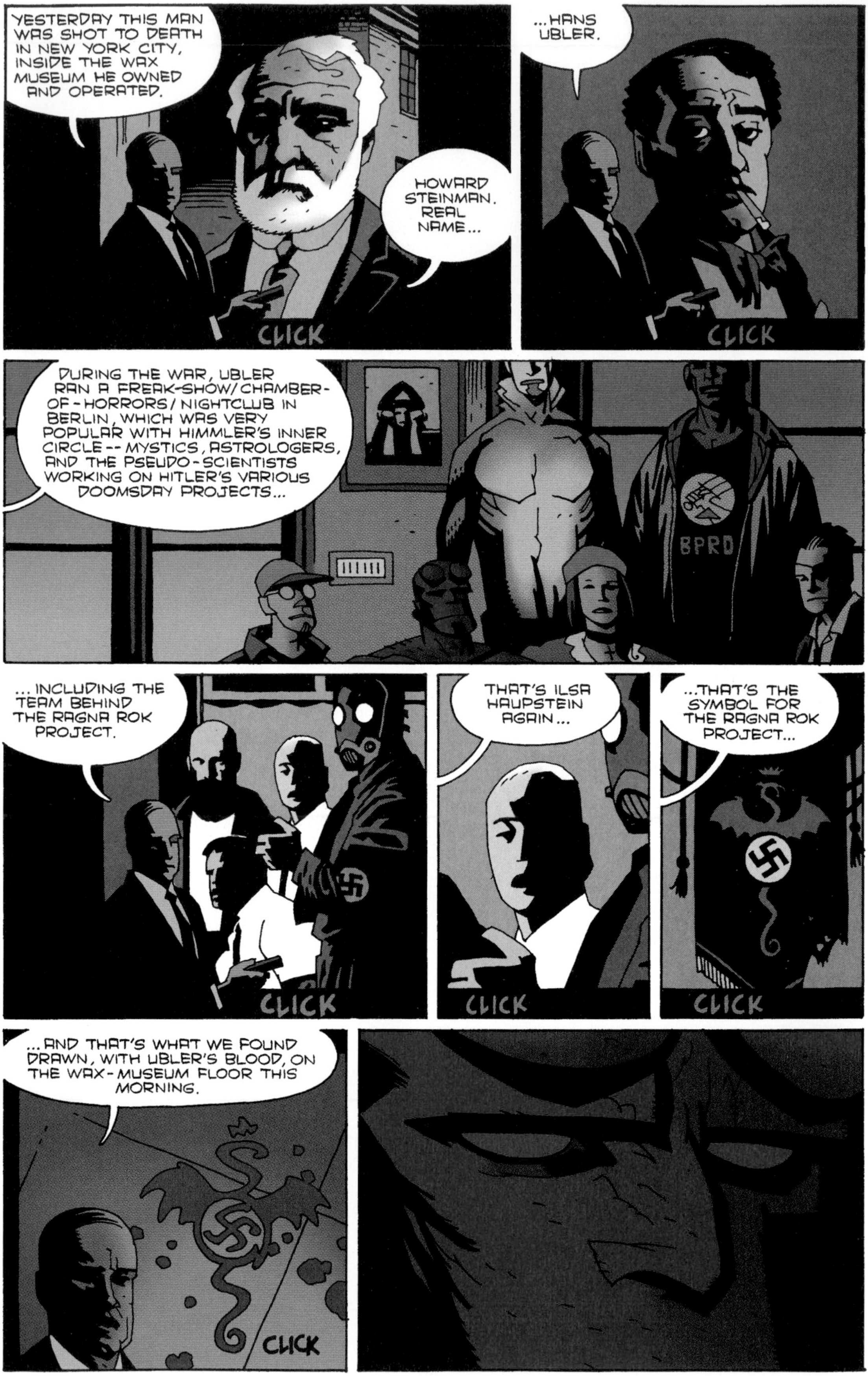
YESTERDAY THIS MAN WAS SHOT TO DEATH IN NEW YORK CITY, INSIDE THE WAX MUSEUM HE OWNED AND OPERATED.
HOWARD STEINMAN. REAL NAME...
CLICK
...HANS UBLER.
CLICK
DURING THE WAR, UBLER RAN A FREAK-SHOW/CHAMBER-OF-HORRORS/NIGHTCLUB IN BERLIN, WHICH WAS VERY POPULAR WITH HIMMLER'S INNER CIRCLE -- MYSTICS, ASTROLOGERS, AND THE PSEUDO-SCIENTISTS WORKING ON HITLER'S VARIOUS DOOMSDAY PROJECTS...
BPRD
...INCLUDING THE TEAM BEHIND THE RAGNA ROK PROJECT.
CLICK
THAT'S ILSA HAUPSTEIN AGAIN...
CLICK
...THAT'S THE SYMBOL FOR THE RAGNA ROK PROJECT...
CLICK
...AND THAT'S WHAT WE FOUND DRAWN, WITH UBLER'S BLOOD, ON THE WAX-MUSEUM FLOOR THIS MORNING.
CLICK

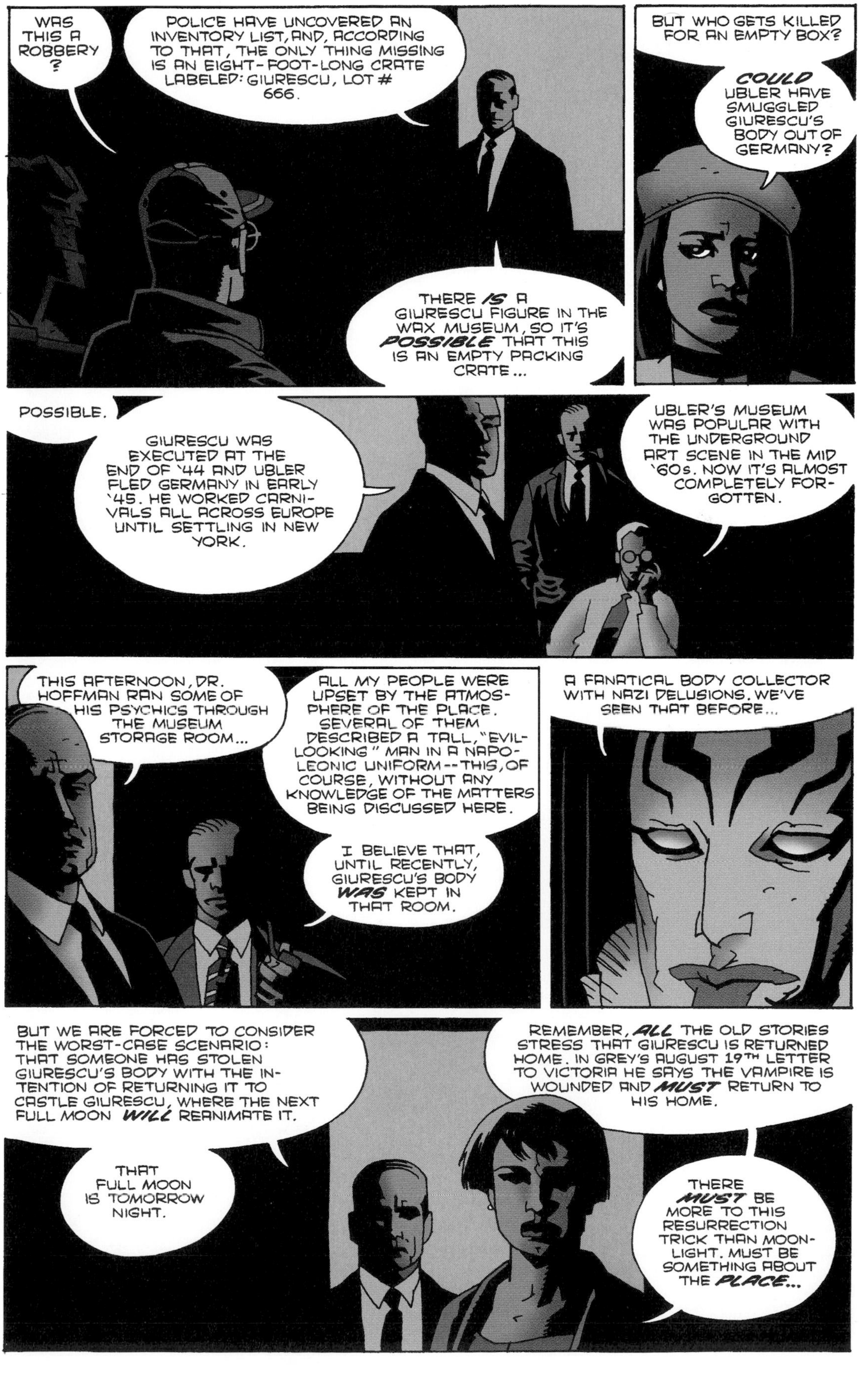
WAS THIS A ROBBERY?
POLICE HAVE UNCOVERED AN INVENTORY LIST, AND, ACCORDING TO THAT, THE ONLY THING MISSING IS AN EIGHT-FOOT-LONG CRATE LABELED: GIURESCU, LOT # 666.
THERE *IS* A GIURESCU FIGURE IN THE WAX MUSEUM, SO IT'S *POSSIBLE* THAT THIS IS AN EMPTY PACKING CRATE...
BUT WHO GETS KILLED FOR AN EMPTY BOX?
COULD UBLER HAVE SMUGGLED GIURESCU'S BODY OUT OF GERMANY?
POSSIBLE.
GIURESCU WAS EXECUTED AT THE END OF '44 AND UBLER FLED GERMANY IN EARLY '45. HE WORKED CARNIVALS ALL ACROSS EUROPE UNTIL SETTLING IN NEW YORK.
UBLER'S MUSEUM WAS POPULAR WITH THE UNDERGROUND ART SCENE IN THE MID '60s. NOW IT'S ALMOST COMPLETELY FORGOTTEN.
THIS AFTERNOON, DR. HOFFMAN RAN SOME OF HIS PSYCHICS THROUGH THE MUSEUM STORAGE ROOM...
ALL MY PEOPLE WERE UPSET BY THE ATMOSPHERE OF THE PLACE. SEVERAL OF THEM DESCRIBED A TALL, "EVIL-LOOKING" MAN IN A NAPOLEONIC UNIFORM -- THIS, OF COURSE, WITHOUT ANY KNOWLEDGE OF THE MATTERS BEING DISCUSSED HERE.
I BELIEVE THAT, UNTIL RECENTLY, GIURESCU'S BODY *WAS* KEPT IN THAT ROOM.
A FANATICAL BODY COLLECTOR WITH NAZI DELUSIONS. WE'VE SEEN THAT BEFORE...
BUT WE ARE FORCED TO CONSIDER THE WORST-CASE SCENARIO: THAT SOMEONE HAS STOLEN GIURESCU'S BODY WITH THE INTENTION OF RETURNING IT TO CASTLE GIURESCU, WHERE THE NEXT FULL MOON *WILL* REANIMATE IT.
THAT FULL MOON IS TOMORROW NIGHT.
REMEMBER, *ALL* THE OLD STORIES STRESS THAT GIURESCU IS RETURNED HOME. IN GREY'S AUGUST 19TH LETTER TO VICTORIA HE SAYS THE VAMPIRE IS WOUNDED AND *MUST* RETURN TO HIS HOME.
THERE *MUST* BE MORE TO THIS RESURRECTION TRICK THAN MOONLIGHT. MUST BE SOMETHING ABOUT THE *PLACE*...

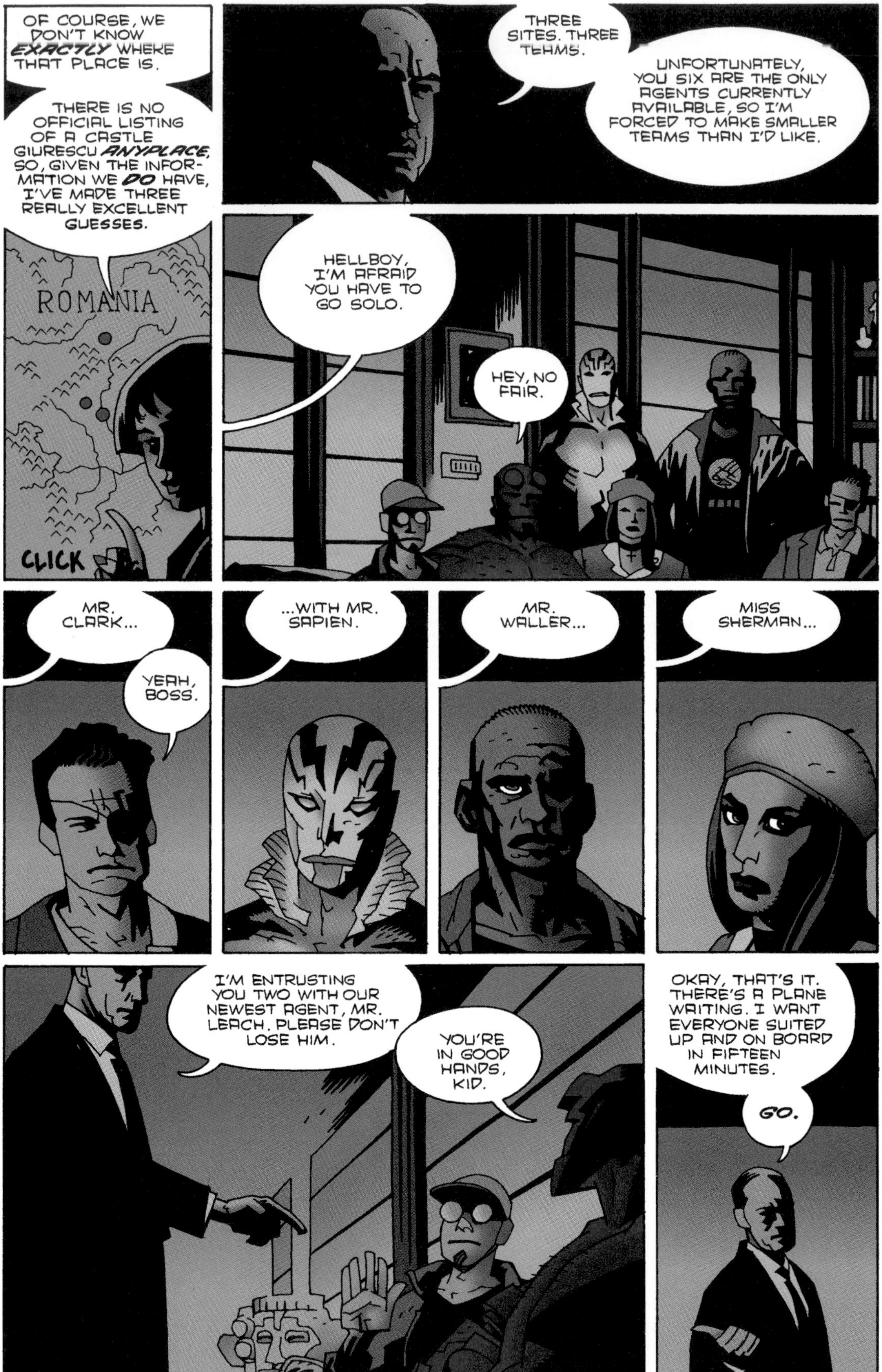
OF COURSE, WE DON'T KNOW EXACTLY WHERE THAT PLACE IS.
THERE IS NO OFFICIAL LISTING OF A CASTLE GIURESCU ANYPLACE, SO, GIVEN THE INFORMATION WE DO HAVE, I'VE MADE THREE REALLY EXCELLENT GUESSES.
ROMANIA
CLICK
THREE SITES. THREE TEAMS.
UNFORTUNATELY, YOU SIX ARE THE ONLY AGENTS CURRENTLY AVAILABLE, SO I'M FORCED TO MAKE SMALLER TEAMS THAN I'D LIKE.
HELLBOY, I'M AFRAID YOU HAVE TO GO SOLO.
HEY, NO FAIR.
MR. CLARK...
YEAH, BOSS.
...WITH MR. SAPIEN.
MR. WALLER...
MISS SHERMAN...
I'M ENTRUSTING YOU TWO WITH OUR NEWEST AGENT, MR. LEACH. PLEASE DON'T LOSE HIM.
YOU'RE IN GOOD HANDS, KID.
OKAY, THAT'S IT. THERE'S A PLANE WAITING. I WANT EVERYONE SUITED UP AND ON BOARD IN FIFTEEN MINUTES.
GO.

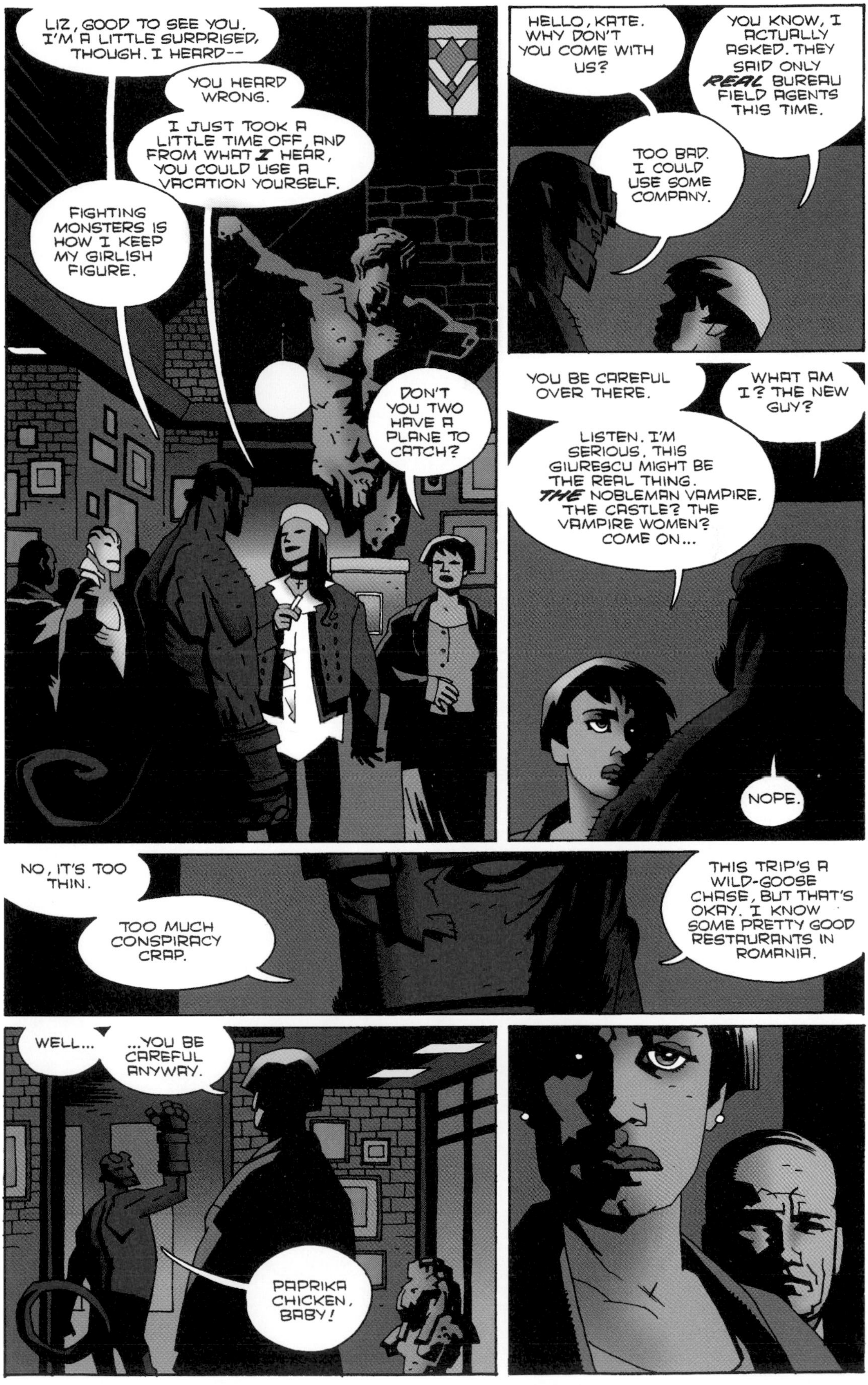
LIZ, GOOD TO SEE YOU. I'M A LITTLE SURPRISED, THOUGH. I HEARD--
YOU HEARD WRONG.
I JUST TOOK A LITTLE TIME OFF, AND FROM WHAT I HEAR, YOU COULD USE A VACATION YOURSELF.
FIGHTING MONSTERS IS HOW I KEEP MY GIRLISH FIGURE.
DON'T YOU TWO HAVE A PLANE TO CATCH?
HELLO, KATE. WHY DON'T YOU COME WITH US?
YOU KNOW, I ACTUALLY ASKED. THEY SAID ONLY REAL BUREAU FIELD AGENTS THIS TIME.
TOO BAD. I COULD USE SOME COMPANY.
YOU BE CAREFUL OVER THERE.
WHAT AM I? THE NEW GUY?
LISTEN. I'M SERIOUS. THIS GIURESCU MIGHT BE THE REAL THING. THE NOBLEMAN VAMPIRE. THE CASTLE? THE VAMPIRE WOMEN? COME ON...
NOPE.
NO, IT'S TOO THIN.
TOO MUCH CONSPIRACY CRAP.
THIS TRIP'S A WILD-GOOSE CHASE, BUT THAT'S OKAY. I KNOW SOME PRETTY GOOD RESTAURANTS IN ROMANIA.
WELL...
...YOU BE CAREFUL ANYWAY.
PAPRIKA CHICKEN, BABY!

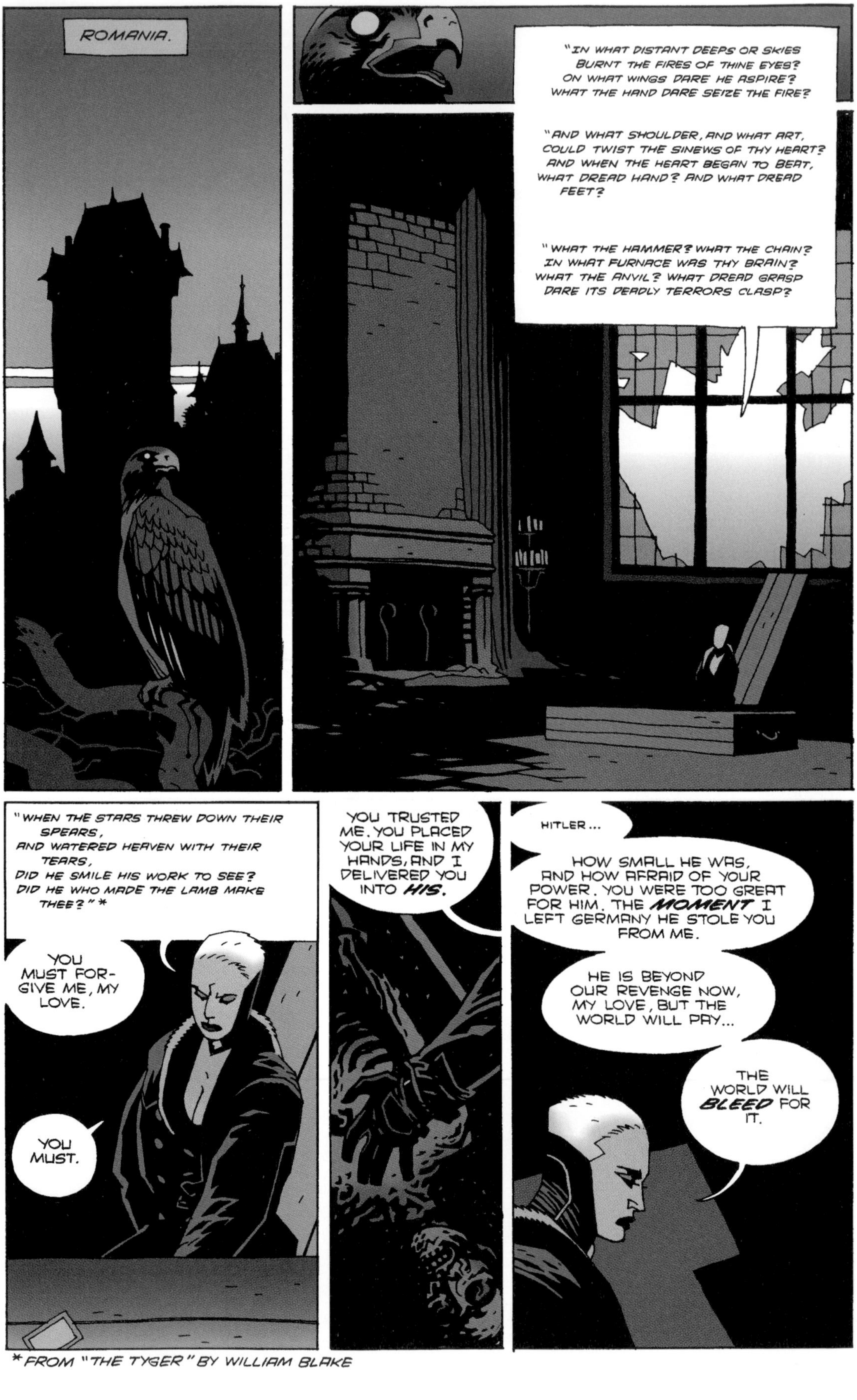
ROMANIA.
"IN WHAT DISTANT DEEPS OR SKIES BURNT THE FIRES OF THINE EYES? ON WHAT WINGS DARE HE ASPIRE? WHAT THE HAND DARE SEIZE THE FIRE?
"AND WHAT SHOULDER, AND WHAT ART, COULD TWIST THE SINEWS OF THY HEART? AND WHEN THE HEART BEGAN TO BEAT, WHAT DREAD HAND? AND WHAT DREAD FEET?
"WHAT THE HAMMER? WHAT THE CHAIN? IN WHAT FURNACE WAS THY BRAIN? WHAT THE ANVIL? WHAT DREAD GRASP DARE ITS DEADLY TERRORS CLASP?
"WHEN THE STARS THREW DOWN THEIR SPEARS, AND WATERED HEAVEN WITH THEIR TEARS, DID HE SMILE HIS WORK TO SEE? DID HE WHO MADE THE LAMB MAKE THEE?" *
YOU MUST FOR-GIVE ME, MY LOVE.
YOU MUST.
YOU TRUSTED ME. YOU PLACED YOUR LIFE IN MY HANDS, AND I DELIVERED YOU INTO HIS.
HITLER...
HOW SMALL HE WAS, AND HOW AFRAID OF YOUR POWER. YOU WERE TOO GREAT FOR HIM. THE MOMENT I LEFT GERMANY HE STOLE YOU FROM ME.
HE IS BEYOND OUR REVENGE NOW, MY LOVE, BUT THE WORLD WILL PAY...
THE WORLD WILL BLEED FOR IT.

*FROM "THE TYGER" BY WILLIAM BLAKE

TWO OF YOU, CARRY THIS BOX DOWNSTAIRS AT ONCE. I HAVE DESCRIBED THE ROOM TO YOU. FIND IT.

I'VE TOLD YOU HOW THE BODY IS TO BE PLACED?

YES, MISTRESS!

GO THEN!

#666

OH, I WOULD CUT OPEN THE WORLD TO SEE IT *BLEED*.

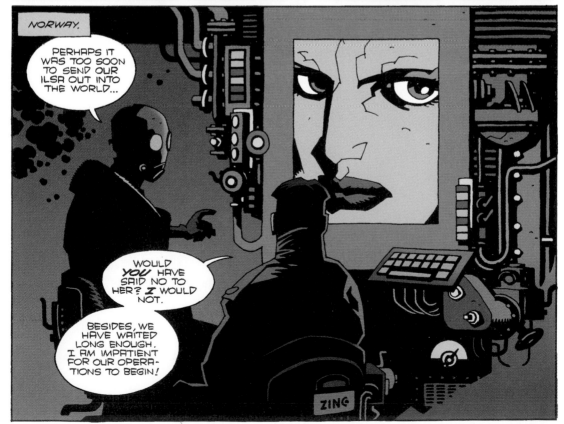

NORWAY.

PERHAPS IT WAS TOO SOON TO SEND OUR ILSA OUT INTO THE WORLD...

WOULD *YOU* HAVE SAID NO TO HER? *I* WOULD NOT.

BESIDES, WE HAVE WAITED LONG ENOUGH. I AM IMPATIENT FOR OUR OPERATIONS TO BEGIN!

ZING

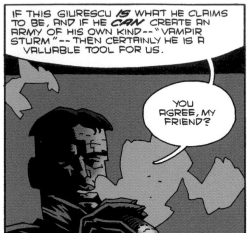

IF THIS GIURESCU *IS* WHAT HE CLAIMS TO BE, AND IF HE *CAN* CREATE AN ARMY OF HIS OWN KIND--"VAMPIR STURM"-- THEN CERTAINLY HE IS A VALUABLE TOOL FOR US.

YOU AGREE, MY FRIEND?

NO, LEOPOLD. NO, I DO NOT.

HMM.

I THINK THIS THING IS AN UGLY AND, ULTIMATELY, UNCONTROLLABLE FORCE.

EVEN THE FÜHRER RECOGNIZED THIS.

NO, I HAVE MORE FAITH...

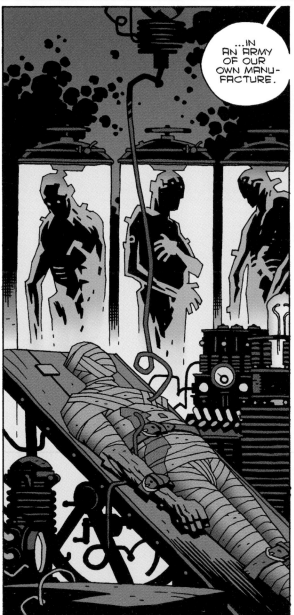

...IN AN ARMY OF OUR OWN MANU-FACTURE.

BUT SHE *IS* FOND OF HIM.

YES. WHAT DO YOU SUPPOSE WENT ON BETWEEN THEM... ALL THOSE YEARS AGO?

SHE NEVER WOULD SPEAK OF IT...

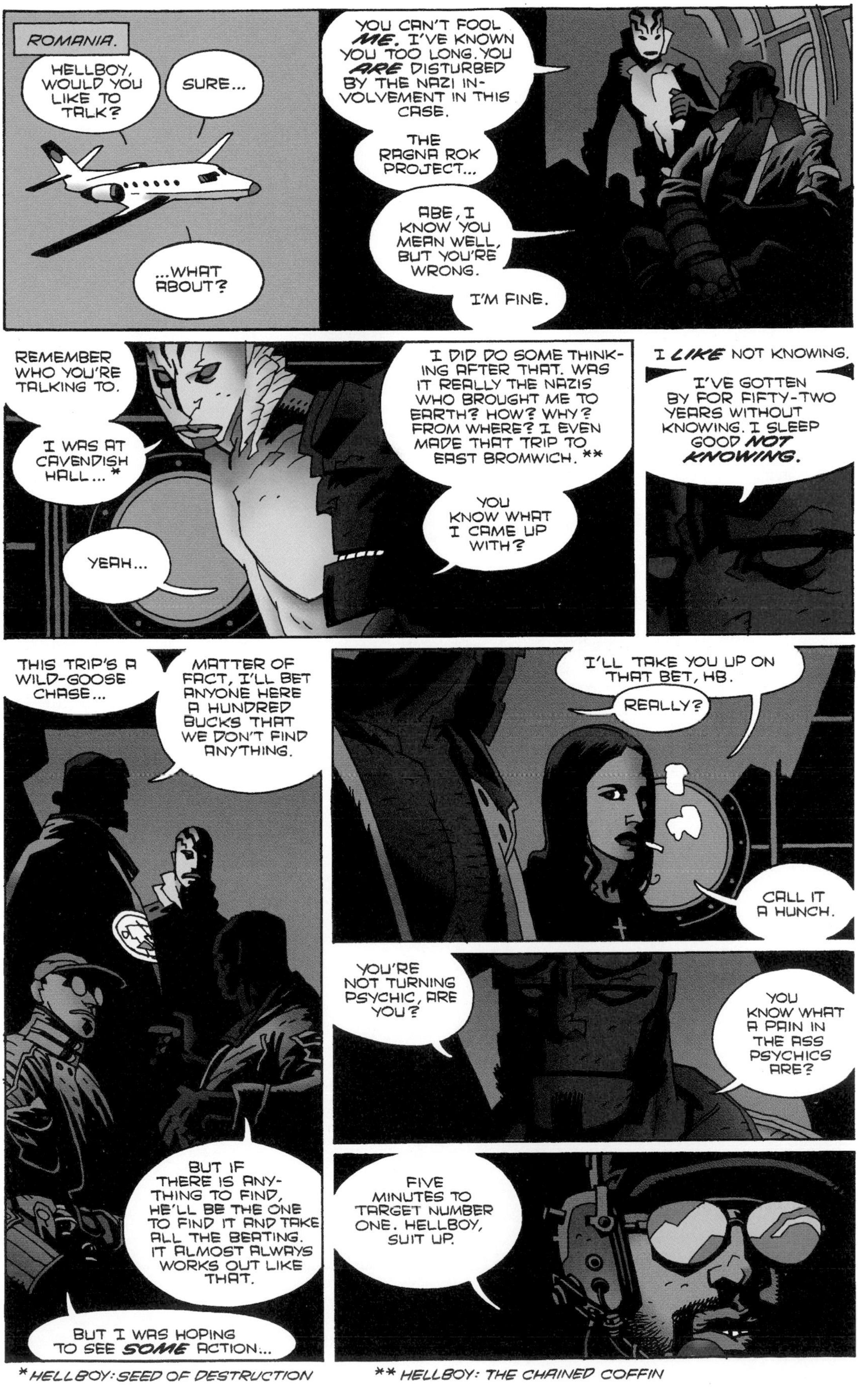
ROMANIA.
HELLBOY, WOULD YOU LIKE TO TALK?
SURE...
...WHAT ABOUT?
YOU CAN'T FOOL ME. I'VE KNOWN YOU TOO LONG. YOU ARE DISTURBED BY THE NAZI INVOLVEMENT IN THIS CASE.
THE RAGNA ROK PROJECT...
ABE, I KNOW YOU MEAN WELL, BUT YOU'RE WRONG.
I'M FINE.
REMEMBER WHO YOU'RE TALKING TO.
I WAS AT CAVENDISH HALL... *
YEAH...
I DID DO SOME THINKING AFTER THAT. WAS IT REALLY THE NAZIS WHO BROUGHT ME TO EARTH? HOW? WHY? FROM WHERE? I EVEN MADE THAT TRIP TO EAST BROMWICH. **
YOU KNOW WHAT I CAME UP WITH?
I LIKE NOT KNOWING.
I'VE GOTTEN BY FOR FIFTY-TWO YEARS WITHOUT KNOWING. I SLEEP GOOD NOT KNOWING.
THIS TRIP'S A WILD-GOOSE CHASE...
MATTER OF FACT, I'LL BET ANYONE HERE A HUNDRED BUCKS THAT WE DON'T FIND ANYTHING.
BUT IF THERE IS ANYTHING TO FIND, HE'LL BE THE ONE TO FIND IT AND TAKE ALL THE BEATING. IT ALMOST ALWAYS WORKS OUT LIKE THAT.
BUT I WAS HOPING TO SEE SOME ACTION...
I'LL TAKE YOU UP ON THAT BET, HB.
REALLY?
CALL IT A HUNCH.
YOU'RE NOT TURNING PSYCHIC, ARE YOU?
YOU KNOW WHAT A PAIN IN THE ASS PSYCHICS ARE?
FIVE MINUTES TO TARGET NUMBER ONE. HELLBOY, SUIT UP.

* HELLBOY: SEED OF DESTRUCTION

** HELLBOY: THE CHAINED COFFIN

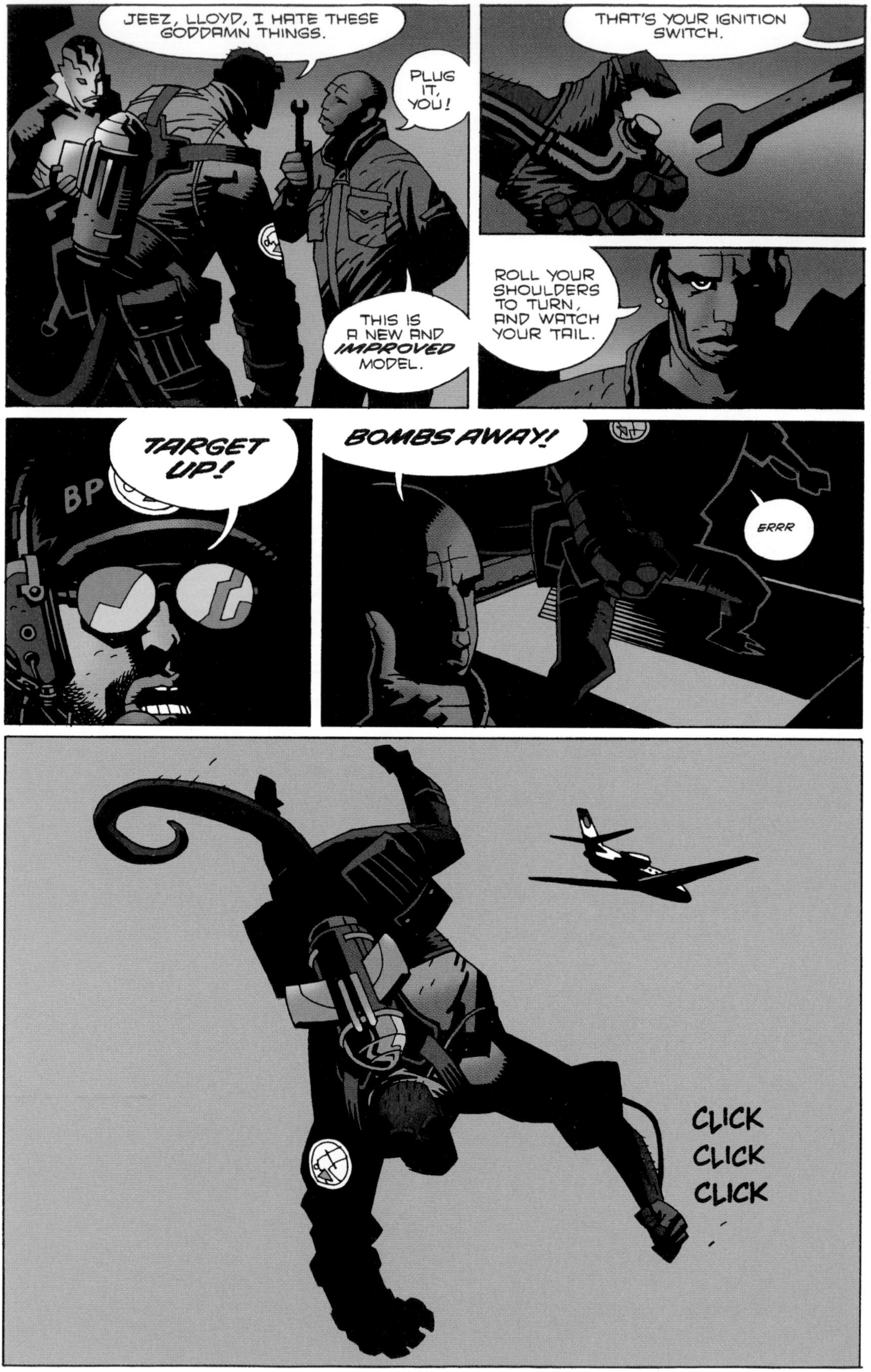
JEEZ, LLOYD, I HATE THESE GODDAMN THINGS.
PLUG IT, YOU!
THIS IS A NEW AND *IMPROVED* MODEL.
THAT'S YOUR IGNITION SWITCH.
ROLL YOUR SHOULDERS TO TURN, AND WATCH YOUR TAIL.
TARGET UP!
BOMBS AWAY!
ERRR
CLICK
CLICK
CLICK

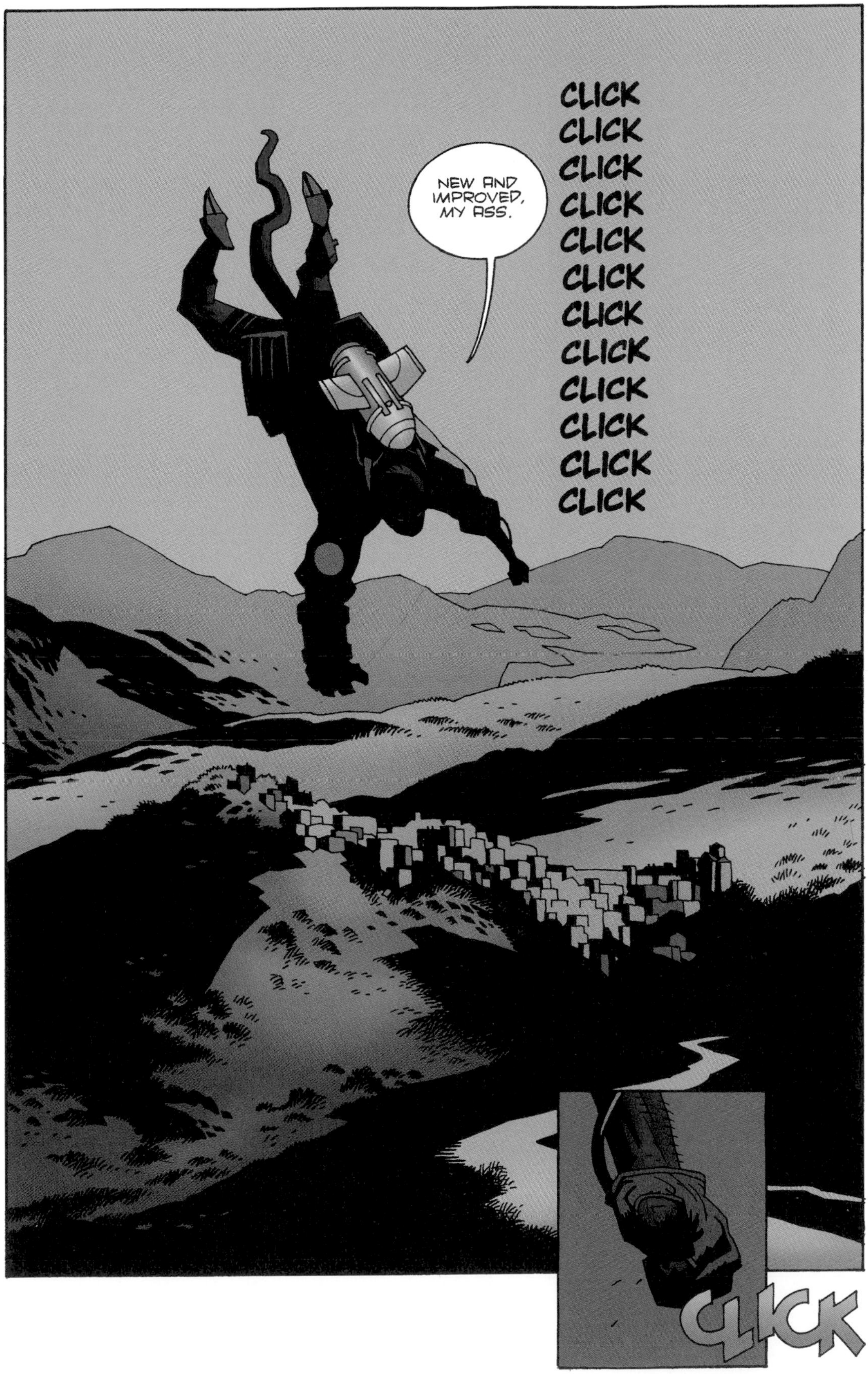
NEW AND IMPROVED, MY ASS.
CLICK
CLICK
CLICK
CLICK
CLICK
CLICK
CLICK
CLICK
CLICK
CLICK
CLICK
CLICK
CLICK

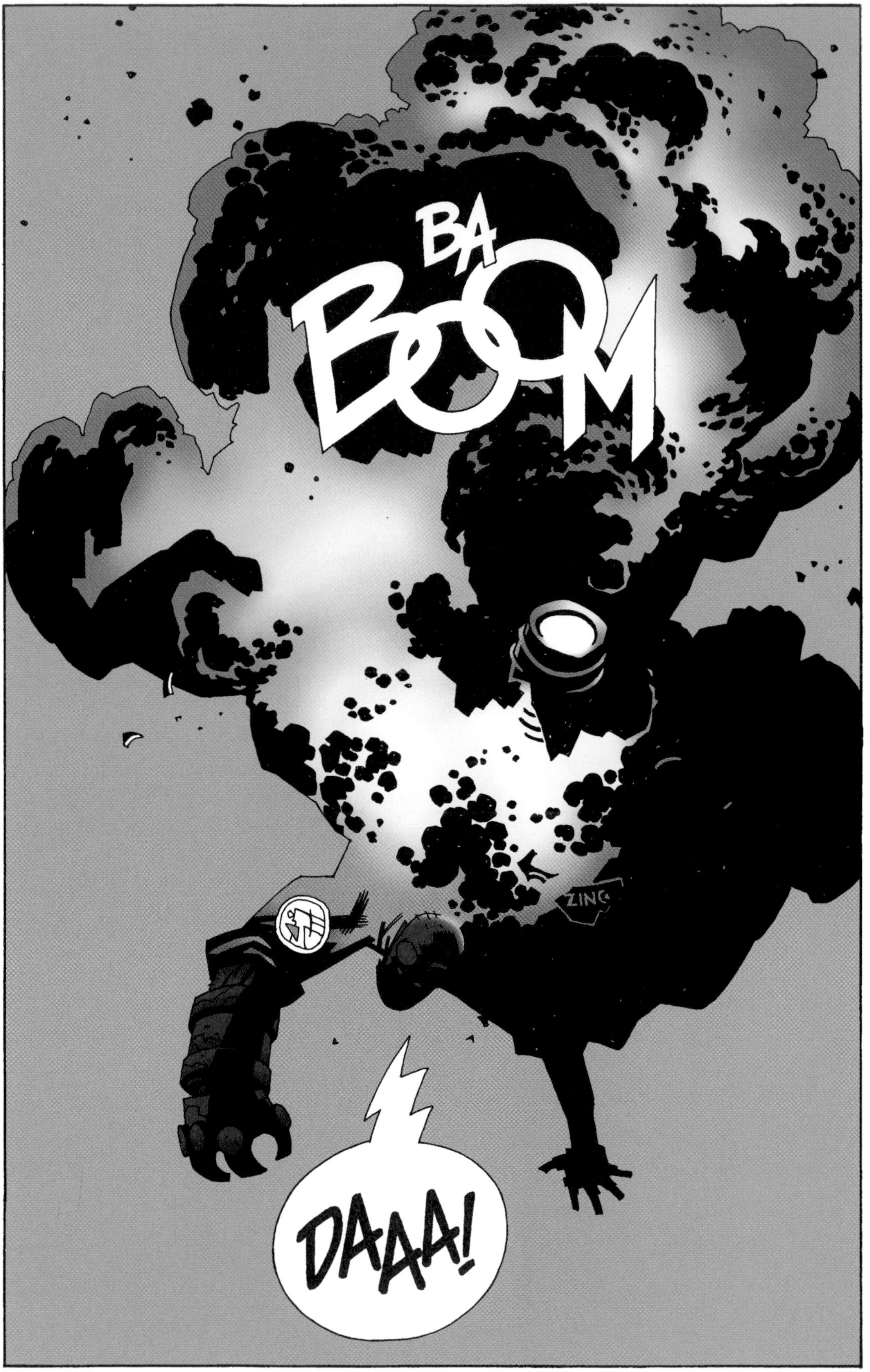
BA
BOOM
ZING
DAAA!

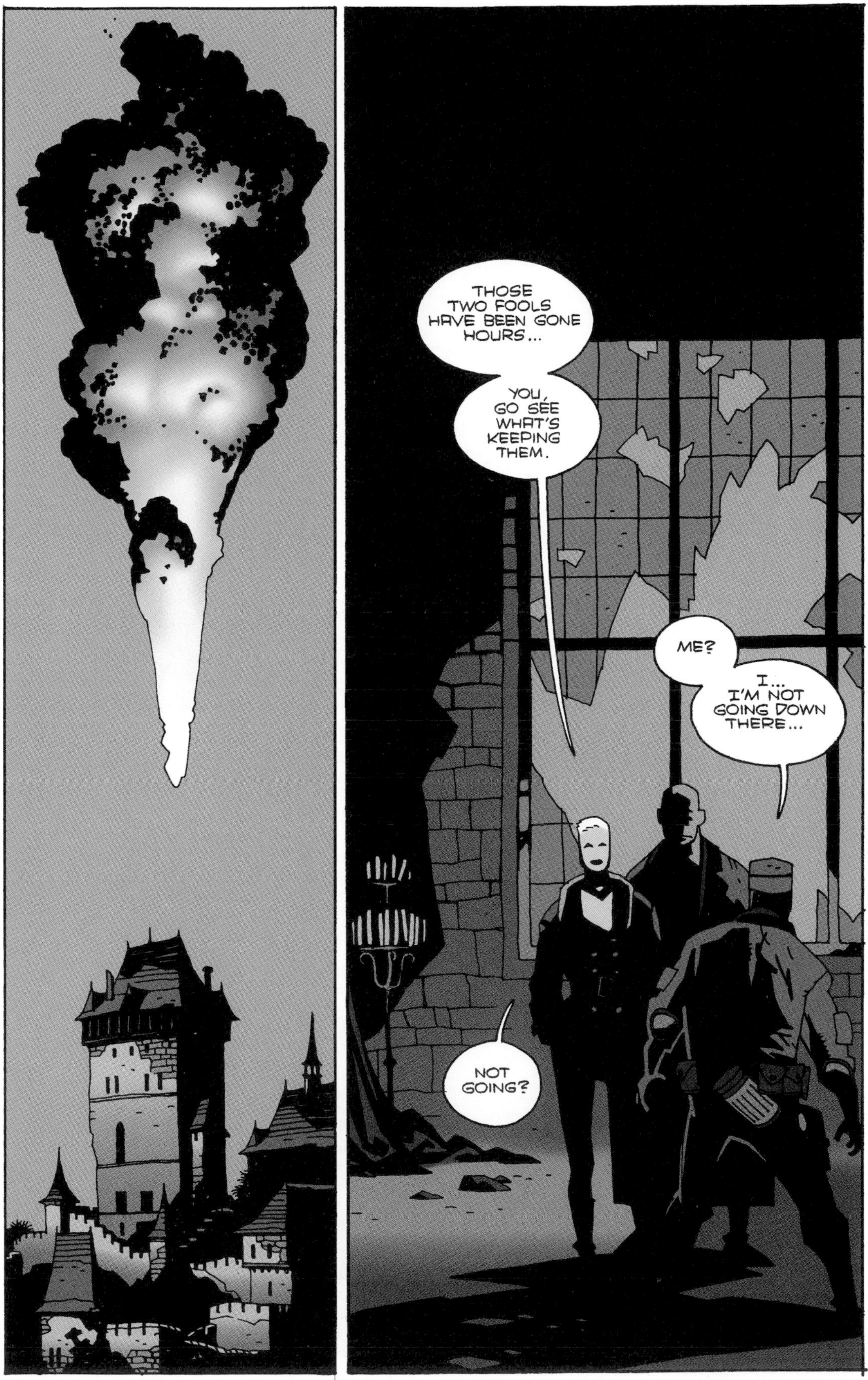
THOSE TWO FOOLS HAVE BEEN GONE HOURS...
YOU, GO SEE WHAT'S KEEPING THEM.
ME?
I... I'M NOT GOING DOWN THERE...
NOT GOING?

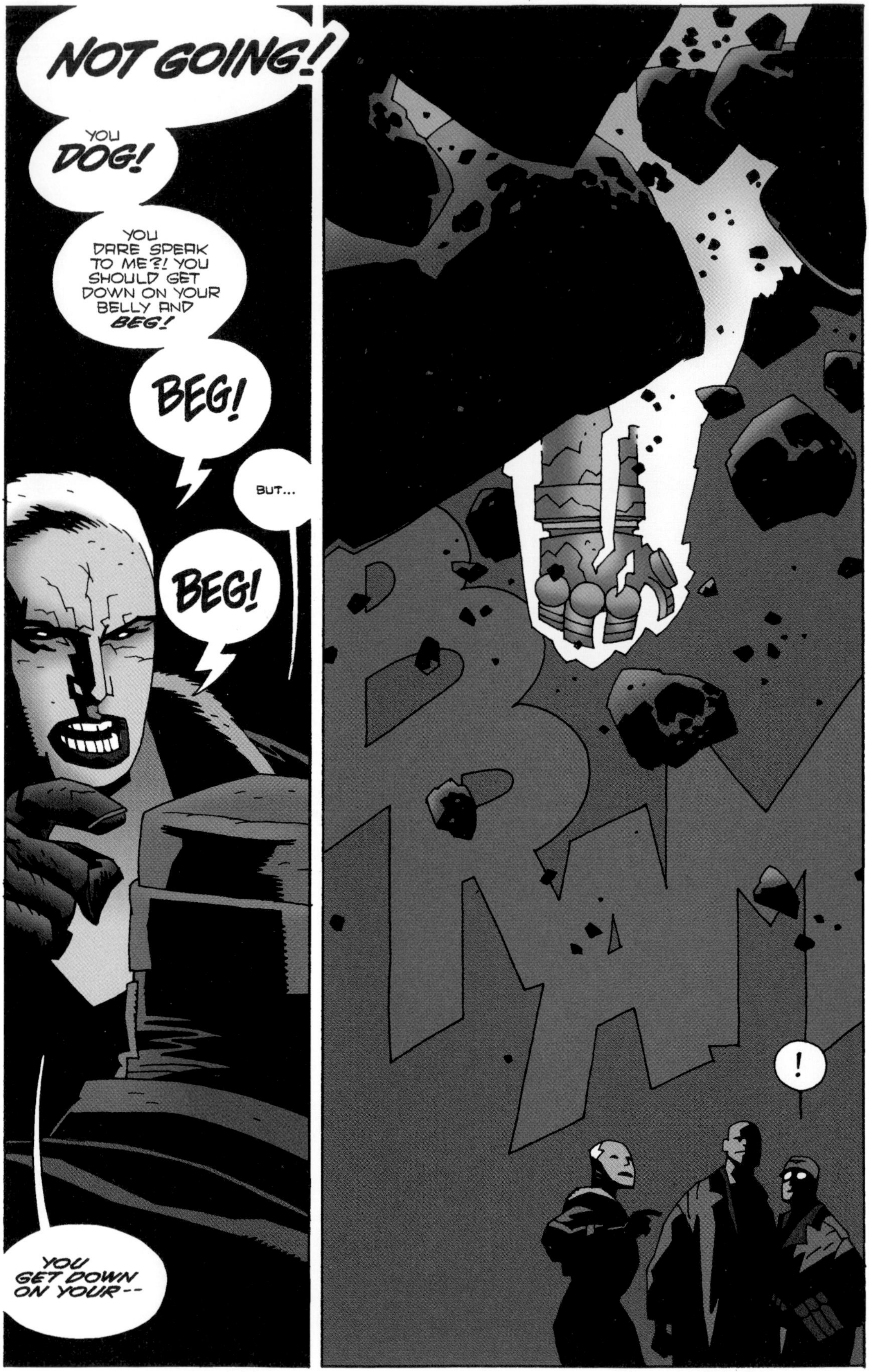
NOT GOING!
YOU DOG!
YOU DARE SPEAK TO ME?! YOU SHOULD GET DOWN ON YOUR BELLY AND BEG!
BEG!
BUT...
BEG!
YOU GET DOWN ON YOUR--
!

CHAPTER TWO

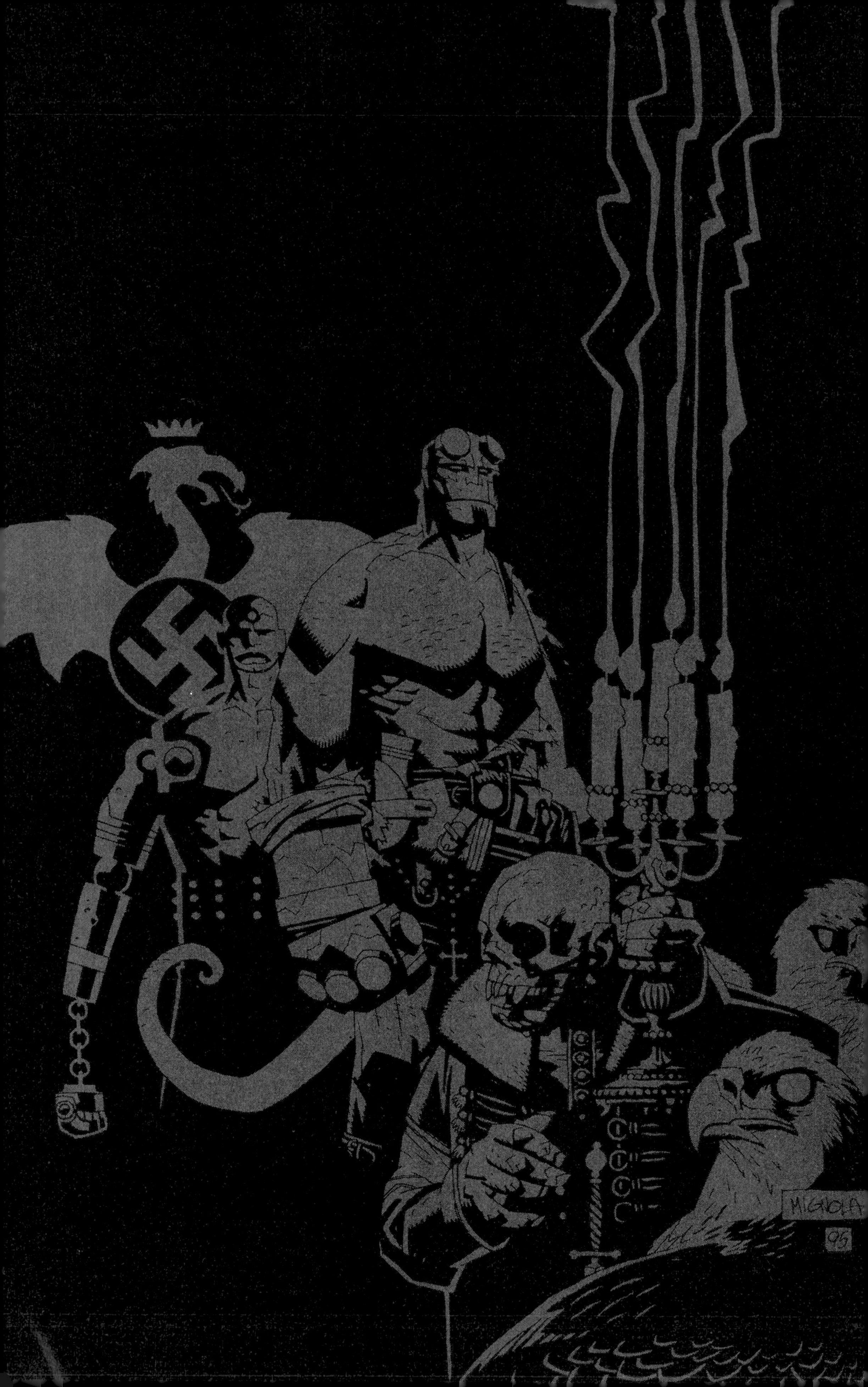
MIGNOLA

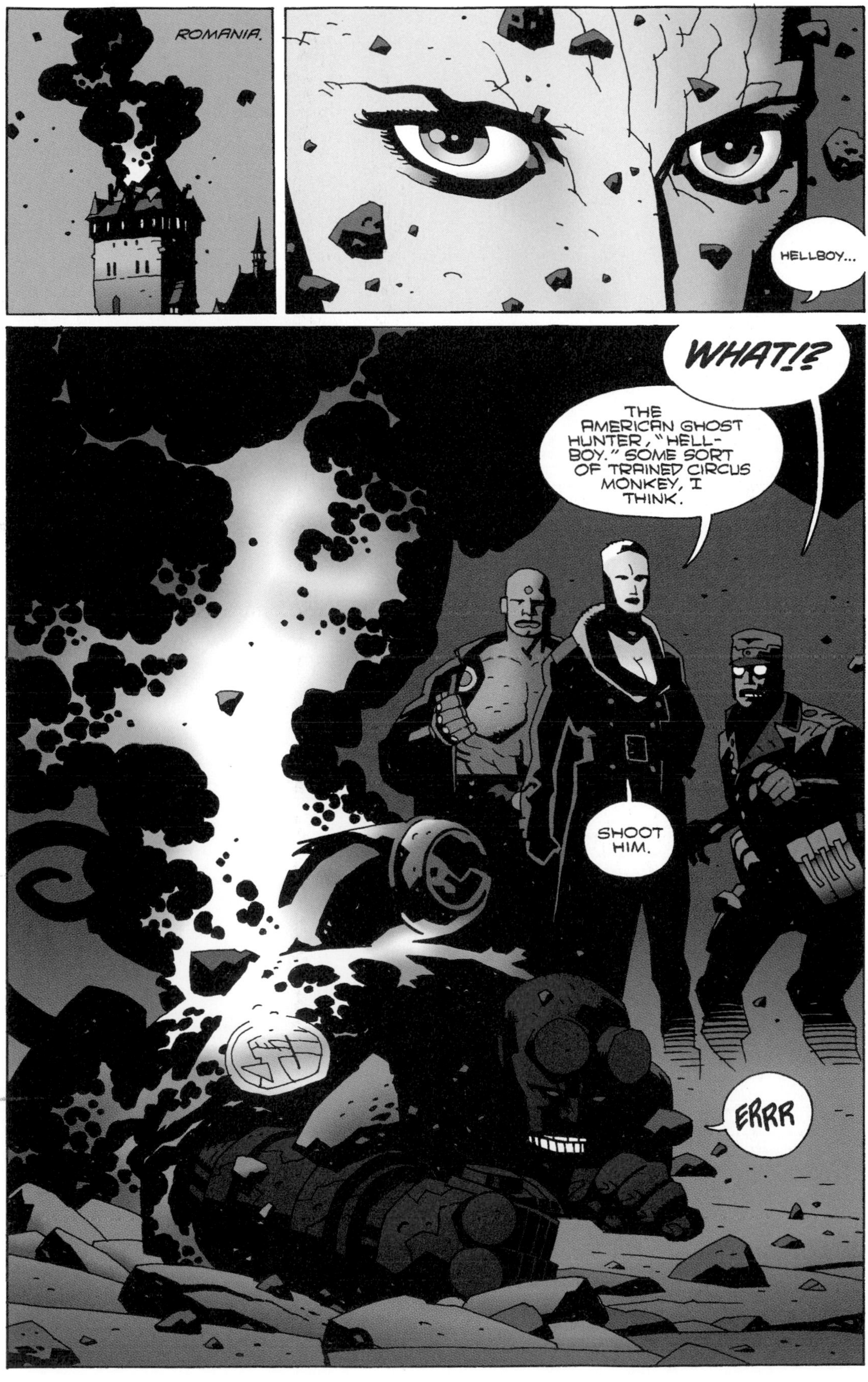
ROMANIA.
HELLBOY...
WHAT!?
THE AMERICAN GHOST HUNTER, "HELL-BOY." SOME SORT OF TRAINED CIRCUS MONKEY, I THINK.
SHOOT HIM.
ERRR

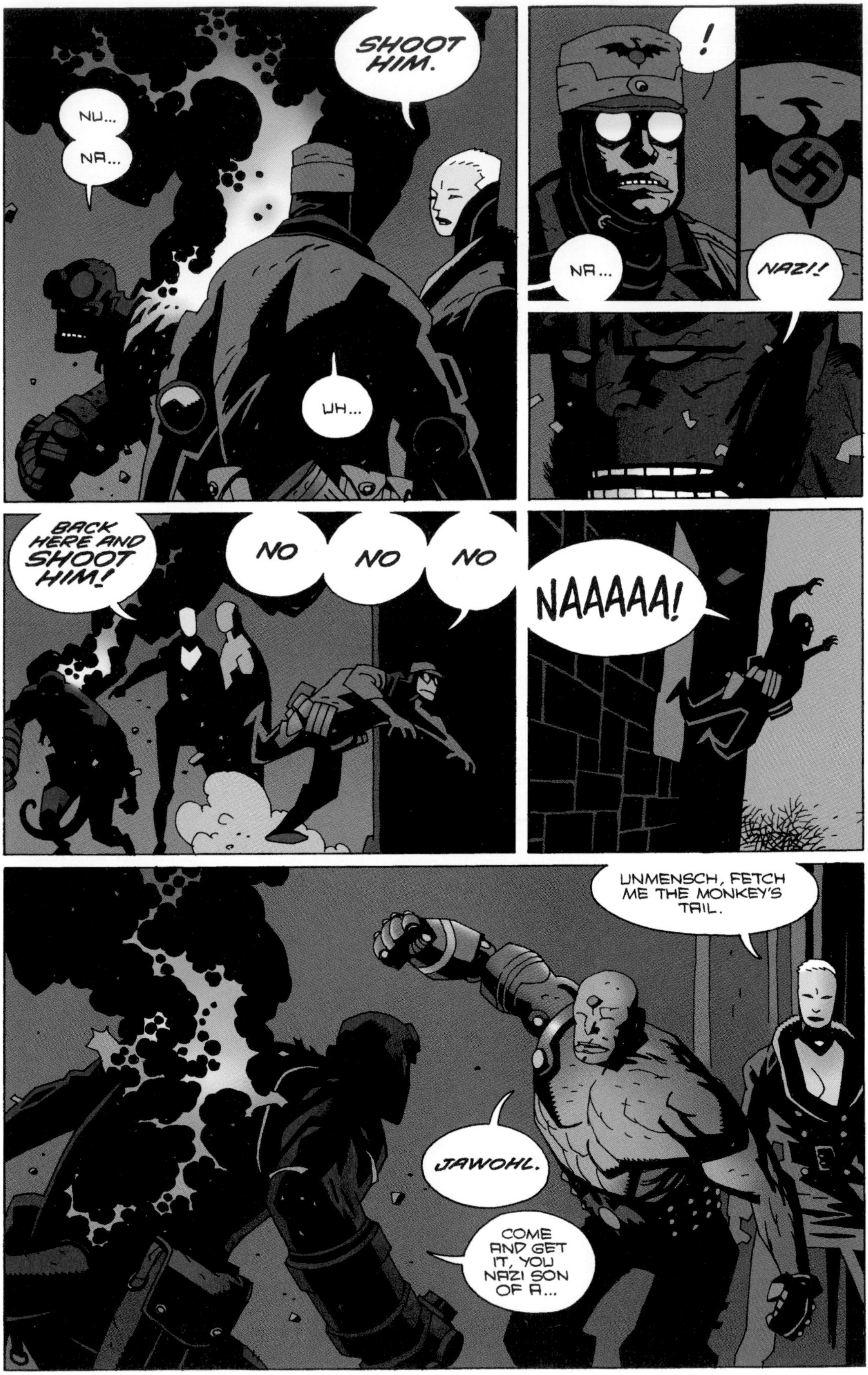
SHOOT HIM.
NU...
NA...
UH...
!
NA...
NAZI!
BACK HERE AND SHOOT HIM!
NO
NO
NO
NAAAAA!
UNMENSCH, FETCH ME THE MONKEY'S TAIL.
JAWOHL.
COME AND GET IT, YOU NAZI SON OF A...

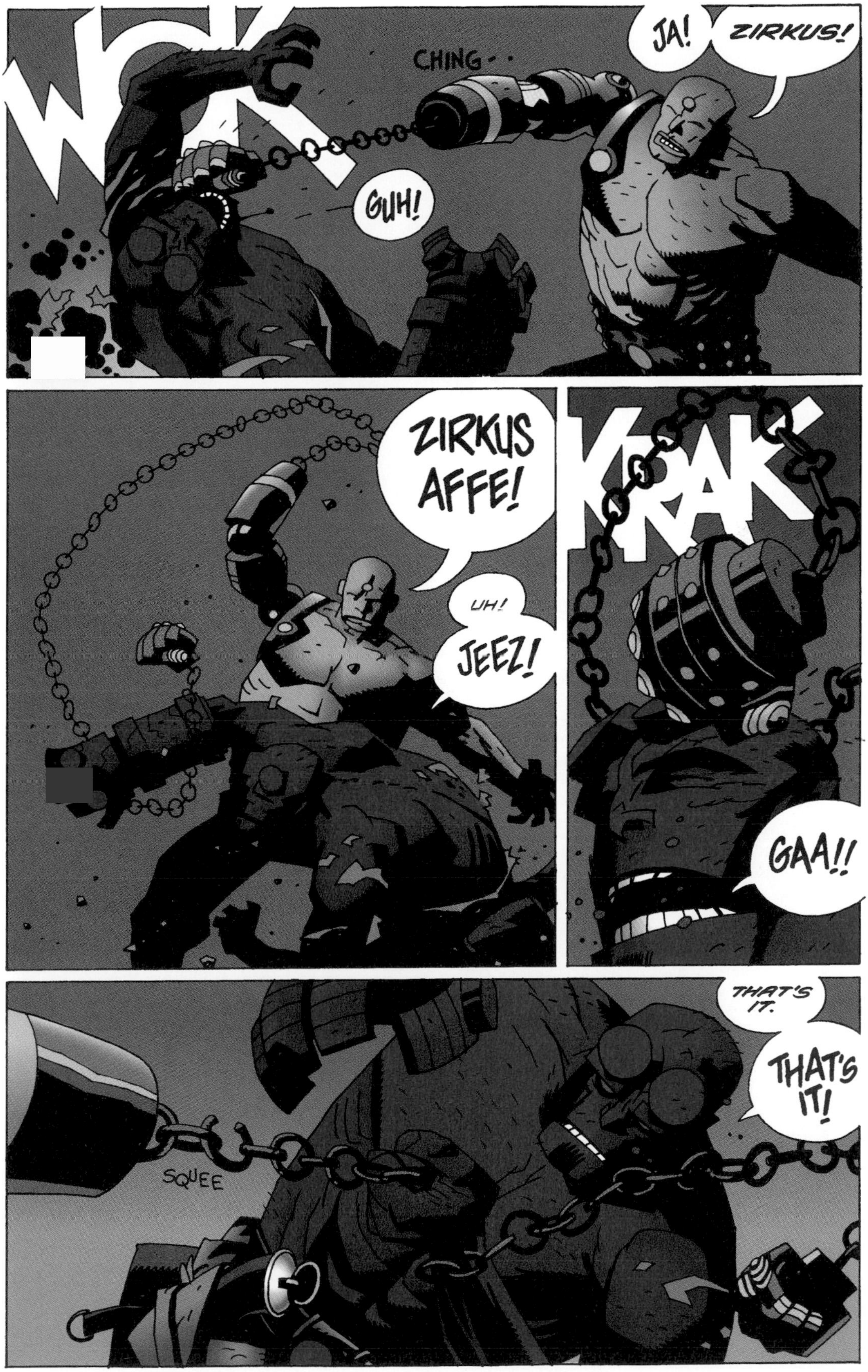
CHING . .
JA!
ZIRKUS!
GUH!
ZIRKUS AFFE!
UH!
JEEZ!
KRAK
GAA!!
THAT'S IT.
THAT'S IT!
SQUEE

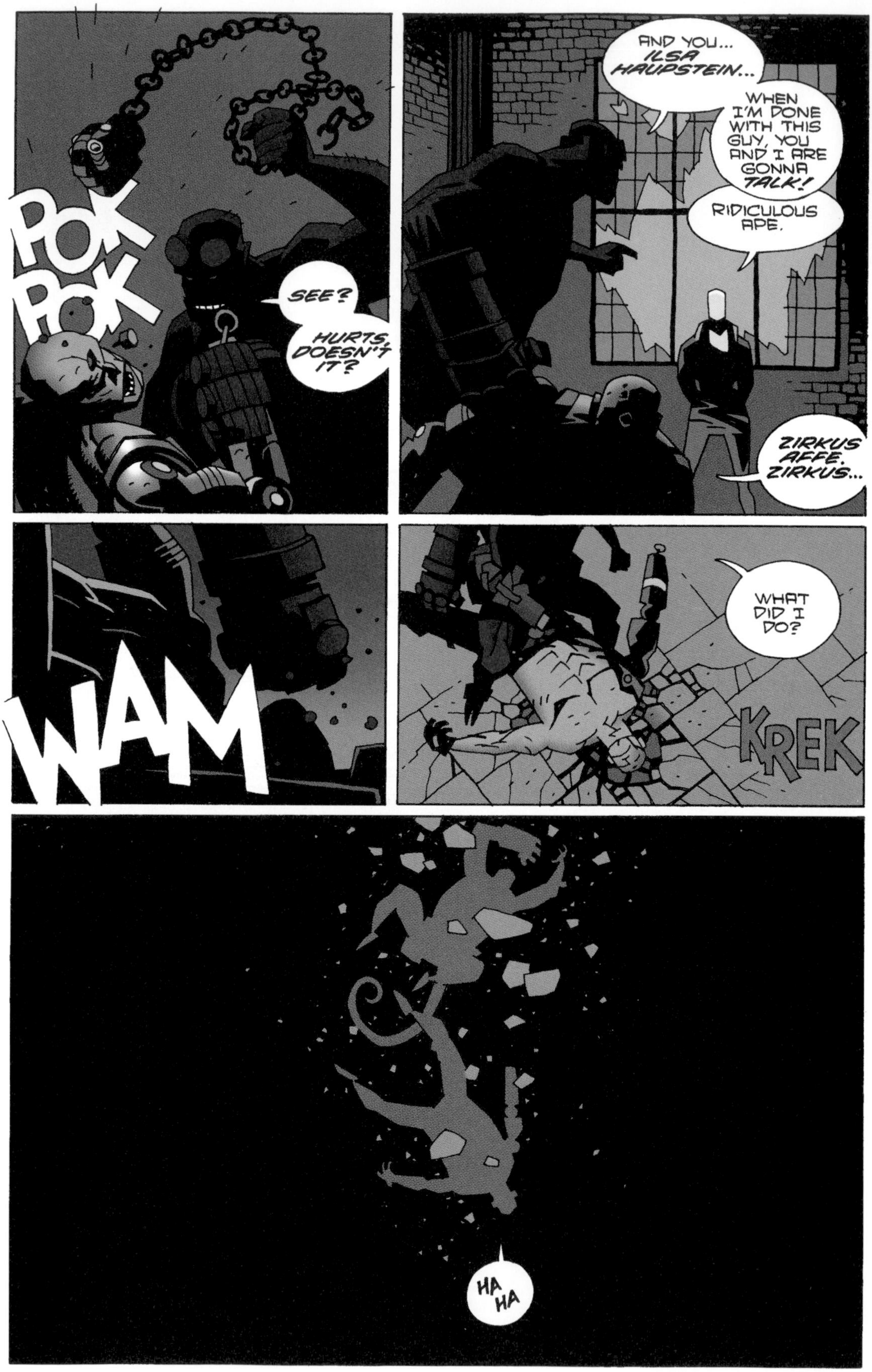
POK POK
SEE?
HURTS, DOESN'T IT?
AND YOU... ILSA HAUPSTEIN...
WHEN I'M DONE WITH THIS GUY, YOU AND I ARE GONNA TALK!
RIDICULOUS APE.
ZIRKUS AFFE. ZIRKUS...
WAM
WHAT DID I DO?
KREK
HA HA

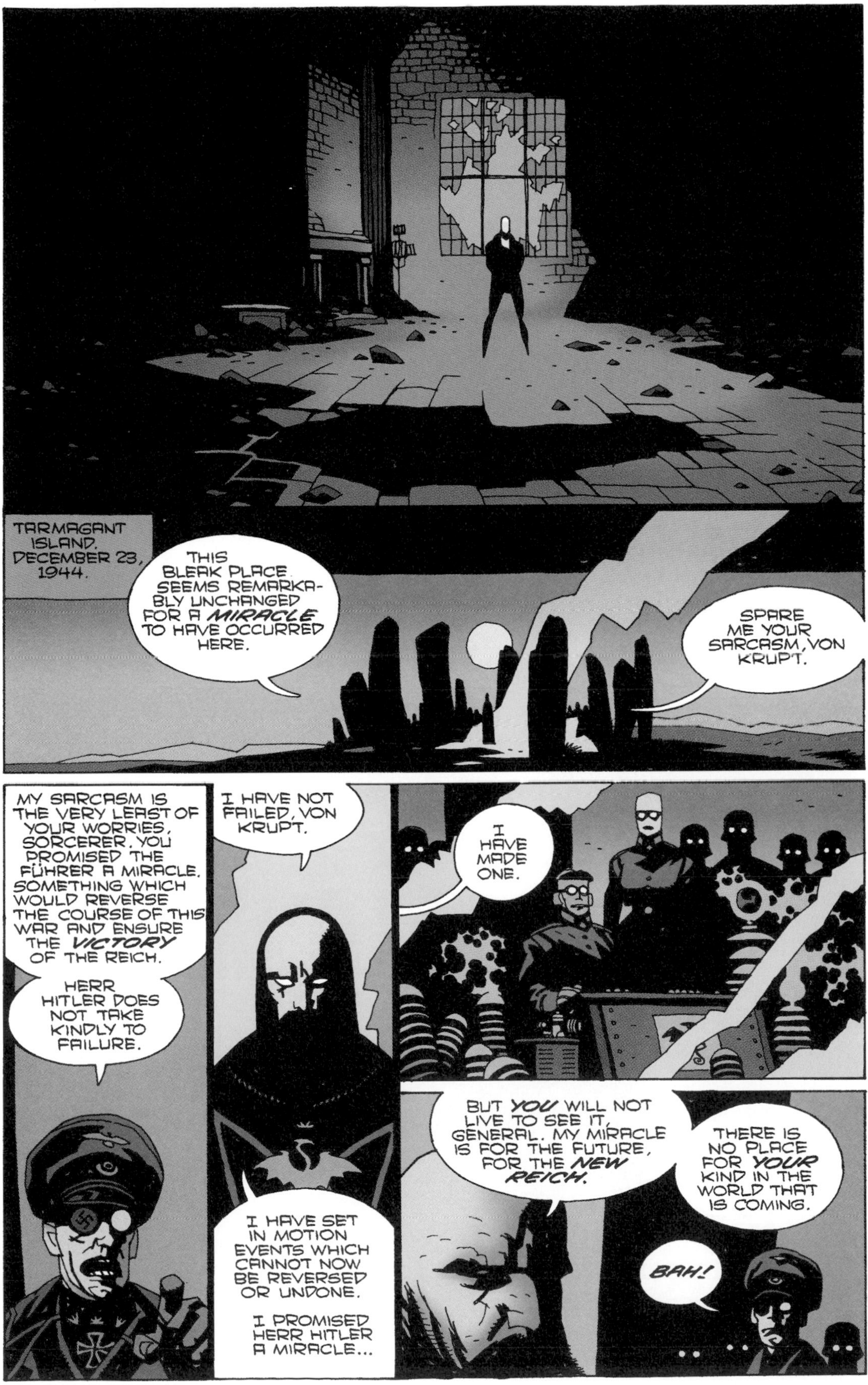
TARMAGANT ISLAND. DECEMBER 23, 1944.
THIS BLEAK PLACE SEEMS REMARKABLY UNCHANGED FOR A *MIRACLE* TO HAVE OCCURRED HERE.
SPARE ME YOUR SARCASM, VON KRUPT.
MY SARCASM IS THE VERY LEAST OF YOUR WORRIES, SORCERER. YOU PROMISED THE FÜHRER A MIRACLE. SOMETHING WHICH WOULD REVERSE THE COURSE OF THIS WAR AND ENSURE THE *VICTORY* OF THE REICH.
HERR HITLER DOES NOT TAKE KINDLY TO FAILURE.
I HAVE NOT FAILED, VON KRUPT.
I HAVE SET IN MOTION EVENTS WHICH CANNOT NOW BE REVERSED OR UNDONE.
I PROMISED HERR HITLER A MIRACLE...
I HAVE MADE ONE.
BUT *YOU* WILL NOT LIVE TO SEE IT, GENERAL. MY MIRACLE IS FOR THE FUTURE, FOR THE *NEW REICH.*
THERE IS NO PLACE FOR *YOUR* KIND IN THE WORLD THAT IS COMING.
BAH!

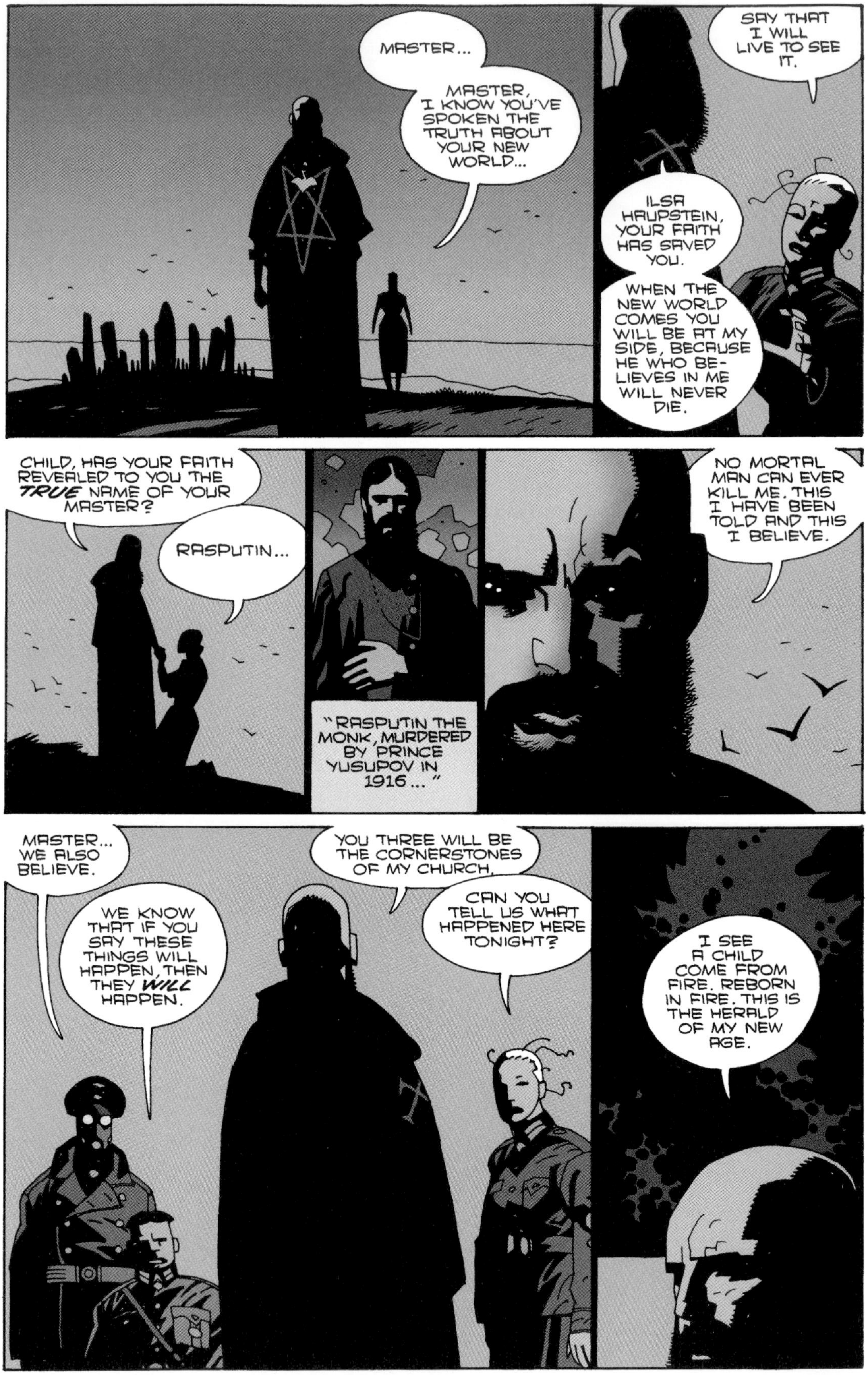
MASTER...
MASTER, I KNOW YOU'VE SPOKEN THE TRUTH ABOUT YOUR NEW WORLD...
SAY THAT I WILL LIVE TO SEE IT.
ILSA HAUPSTEIN, YOUR FAITH HAS SAVED YOU.
WHEN THE NEW WORLD COMES YOU WILL BE AT MY SIDE, BECAUSE HE WHO BE-LIEVES IN ME WILL NEVER DIE.
CHILD, HAS YOUR FAITH REVEALED TO YOU THE TRUE NAME OF YOUR MASTER?
RASPUTIN...
"RASPUTIN THE MONK, MURDERED BY PRINCE YUSUPOV IN 1916..."
NO MORTAL MAN CAN EVER KILL ME. THIS I HAVE BEEN TOLD AND THIS I BELIEVE.
MASTER... WE ALSO BELIEVE.
WE KNOW THAT IF YOU SAY THESE THINGS WILL HAPPEN, THEN THEY WILL HAPPEN.
YOU THREE WILL BE THE CORNERSTONES OF MY CHURCH.
CAN YOU TELL US WHAT HAPPENED HERE TONIGHT?
I SEE A CHILD COME FROM FIRE. REBORN IN FIRE. THIS IS THE HERALD OF MY NEW AGE.

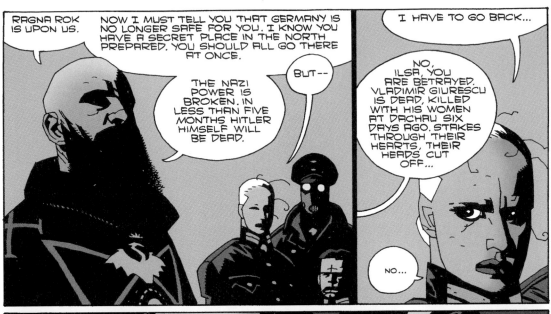

RAGNA ROK IS UPON US.

NOW I MUST TELL YOU THAT GERMANY IS NO LONGER SAFE FOR YOU. I KNOW YOU HAVE A SECRET PLACE IN THE NORTH PREPARED. YOU SHOULD ALL GO THERE AT ONCE.

THE NAZI POWER IS BROKEN. IN LESS THAN FIVE MONTHS HITLER HIMSELF WILL BE DEAD.

BUT--

I HAVE TO GO BACK...

NO, ILSA, YOU ARE BETRAYED. VLADIMIR GIURESCU IS DEAD, KILLED WITH HIS WOMEN AT DACHAU SIX DAYS AGO. STAKES THROUGH THEIR HEARTS, THEIR HEADS CUT OFF...

NO...

ROMANIA. NOW.

MY LOVE, FORGIVE ME...

ILSA...

DO NOT TORTURE YOURSELF FOR THE VAMPIRE...

MASTER?!

MASTER, I--

DO NOT TOUCH ME.

I AM NO LONGER FLESH AND BLOOD, BUT SPIRIT ONLY, AND I HAVE LIVED AMONG SPIRITS...

I DON'T KNOW WHAT TO--

COME.

WALK WITH ME A WHILE. IN THE SUN-LIGHT.

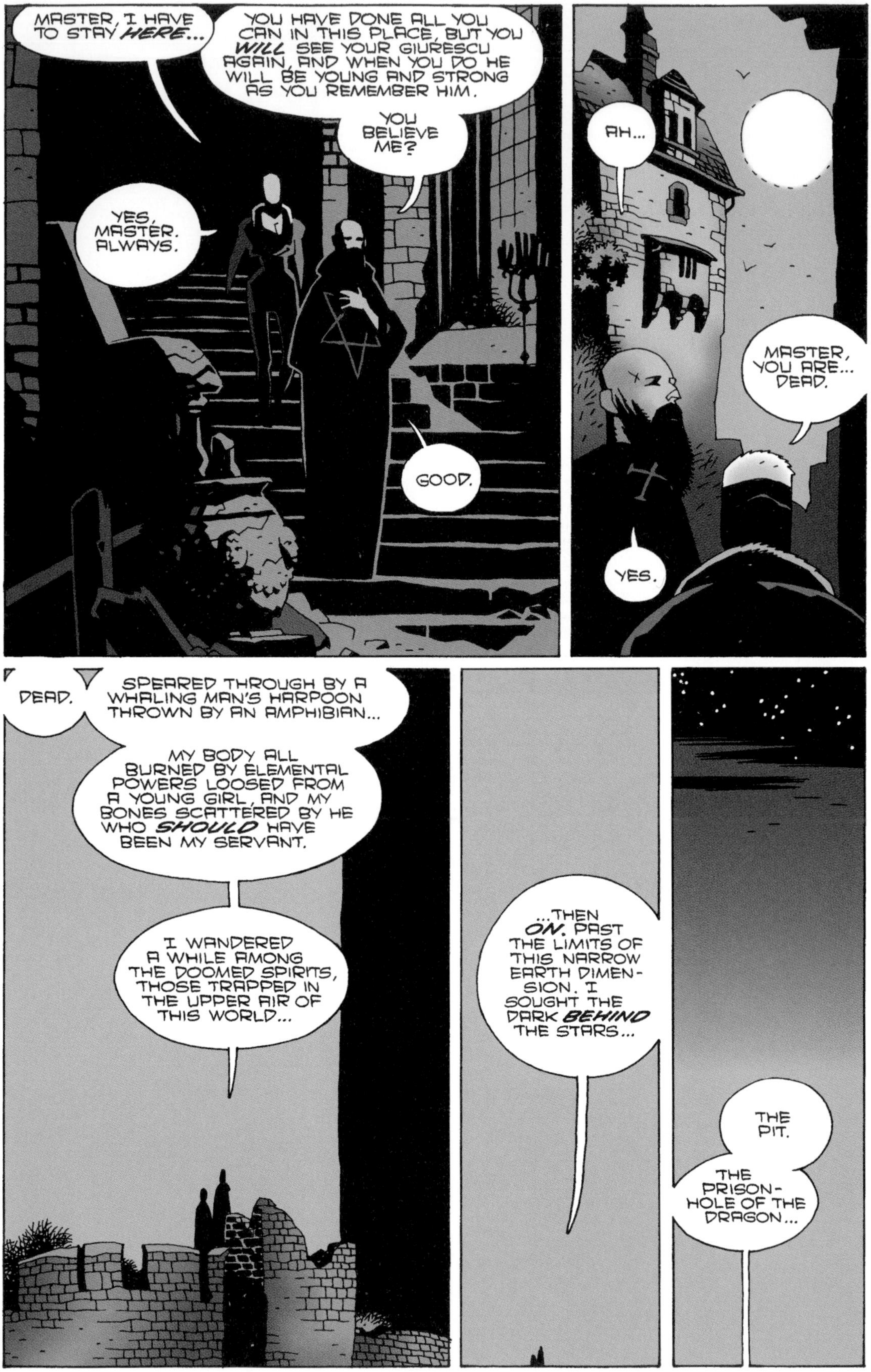
MASTER, I HAVE TO STAY HERE...
YOU HAVE DONE ALL YOU CAN IN THIS PLACE, BUT YOU WILL SEE YOUR GIURESCU AGAIN, AND WHEN YOU DO HE WILL BE YOUNG AND STRONG AS YOU REMEMBER HIM.
YOU BELIEVE ME?
YES, MASTER. ALWAYS.
GOOD.
AH...
MASTER, YOU ARE... DEAD.
YES.
DEAD.
SPEARED THROUGH BY A WHALING MAN'S HARPOON THROWN BY AN AMPHIBIAN...
MY BODY ALL BURNED BY ELEMENTAL POWERS LOOSED FROM A YOUNG GIRL, AND MY BONES SCATTERED BY HE WHO SHOULD HAVE BEEN MY SERVANT.
I WANDERED A WHILE AMONG THE DOOMED SPIRITS, THOSE TRAPPED IN THE UPPER AIR OF THIS WORLD...
...THEN ON. PAST THE LIMITS OF THIS NARROW EARTH DIMENSION. I SOUGHT THE DARK BEHIND THE STARS...
THE PIT.
THE PRISON-HOLE OF THE DRAGON...

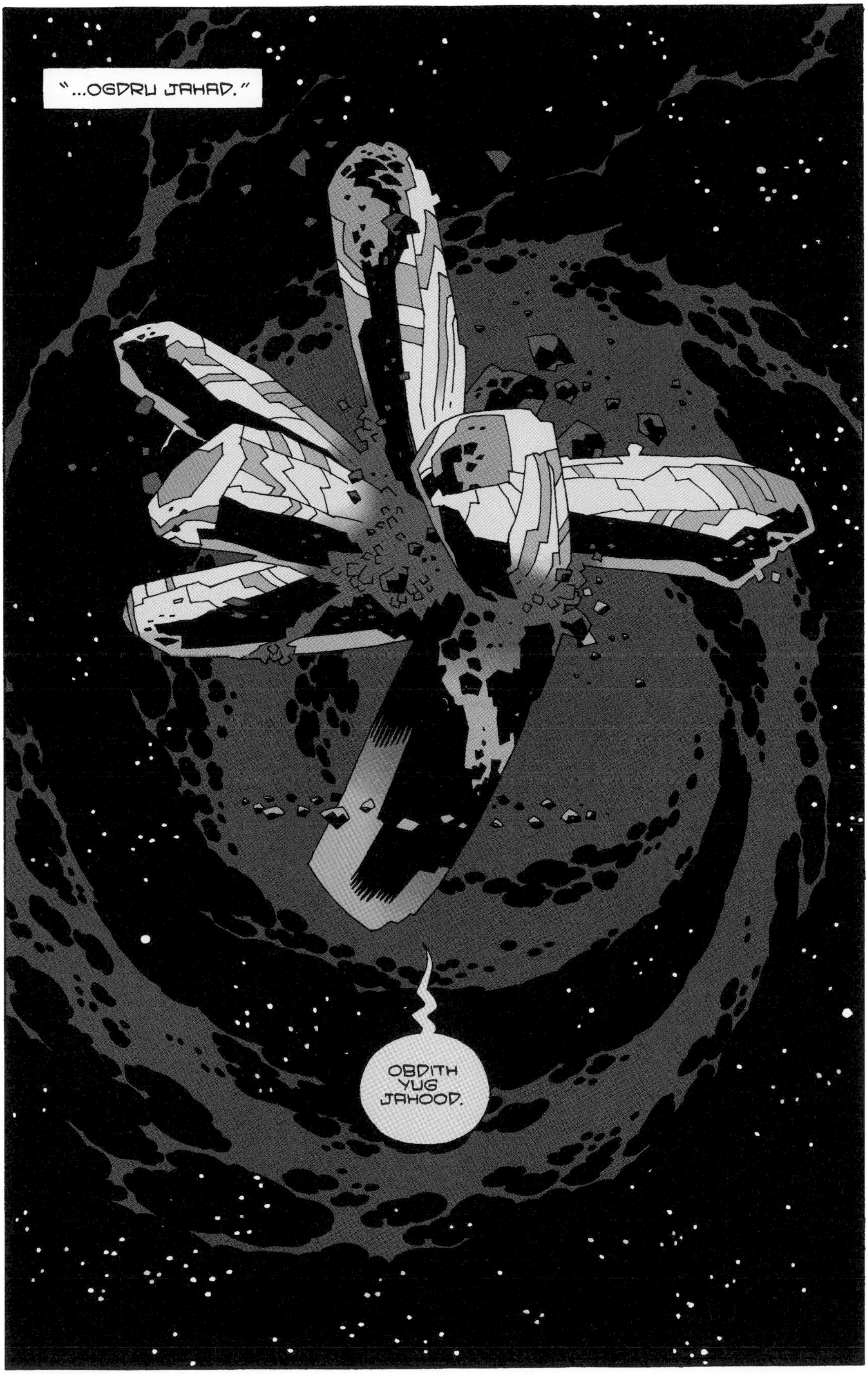
"...OGDRU JAHAD."
OBDITH YUG JAHOOD.

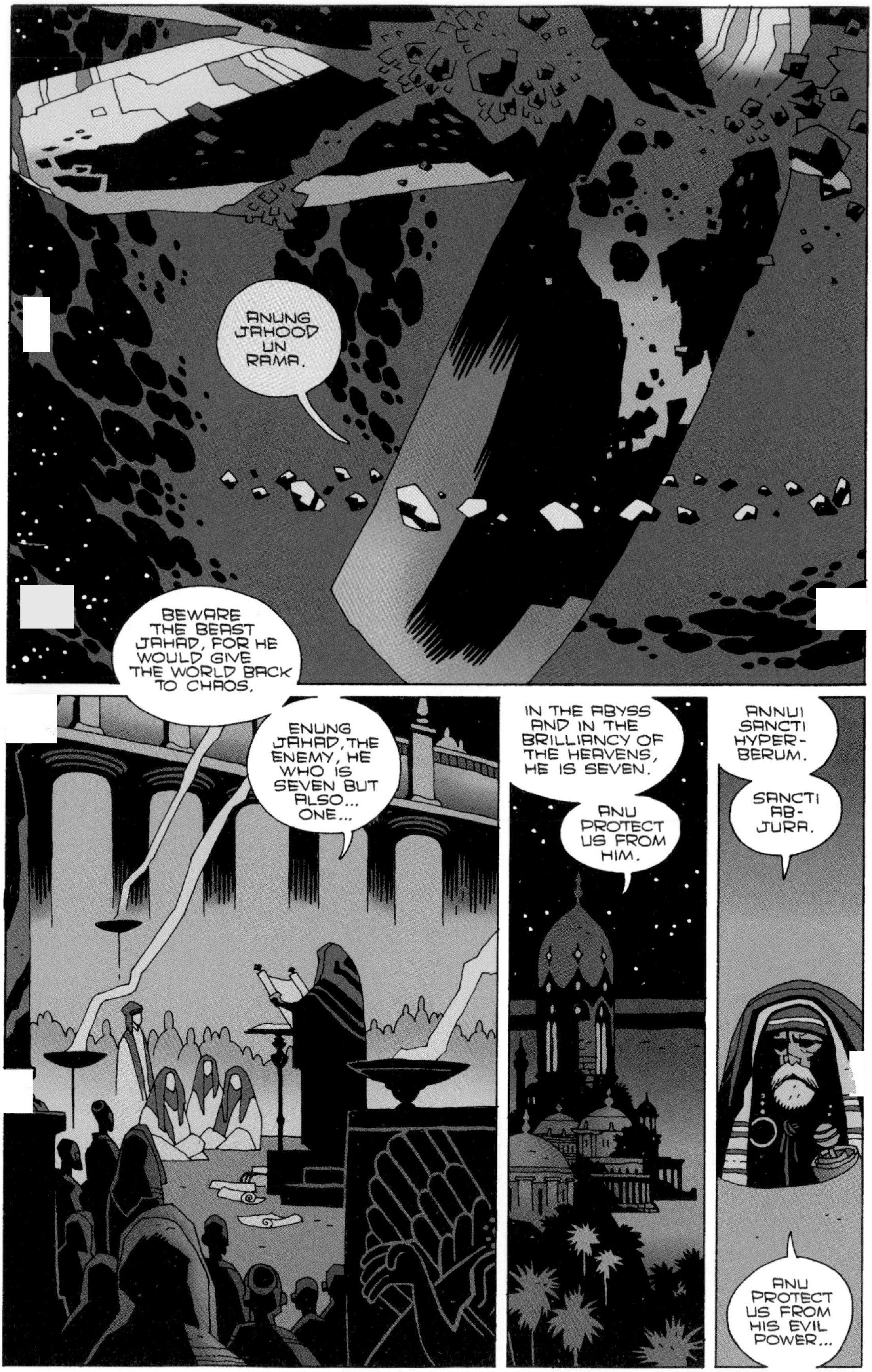
ANUNG JAHOOD UN RAMA.
BEWARE THE BEAST JAHAD, FOR HE WOULD GIVE THE WORLD BACK TO CHAOS.
ENUNG JAHAD, THE ENEMY, HE WHO IS SEVEN BUT ALSO... ONE...
IN THE ABYSS AND IN THE BRILLIANCY OF THE HEAVENS, HE IS SEVEN.
ANU PROTECT US FROM HIM.
ANNUI SANCTI HYPER-BERUM.
SANCTI AB-JURA.
ANU PROTECT US FROM HIS EVIL POWER...

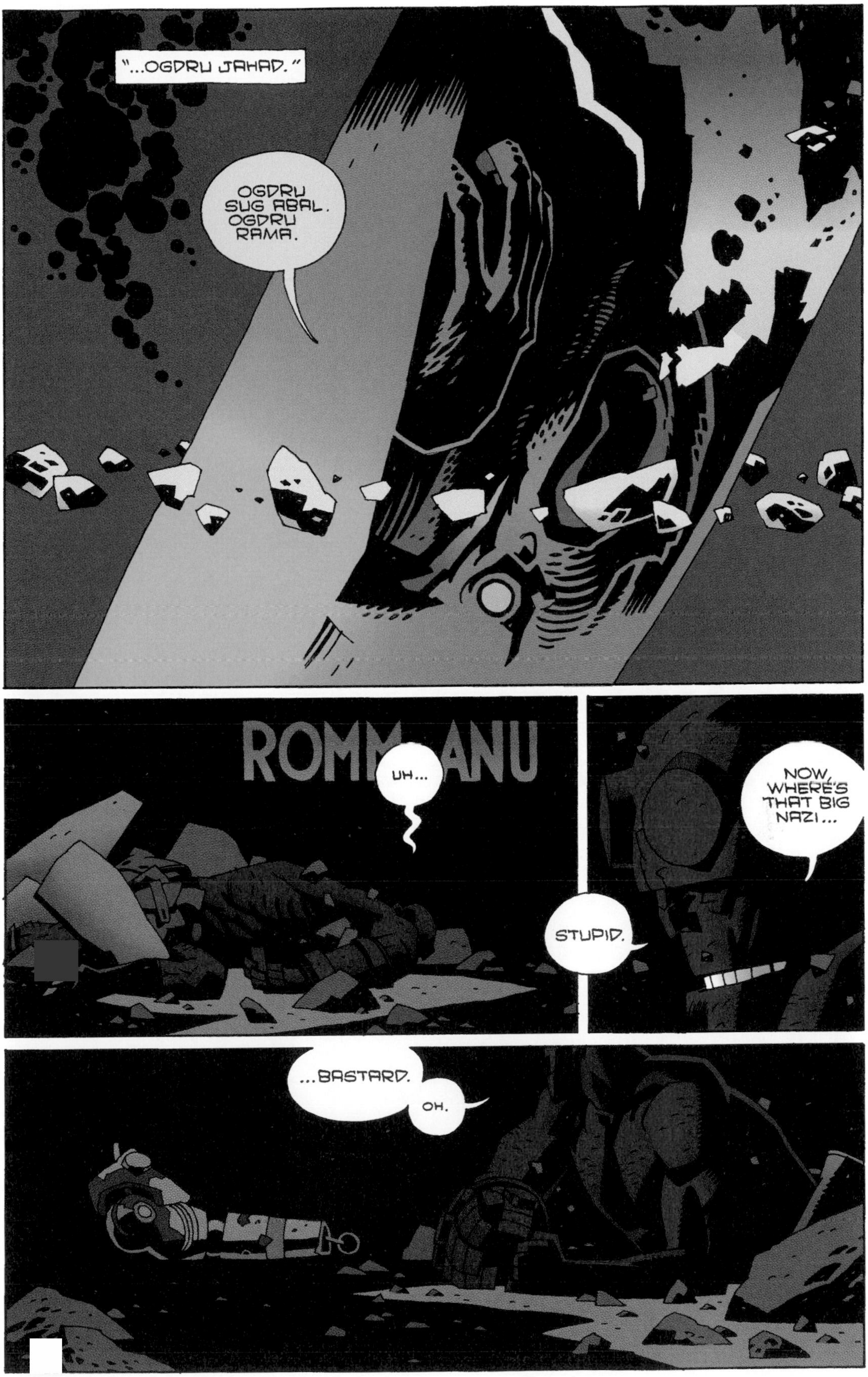
"...OGDRU JAHAD."
OGDRU SUG ABAL. OGDRU RAMA.
ROMM ANU
UH...
NOW, WHERE'S THAT BIG NAZI...
STUPID.
...BASTARD.
OH.

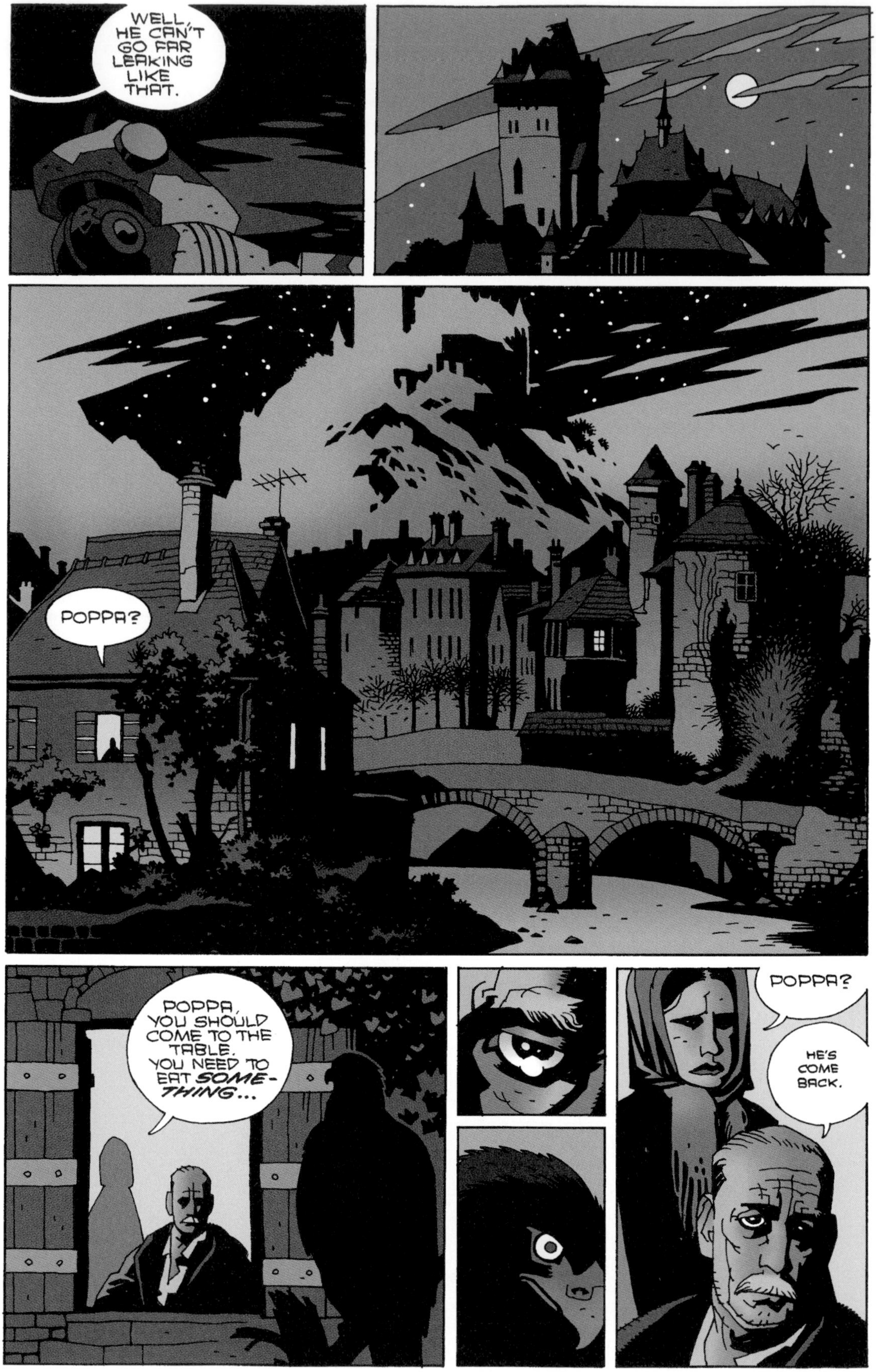
WELL, HE CAN'T GO FAR LEAKING LIKE THAT.
POPPA?
POPPA, YOU SHOULD COME TO THE TABLE. YOU NEED TO EAT SOME-THING...
POPPA?
HE'S COME BACK.

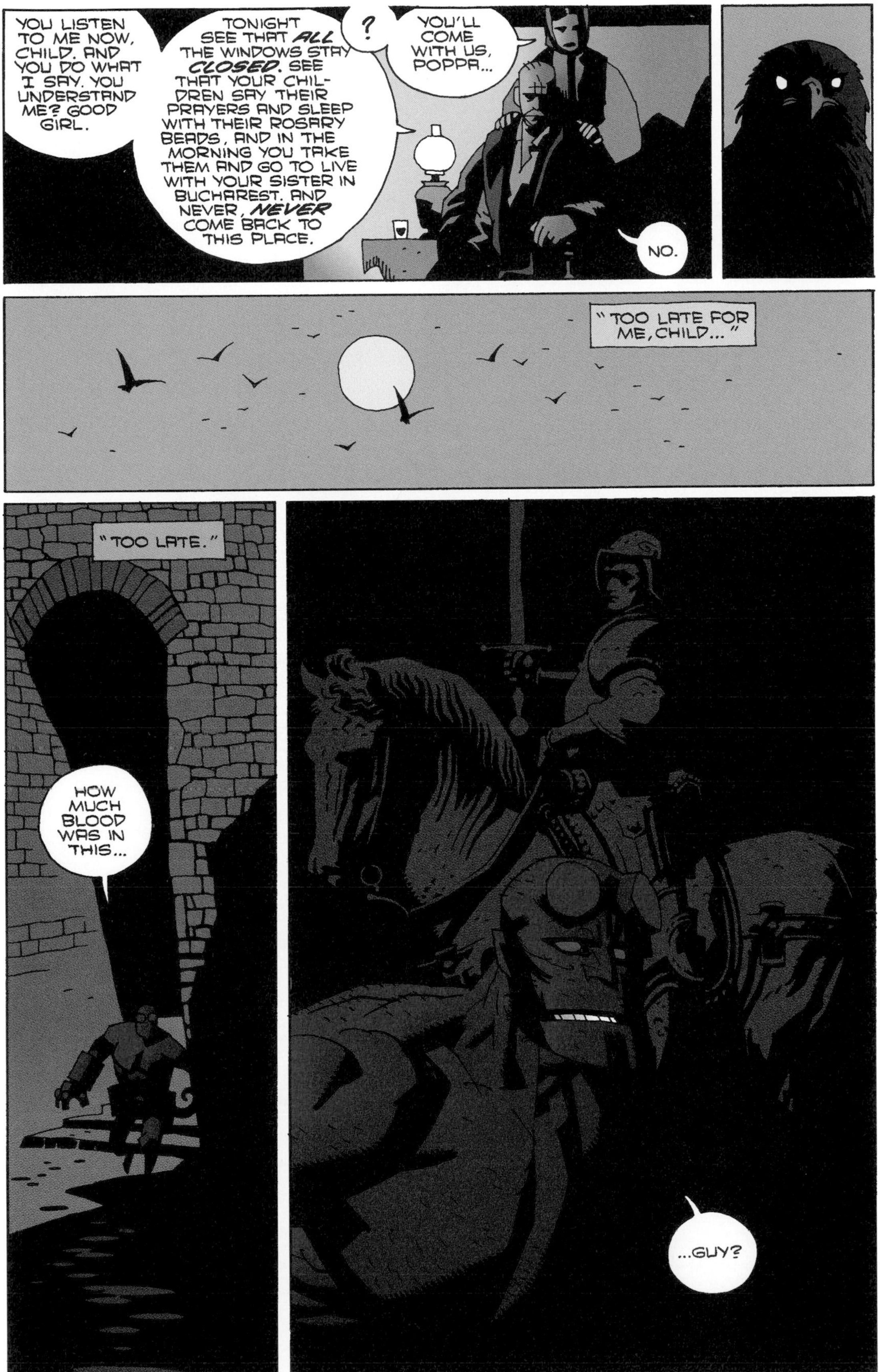
YOU LISTEN TO ME NOW, CHILD. AND YOU DO WHAT I SAY. YOU UNDERSTAND ME? GOOD GIRL.
TONIGHT SEE THAT ALL THE WINDOWS STAY CLOSED. SEE THAT YOUR CHILDREN SAY THEIR PRAYERS AND SLEEP WITH THEIR ROSARY BEADS, AND IN THE MORNING YOU TAKE THEM AND GO TO LIVE WITH YOUR SISTER IN BUCHAREST. AND NEVER, NEVER COME BACK TO THIS PLACE.
?
YOU'LL COME WITH US, POPPA...
NO.
"TOO LATE FOR ME, CHILD..."
"TOO LATE."
HOW MUCH BLOOD WAS IN THIS...
...GUY?

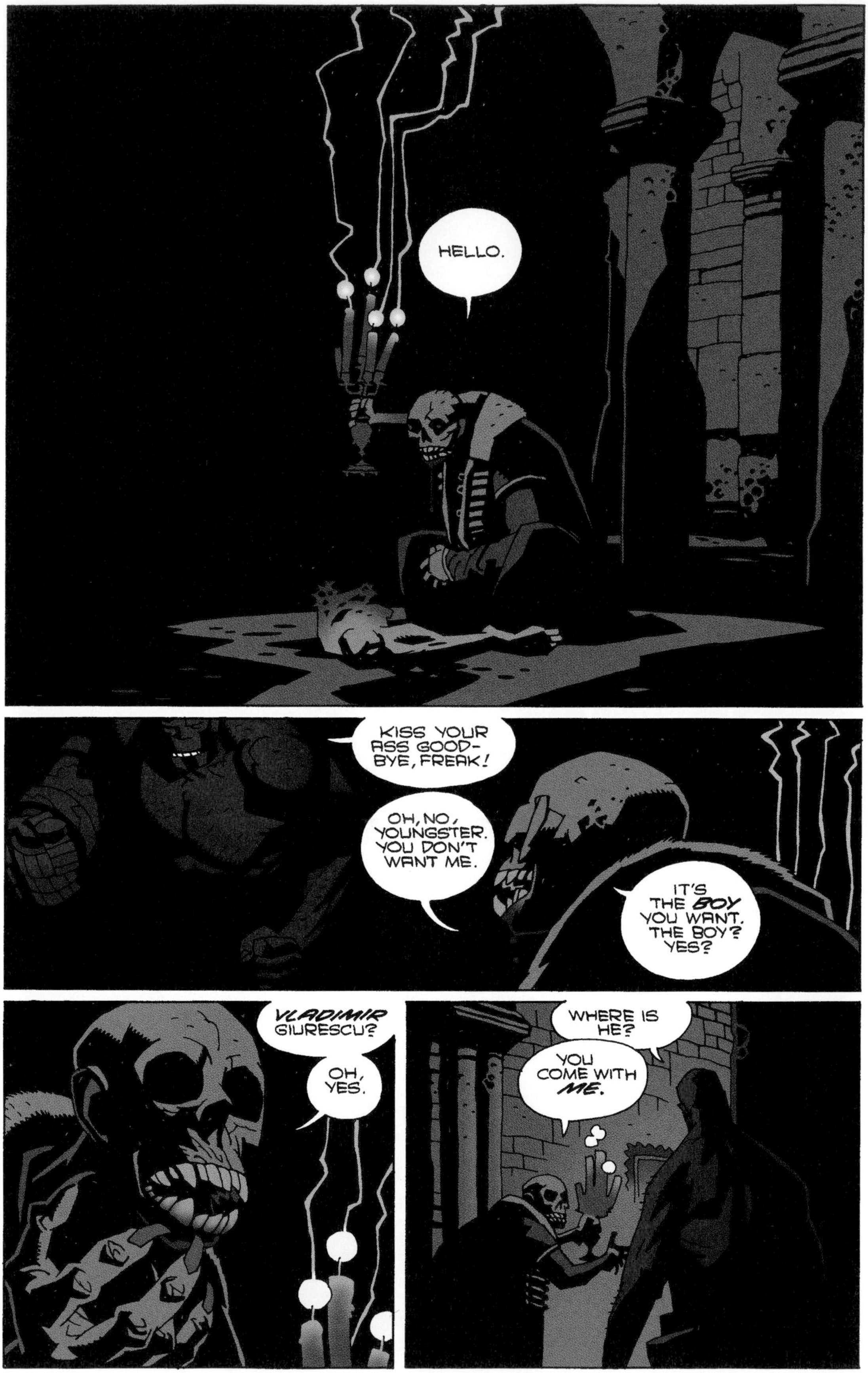
HELLO.
KISS YOUR ASS GOOD-BYE, FREAK!
OH, NO, YOUNGSTER. YOU DON'T WANT ME.
IT'S THE *BOY* YOU WANT. THE BOY? YES?
VLADIMIR GIURESCU?
OH, YES.
WHERE IS HE?
YOU COME WITH *ME.*

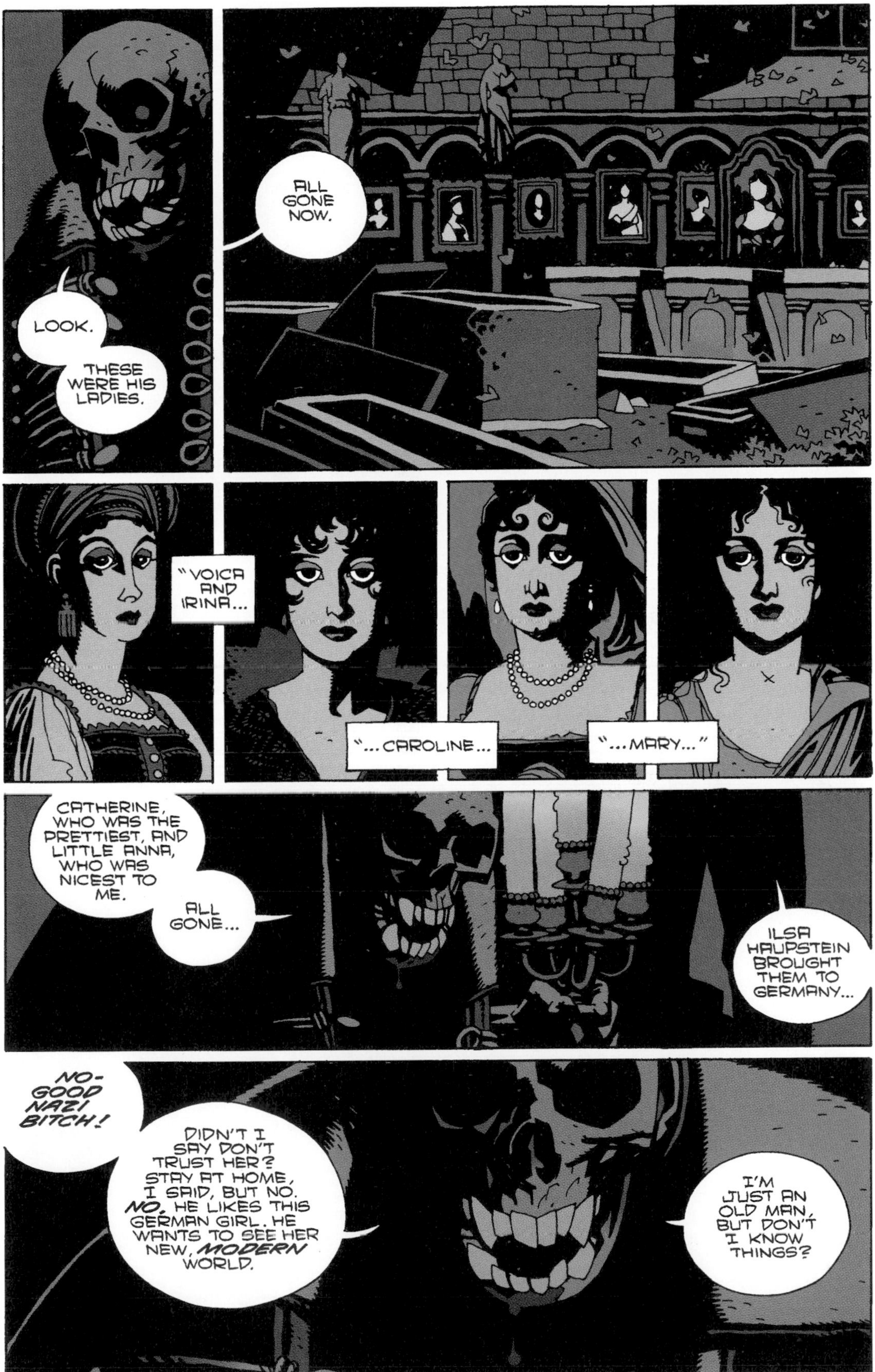

LOOK.
THESE WERE HIS LADIES.
ALL GONE NOW.
"VOICA AND IRINA...
"...CAROLINE...
"...MARY..."
CATHERINE, WHO WAS THE PRETTIEST, AND LITTLE ANNA, WHO WAS NICEST TO ME.
ALL GONE...
ILSA HAUPSTEIN BROUGHT THEM TO GERMANY...
NO-GOOD NAZI BITCH!
DIDN'T I SAY DON'T TRUST HER? STAY AT HOME, I SAID, BUT NO. NO. HE LIKES THIS GERMAN GIRL. HE WANTS TO SEE HER NEW, MODERN WORLD.
I'M JUST AN OLD MAN, BUT DON'T I KNOW THINGS?

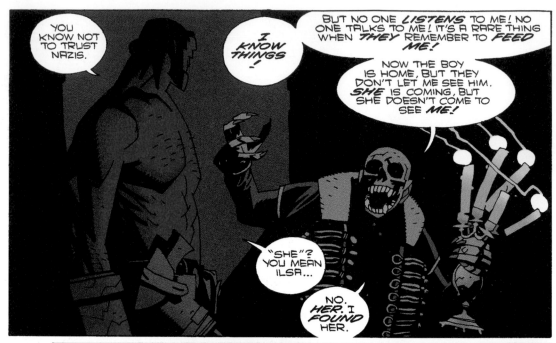

YOU KNOW NOT TO TRUST NAZIS.

I KNOW THINGS!

BUT NO ONE *LISTENS* TO ME! NO ONE TALKS TO ME! IT'S A RARE THING WHEN *THEY* REMEMBER TO *FEED ME!*

NOW THE BOY IS HOME, BUT THEY DON'T LET ME SEE HIM. *SHE* IS COMING, BUT SHE DOESN'T COME TO SEE *ME!*

"SHE"? YOU MEAN ILSA...

NO. *HER.* I *FOUND* HER.

I SAVED HER. THOSE GREEK FISHERMEN PULLED HER OUT OF THAT CAVE ALL WITHERED AND HARD, AND WOULD HAVE PUT HER, LOG-LIKE, INTO THEIR FIRE, BUT I WAS THERE AND THEY SOLD HER TO *ME.*

WHY NOT?

THEY THOUGHT THAT SHE WAS DEAD.

I KNEW BETTER.

SUCH AS SHE DOES NOT DIE AS A MAN DIES, BUT SOMETIMES SLEEPS FOR A THOUSAND YEARS...

I BROUGHT HER HERE. BATHED HER IN OX BLOOD AND MILK, HONEY AND OILS, UNTIL SHE WAS... FLEXIBLE AGAIN. BUILT FOR HER A NEW TEMPLE...

THAT WAS THE YEAR JOHN HUNYADI DROVE THE TURK OUT OF WALLACHIA.*

LONG TIME AGO.

TIME?

*1492

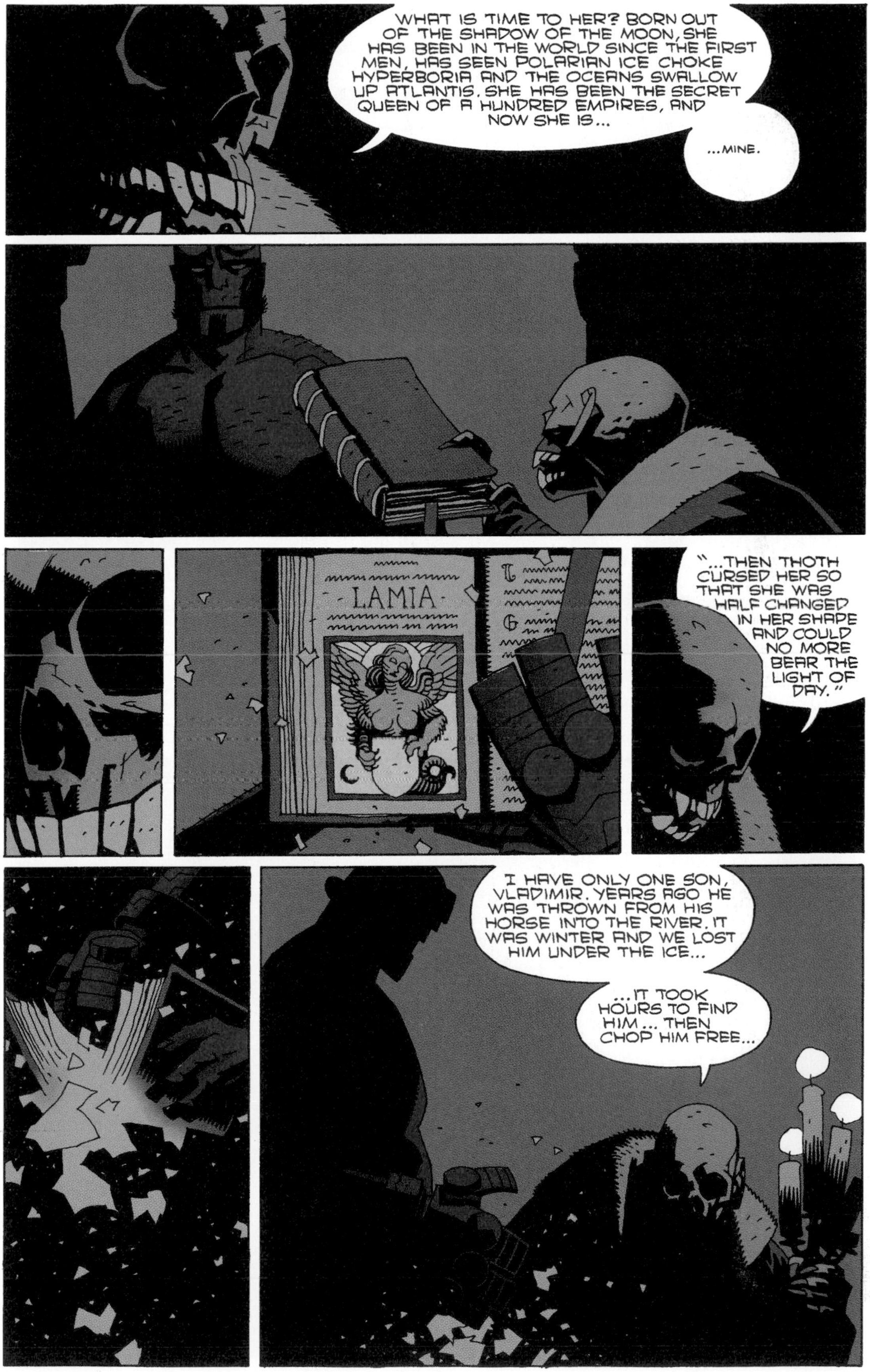

WHAT IS TIME TO HER? BORN OUT OF THE SHADOW OF THE MOON, SHE HAS BEEN IN THE WORLD SINCE THE FIRST MEN, HAS SEEN POLARIAN ICE CHOKE HYPERBORIA AND THE OCEANS SWALLOW UP ATLANTIS. SHE HAS BEEN THE SECRET QUEEN OF A HUNDRED EMPIRES, AND NOW SHE IS...
...MINE.
LAMIA
"...THEN THOTH CURSED HER SO THAT SHE WAS HALF CHANGED IN HER SHAPE AND COULD NO MORE BEAR THE LIGHT OF DAY."
I HAVE ONLY ONE SON, VLADIMIR. YEARS AGO HE WAS THROWN FROM HIS HORSE INTO THE RIVER. IT WAS WINTER AND WE LOST HIM UNDER THE ICE...
...IT TOOK HOURS TO FIND HIM... THEN CHOP HIM FREE...

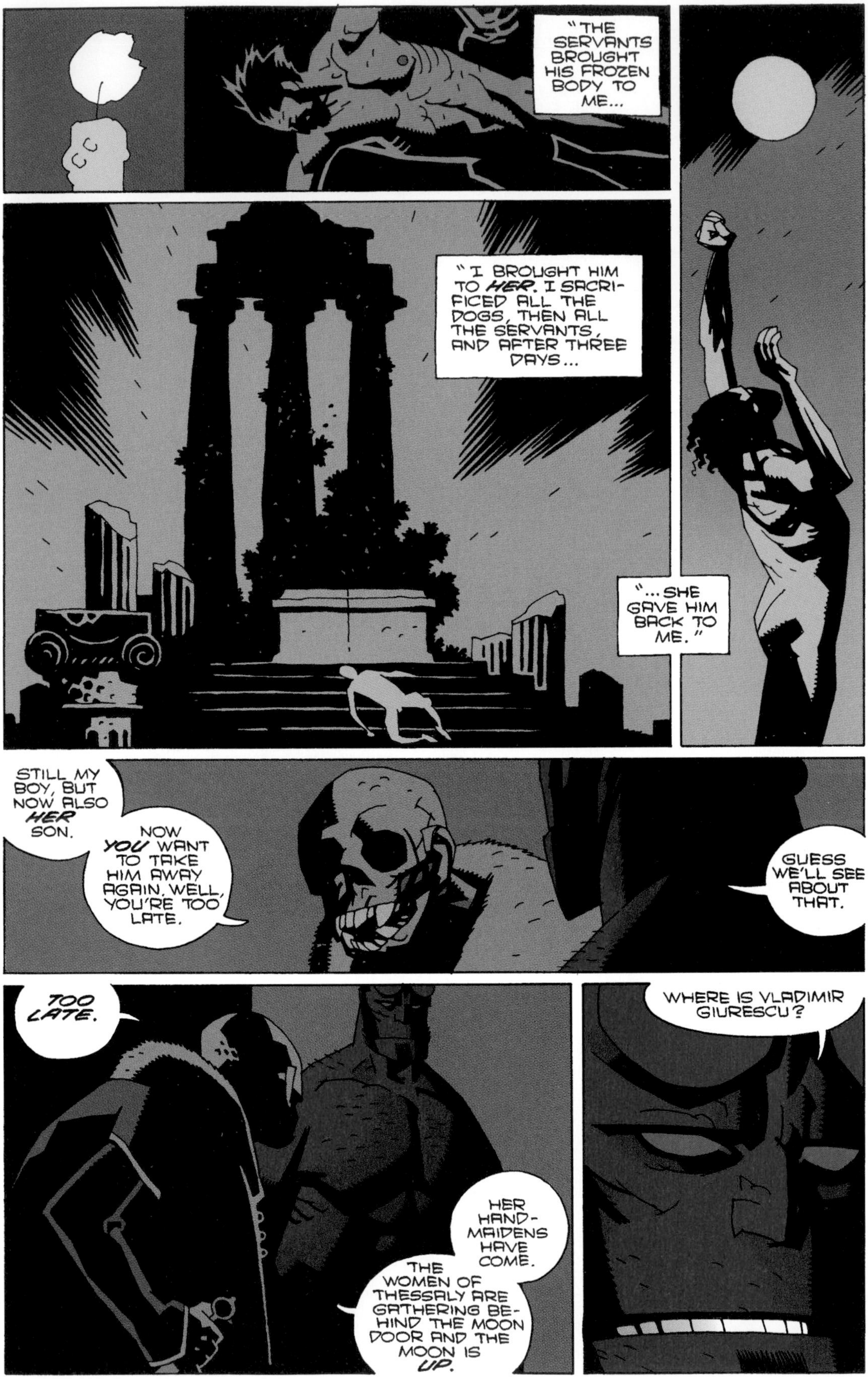
"THE SERVANTS BROUGHT HIS FROZEN BODY TO ME...
"I BROUGHT HIM TO HER. I SACRIFICED ALL THE DOGS, THEN ALL THE SERVANTS, AND AFTER THREE DAYS...
"...SHE GAVE HIM BACK TO ME."
STILL MY BOY, BUT NOW ALSO HER SON.
NOW YOU WANT TO TAKE HIM AWAY AGAIN. WELL, YOU'RE TOO LATE.
GUESS WE'LL SEE ABOUT THAT.
TOO LATE.
HER HAND-MAIDENS HAVE COME.
THE WOMEN OF THESSALY ARE GATHERING BEHIND THE MOON DOOR AND THE MOON IS UP.
WHERE IS VLADIMIR GIURESCU?

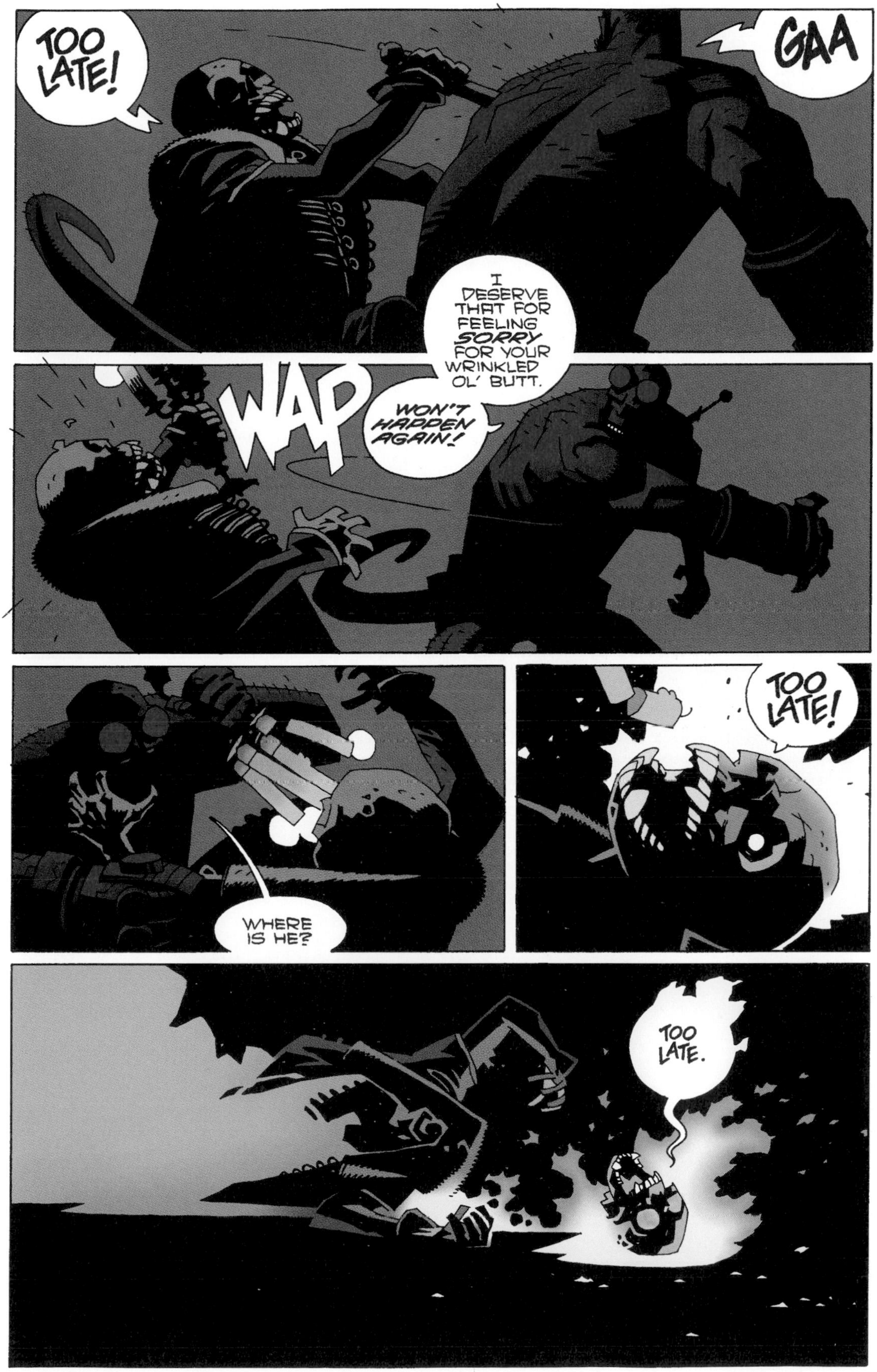
TOO LATE!
GAA
I DESERVE THAT FOR FEELING SORRY FOR YOUR WRINKLED OL' BUTT.
WAP
WON'T HAPPEN AGAIN!
WHERE IS HE?
TOO LATE!
TOO LATE.

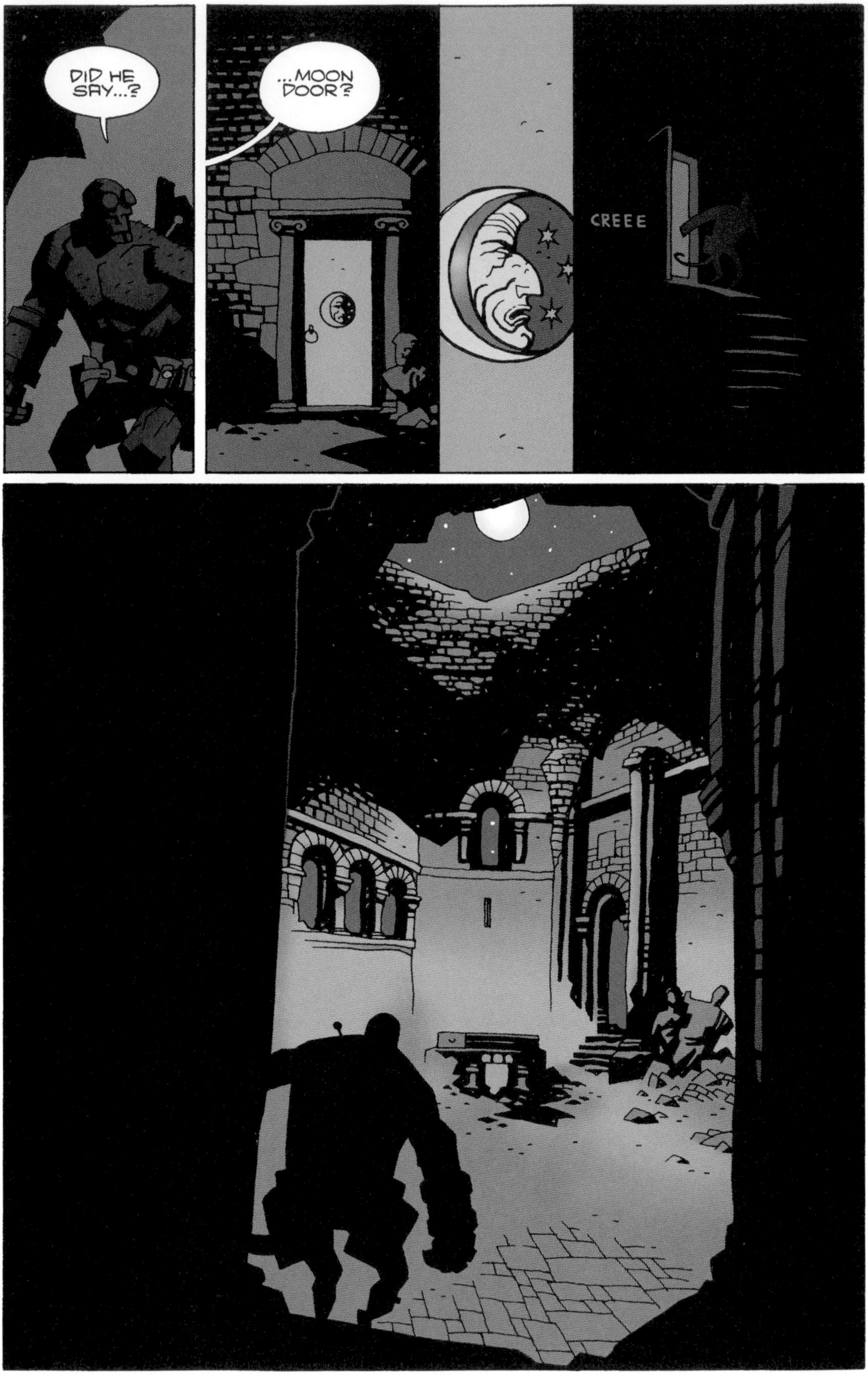
DID HE SAY...?
...MOON DOOR?
CREEE

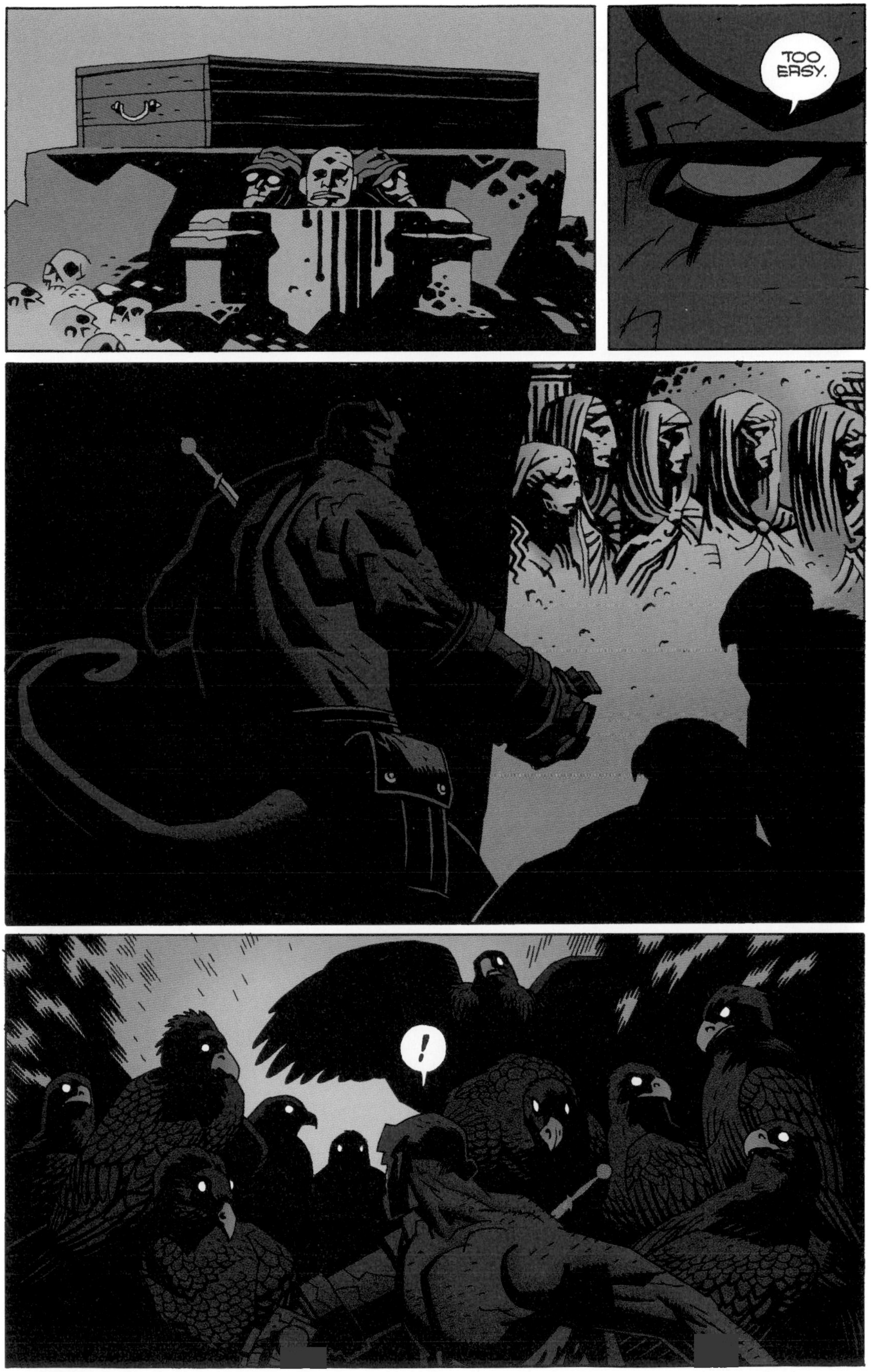
TOO EASY.
!

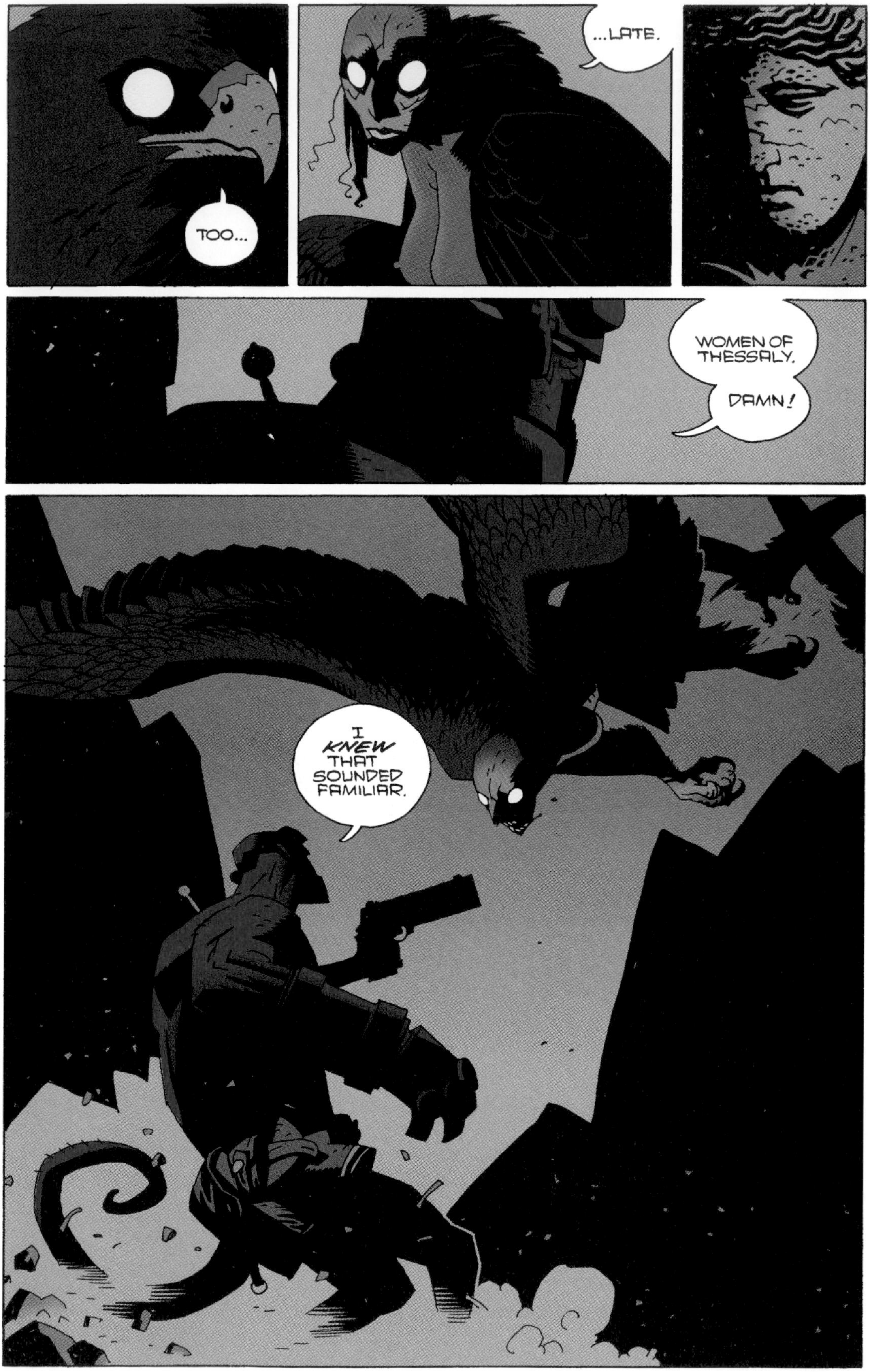
TOO...
...LATE.
WOMEN OF THESSALY.
DAMN!
I KNEW THAT SOUNDED FAMILIAR.

CHAPTER THREE

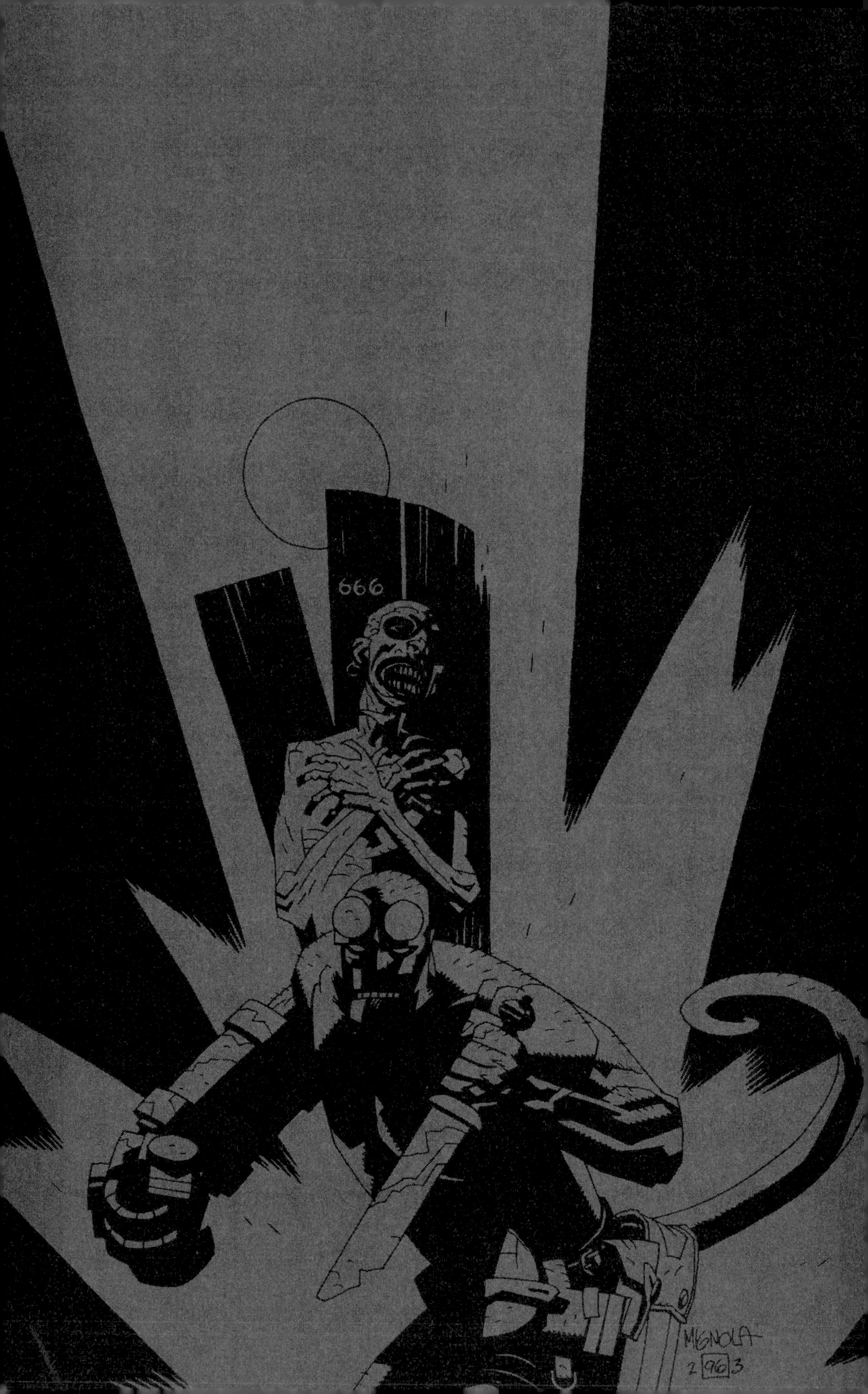
666
MIGNOLA
2 96 3

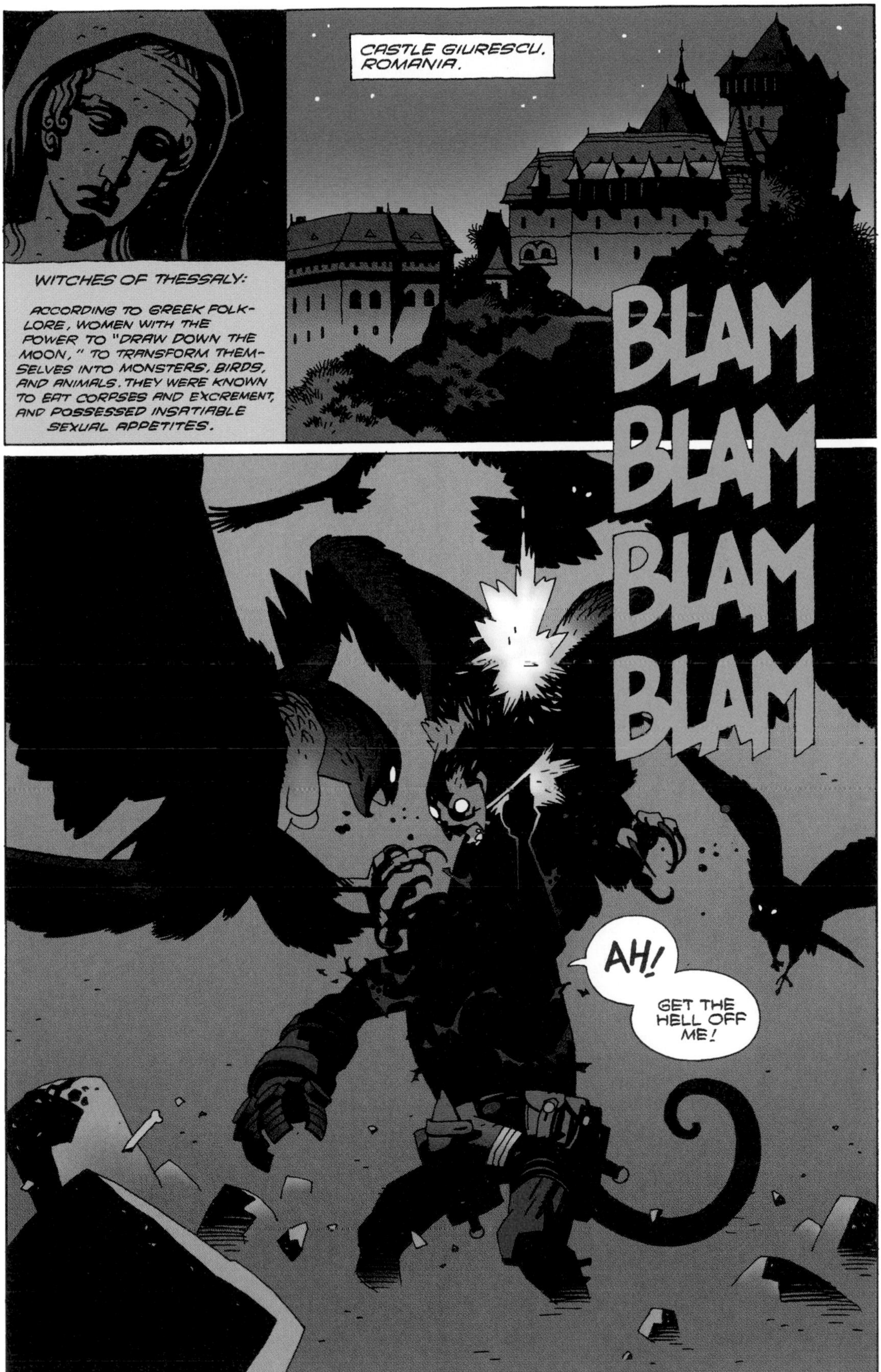
WITCHES OF THESSALY:
ACCORDING TO GREEK FOLK-LORE, WOMEN WITH THE POWER TO "DRAW DOWN THE MOON," TO TRANSFORM THEMSELVES INTO MONSTERS, BIRDS, AND ANIMALS. THEY WERE KNOWN TO EAT CORPSES AND EXCREMENT, AND POSSESSED INSATIABLE SEXUAL APPETITES.
CASTLE GIURESCU, ROMANIA.
BLAM BLAM BLAM BLAM
AH!
GET THE HELL OFF ME!

I'M NOT KIDDING!

I WILL *NOT* BE FOOD FOR BIRD WOMEN!

CLICK CLICK

WAM

YOU TOO, LADY! *BLOW!*

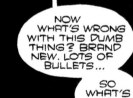

NOW WHAT'S WRONG WITH THIS DUMB THING? BRAND NEW. LOTS OF BULLETS...

SO WHAT'S THE...

CLICK CLICK

CLICK

ZING

GUH!

BLAM

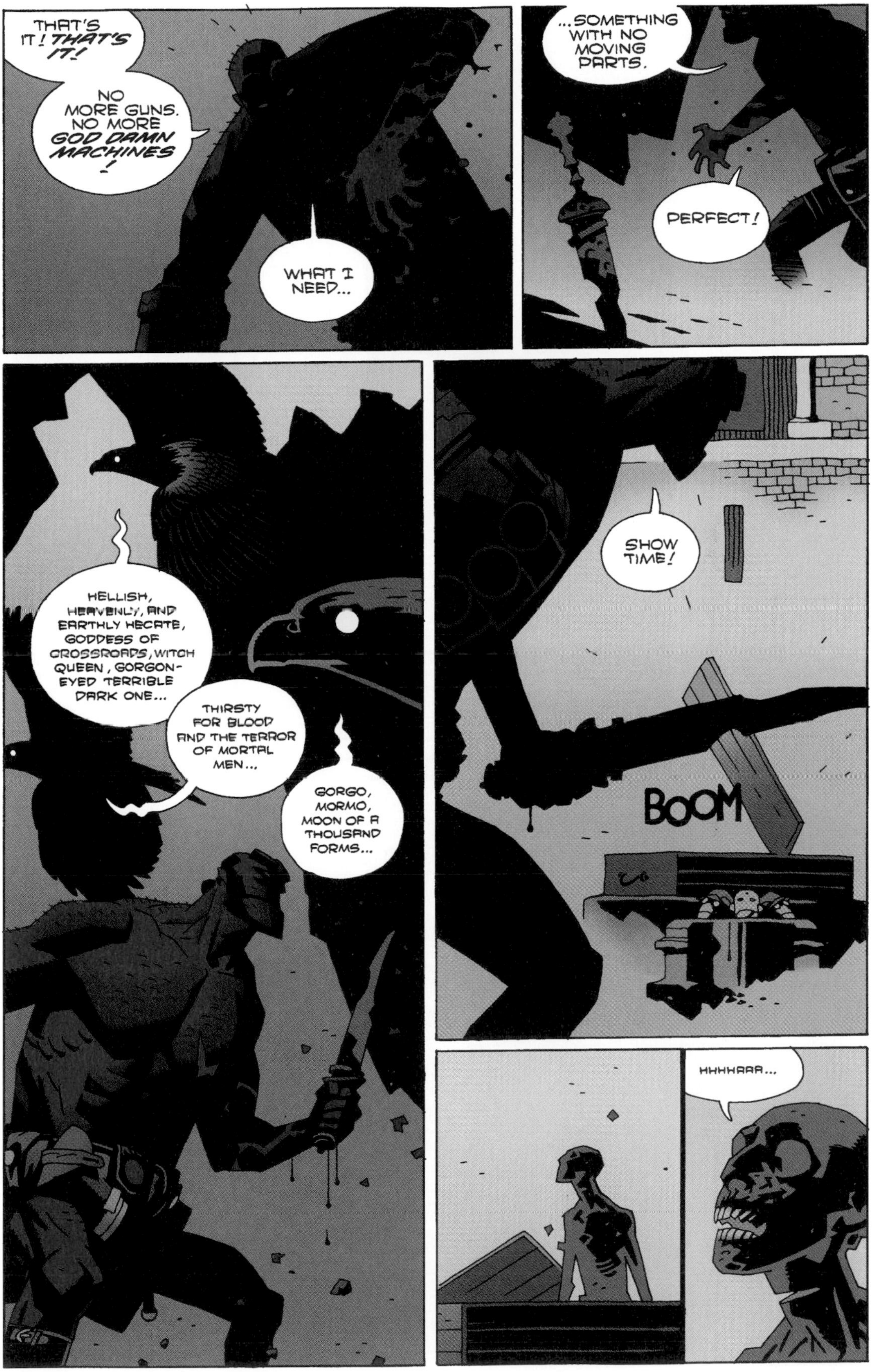
THAT'S IT! THAT'S IT!
NO MORE GUNS. NO MORE GOD DAMN MACHINES!
WHAT I NEED...
...SOMETHING WITH NO MOVING PARTS.
PERFECT!
HELLISH, HEAVENLY, AND EARTHLY HECATE, GODDESS OF CROSSROADS, WITCH QUEEN, GORGON-EYED TERRIBLE DARK ONE...
THIRSTY FOR BLOOD AND THE TERROR OF MORTAL MEN...
GORGO, MORMO, MOON OF A THOUSAND FORMS...
SHOW TIME!
BOOM
HHHHAAA...

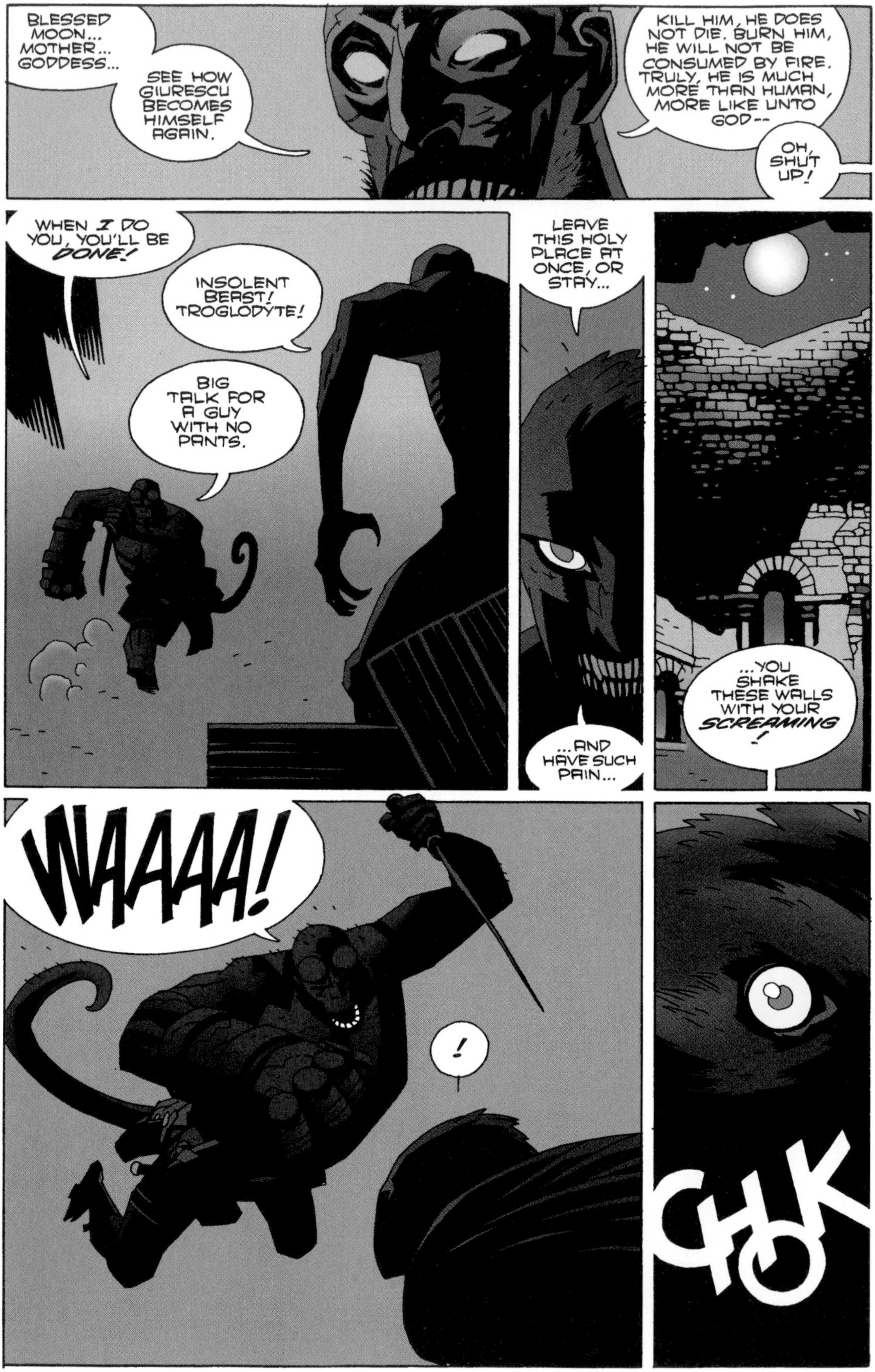
BLESSED MOON... MOTHER... GODDESS...
SEE HOW GIURESCU BECOMES HIMSELF AGAIN.
KILL HIM, HE DOES NOT DIE. BURN HIM, HE WILL NOT BE CONSUMED BY FIRE. TRULY, HE IS MUCH MORE THAN HUMAN, MORE LIKE UNTO GOD--
OH, SHUT UP!
WHEN I DO YOU, YOU'LL BE DONE!
INSOLENT BEAST! TROGLODYTE!
BIG TALK FOR A GUY WITH NO PANTS.
LEAVE THIS HOLY PLACE AT ONCE, OR STAY...
...AND HAVE SUCH PAIN...
...YOU SHAKE THESE WALLS WITH YOUR SCREAMING!
WAAAAA!
!
CHUK

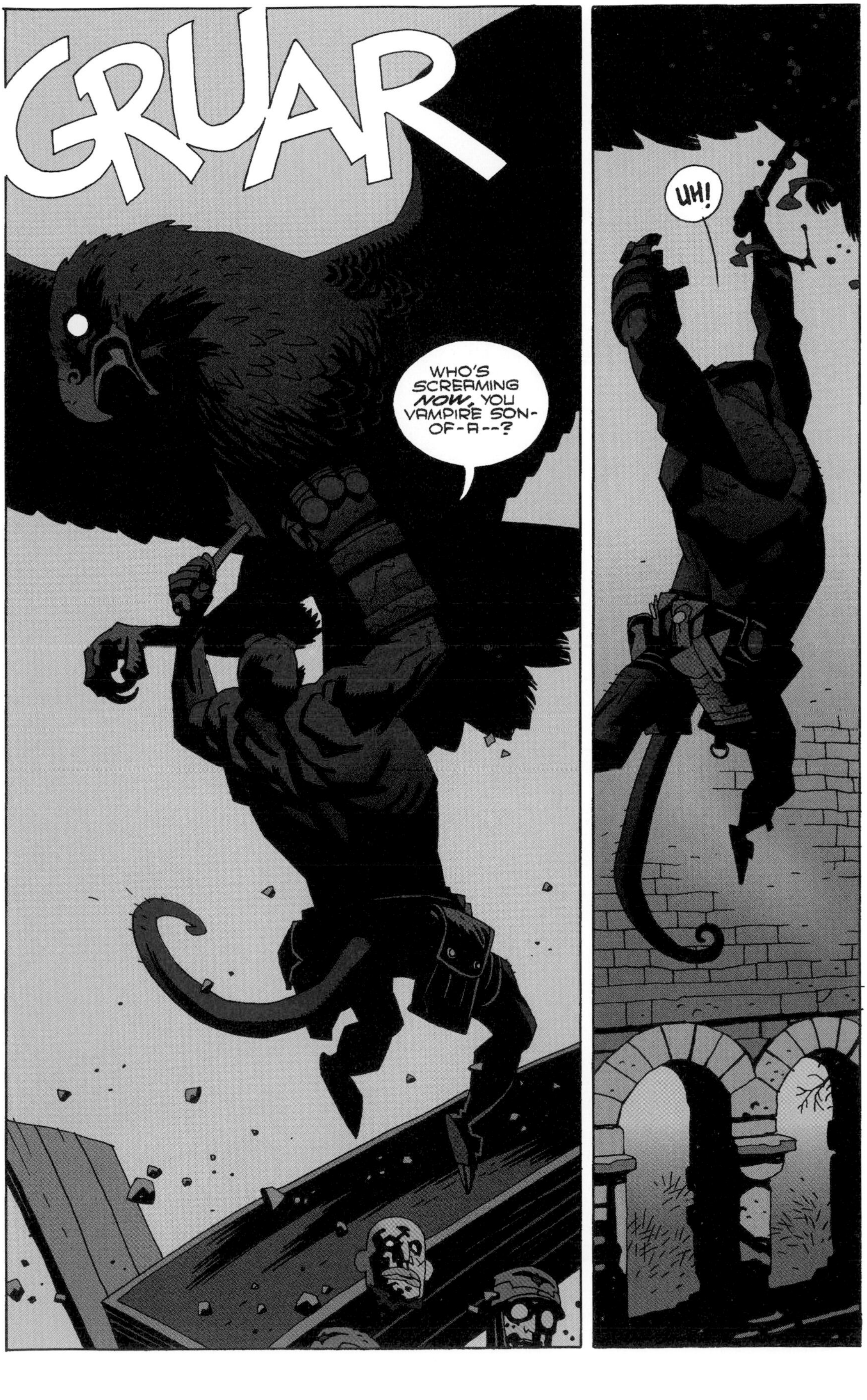
GRUAR
WHO'S SCREAMING NOW, YOU VAMPIRE SON-OF-A--?
UH!

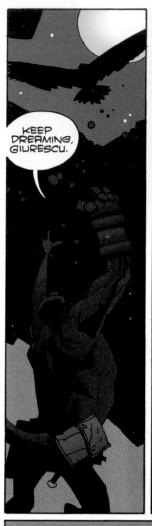

KEEP
DREAMING,
GIURESCU.

YOU'RE
GETTING
AWAY?

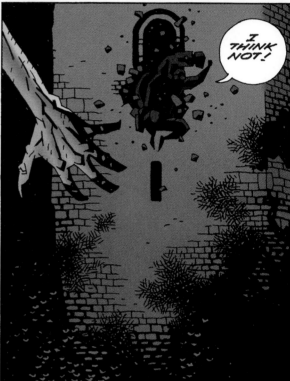

I
THINK
NOT!

KRAK

JEEZ!

GOT
TO GIVE
YOU CREDIT
FOR TRY-
ING.

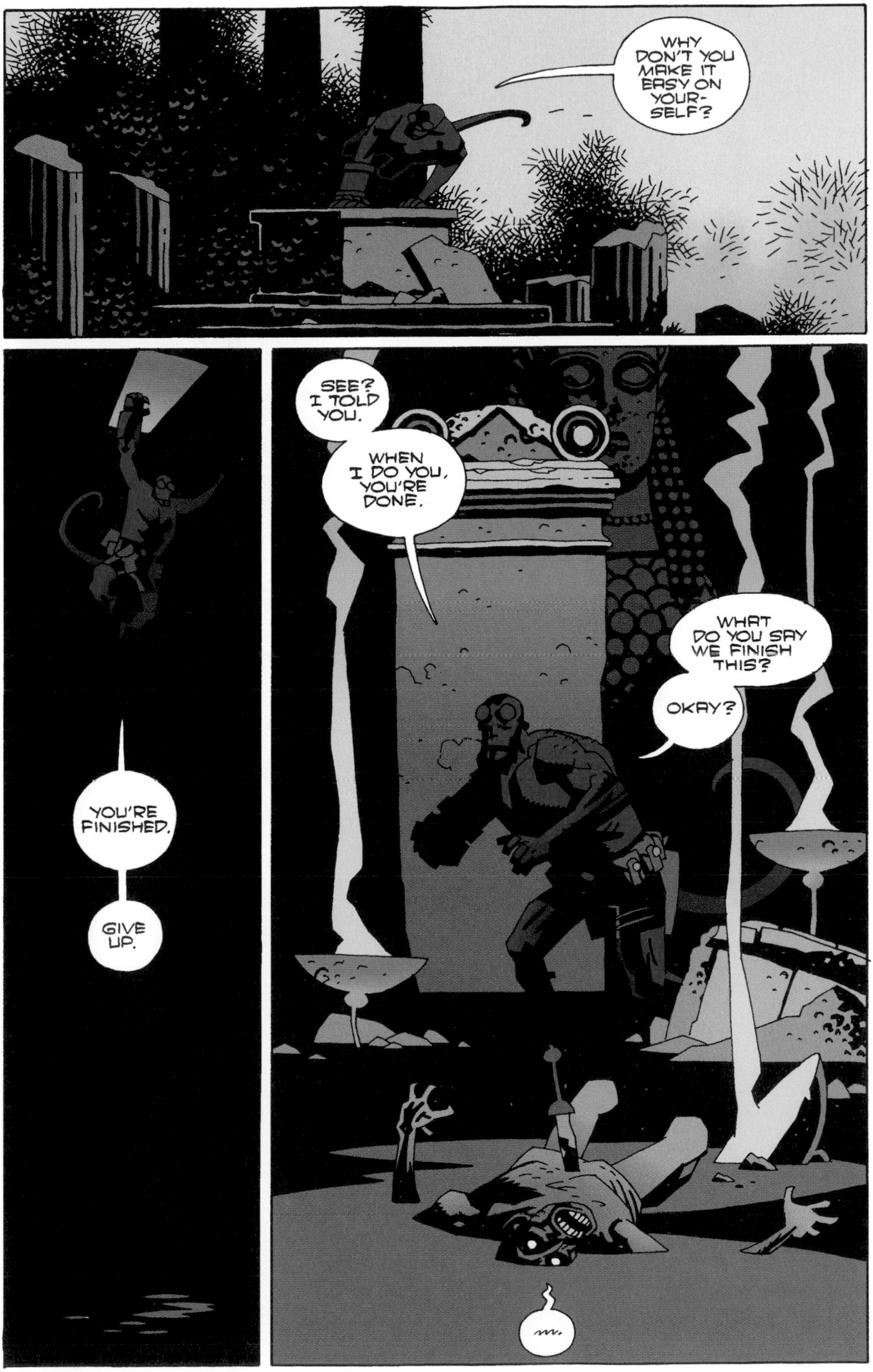
WHY DON'T YOU MAKE IT EASY ON YOUR-SELF?
YOU'RE FINISHED.
GIVE UP.
SEE? I TOLD YOU.
WHEN I DO YOU, YOU'RE DONE.
WHAT DO YOU SAY WE FINISH THIS?
OKAY?
...nn.

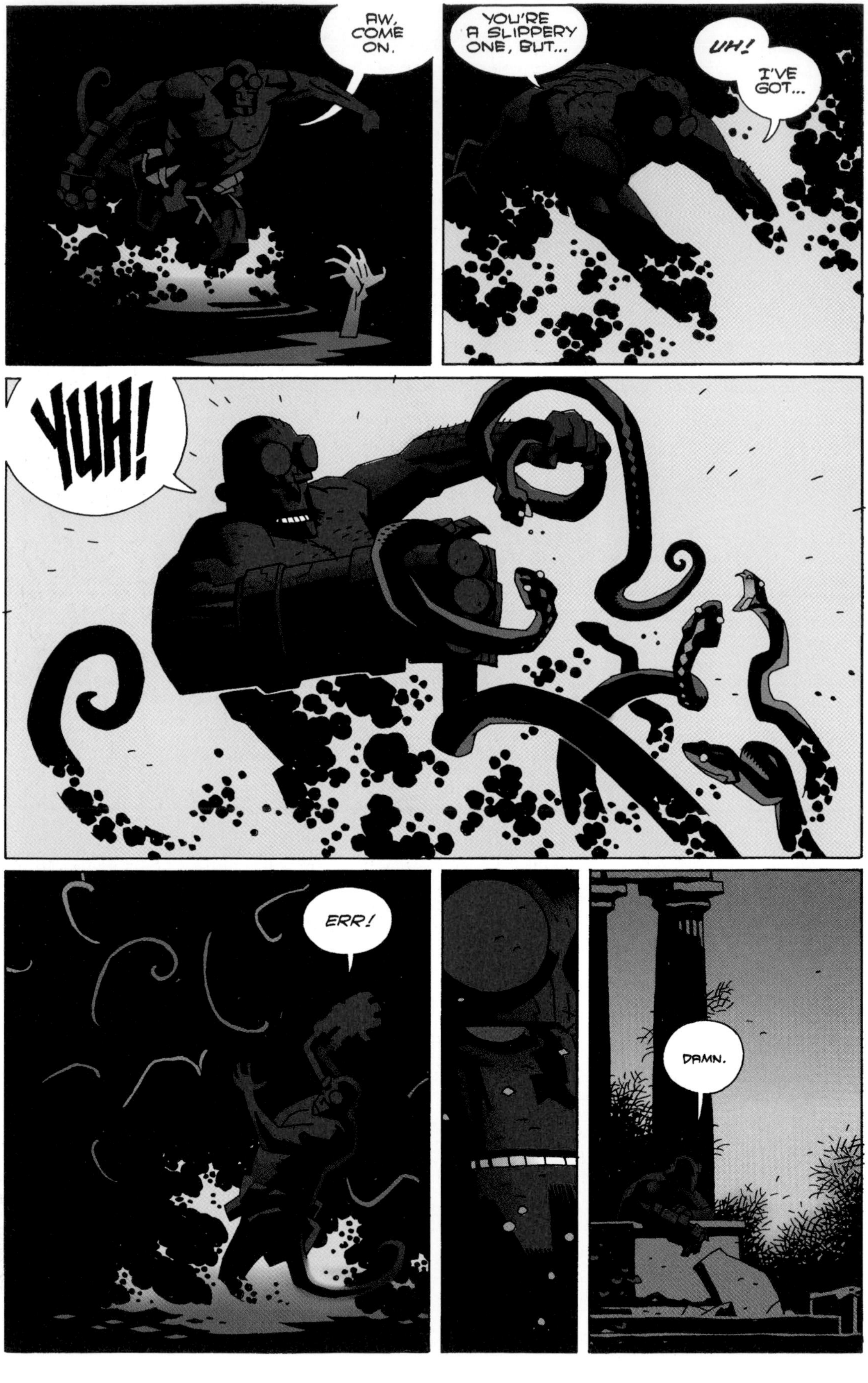
AW, COME ON.
YOU'RE A SLIPPERY ONE, BUT...
UH!
I'VE GOT...
YUH!
ERR!
DAMN.

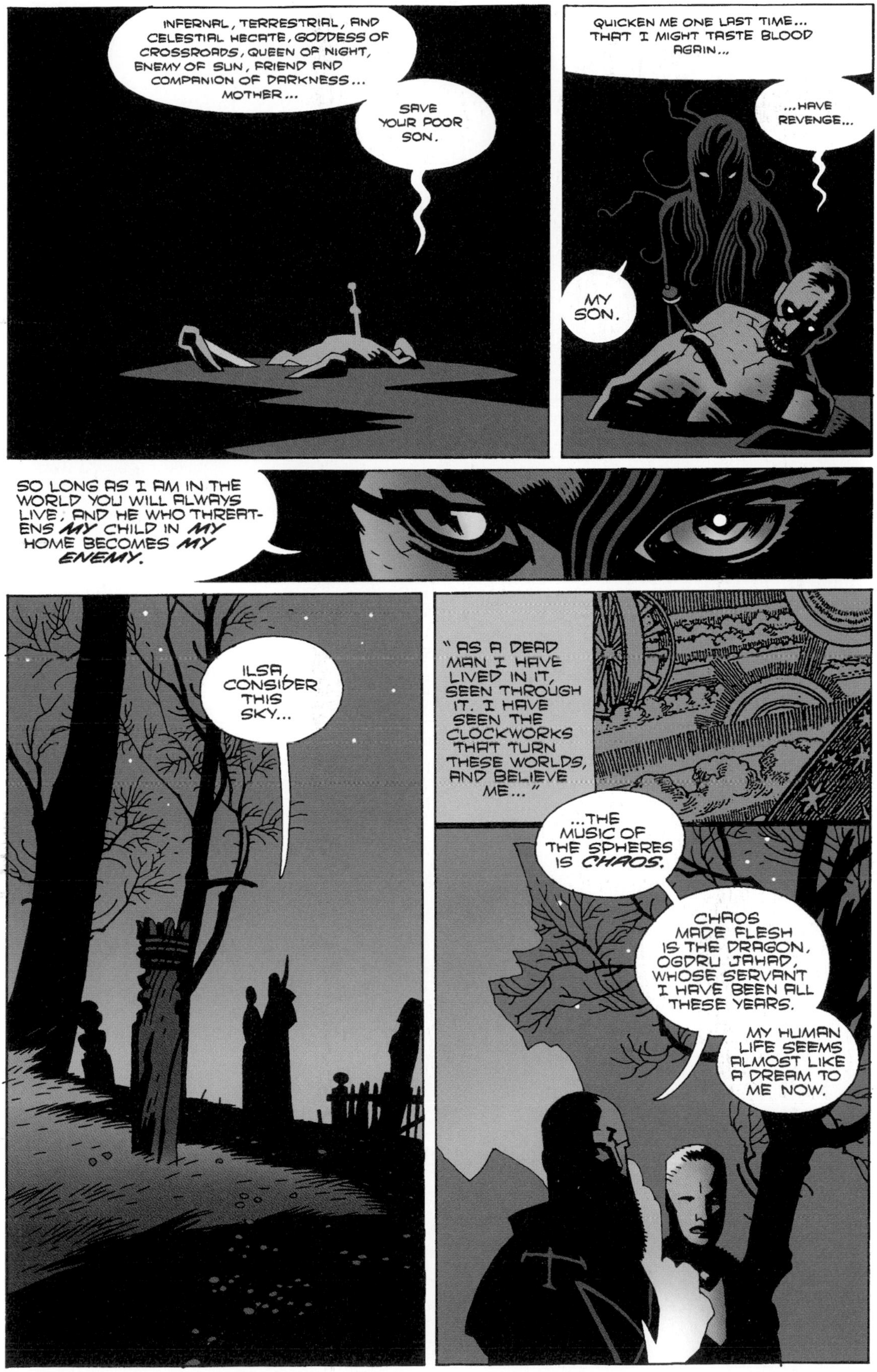

INFERNAL, TERRESTRIAL, AND CELESTIAL HECATE, GODDESS OF CROSSROADS, QUEEN OF NIGHT, ENEMY OF SUN, FRIEND AND COMPANION OF DARKNESS... MOTHER...
SAVE YOUR POOR SON.
QUICKEN ME ONE LAST TIME... THAT I MIGHT TASTE BLOOD AGAIN...
...HAVE REVENGE...
MY SON.
SO LONG AS I AM IN THE WORLD YOU WILL ALWAYS LIVE, AND HE WHO THREATENS MY CHILD IN MY HOME BECOMES MY ENEMY.
ILSA, CONSIDER THIS SKY...
"AS A DEAD MAN I HAVE LIVED IN IT, SEEN THROUGH IT. I HAVE SEEN THE CLOCKWORKS THAT TURN THESE WORLDS, AND BELIEVE ME..."
...THE MUSIC OF THE SPHERES IS CHAOS.
CHAOS MADE FLESH IS THE DRAGON, OGDRU JAHAD, WHOSE SERVANT I HAVE BEEN ALL THESE YEARS.
MY HUMAN LIFE SEEMS ALMOST LIKE A DREAM TO ME NOW.

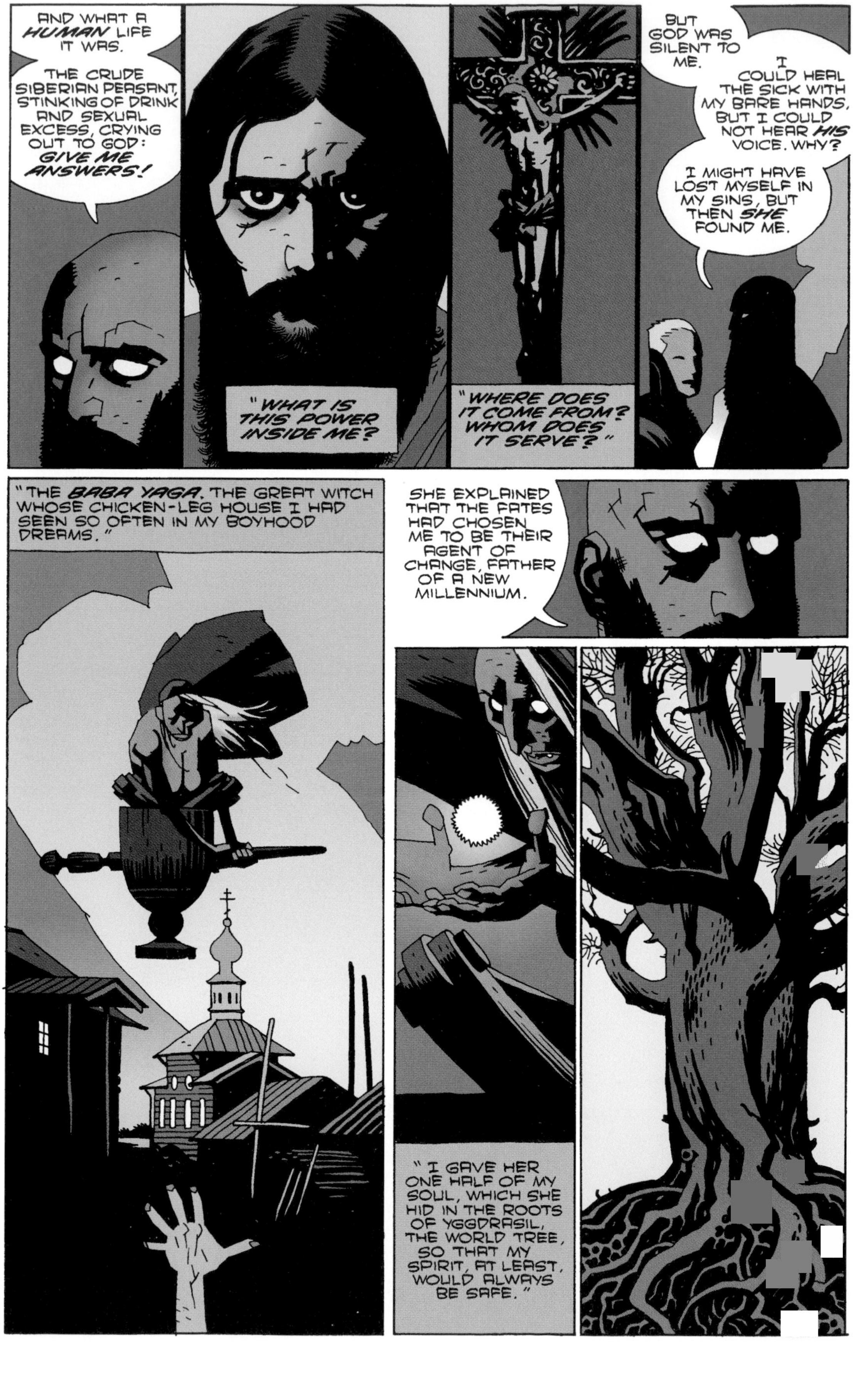
AND WHAT A HUMAN LIFE IT WAS.
THE CRUDE SIBERIAN PEASANT, STINKING OF DRINK AND SEXUAL EXCESS, CRYING OUT TO GOD: GIVE ME ANSWERS!
"WHAT IS THIS POWER INSIDE ME?
"WHERE DOES IT COME FROM? WHOM DOES IT SERVE?"
BUT GOD WAS SILENT TO ME.
I COULD HEAL THE SICK WITH MY BARE HANDS, BUT I COULD NOT HEAR HIS VOICE. WHY?
I MIGHT HAVE LOST MYSELF IN MY SINS, BUT THEN SHE FOUND ME.
"THE BABA YAGA. THE GREAT WITCH WHOSE CHICKEN-LEG HOUSE I HAD SEEN SO OFTEN IN MY BOYHOOD DREAMS."
SHE EXPLAINED THAT THE FATES HAD CHOSEN ME TO BE THEIR AGENT OF CHANGE, FATHER OF A NEW MILLENNIUM.
"I GAVE HER ONE HALF OF MY SOUL, WHICH SHE HID IN THE ROOTS OF YGGDRASIL, THE WORLD TREE, SO THAT MY SPIRIT, AT LEAST, WOULD ALWAYS BE SAFE."

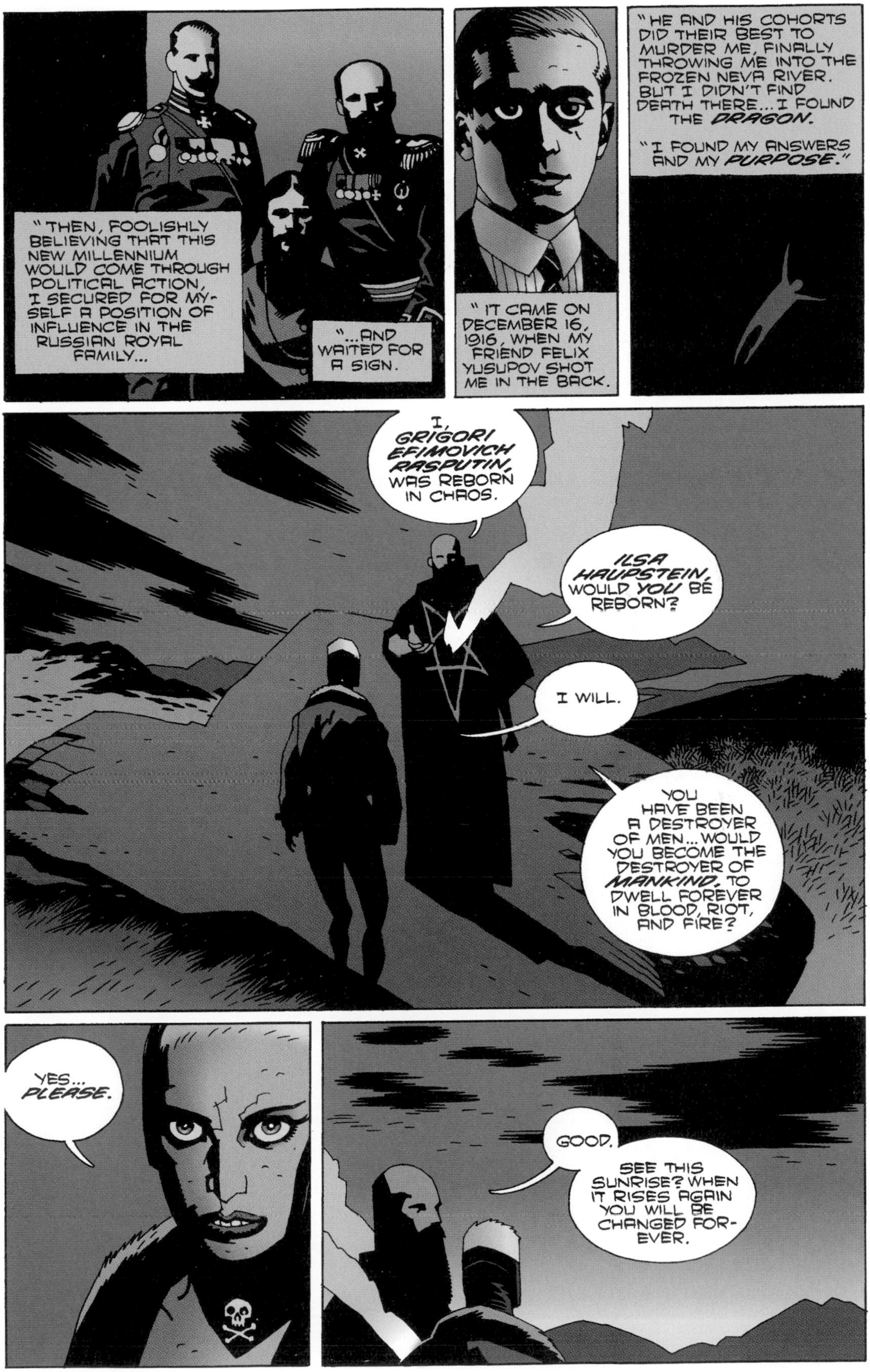
"THEN, FOOLISHLY BELIEVING THAT THIS NEW MILLENNIUM WOULD COME THROUGH POLITICAL ACTION, I SECURED FOR MYSELF A POSITION OF INFLUENCE IN THE RUSSIAN ROYAL FAMILY...
"...AND WAITED FOR A SIGN.
"IT CAME ON DECEMBER 16, 1916, WHEN MY FRIEND FELIX YUSUPOV SHOT ME IN THE BACK.
"HE AND HIS COHORTS DID THEIR BEST TO MURDER ME, FINALLY THROWING ME INTO THE FROZEN NEVA RIVER. BUT I DIDN'T FIND DEATH THERE... I FOUND THE DRAGON.
"I FOUND MY ANSWERS AND MY PURPOSE."
I, GRIGORI EFIMOVICH RASPUTIN, WAS REBORN IN CHAOS.
ILSA HAUPSTEIN, WOULD YOU BE REBORN?
I WILL.
YOU HAVE BEEN A DESTROYER OF MEN... WOULD YOU BECOME THE DESTROYER OF MANKIND, TO DWELL FOREVER IN BLOOD, RIOT, AND FIRE?
YES... PLEASE.
GOOD.
SEE THIS SUNRISE? WHEN IT RISES AGAIN YOU WILL BE CHANGED FOREVER.

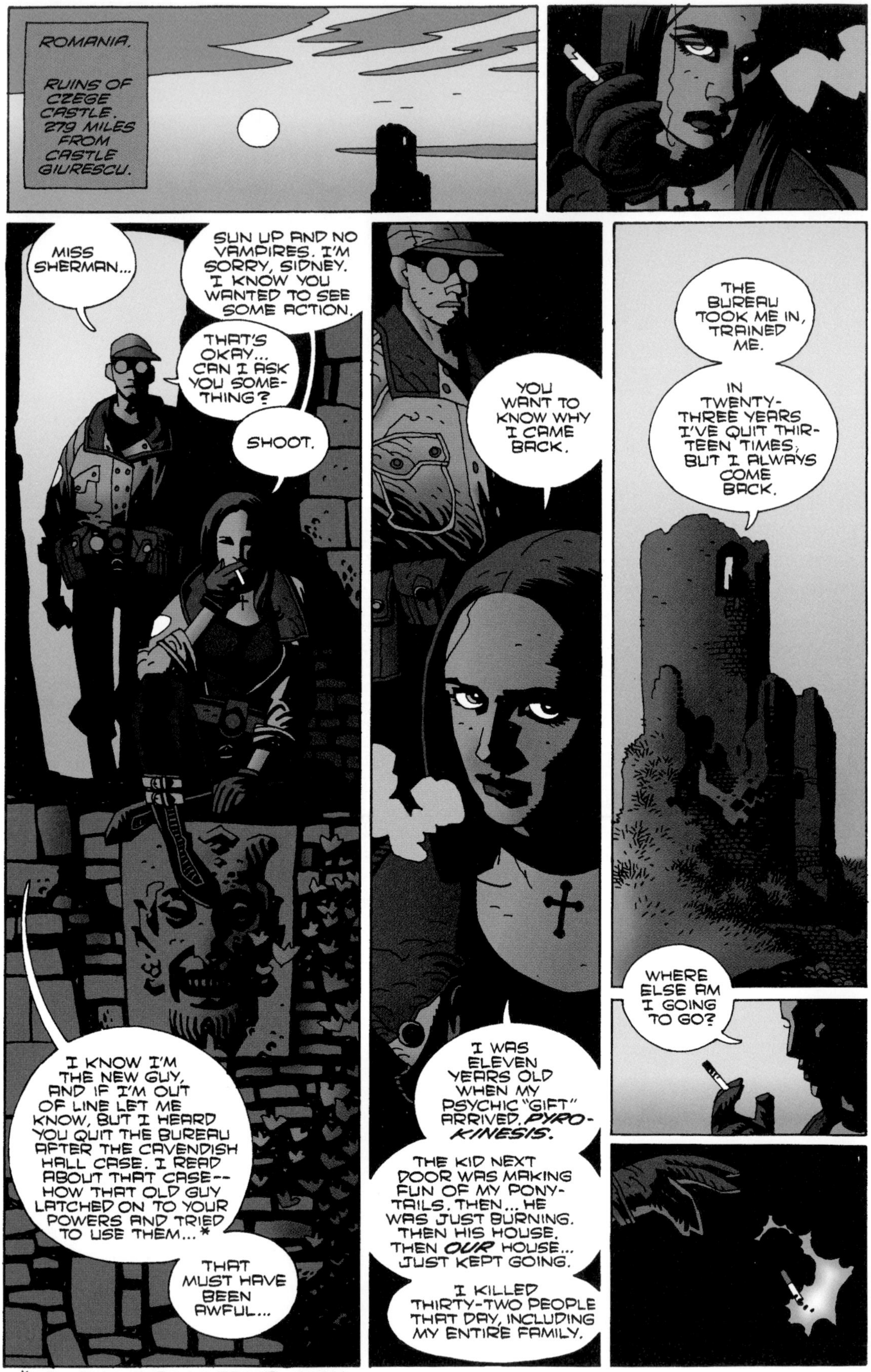
ROMANIA.
RUINS OF CZEGE CASTLE. 279 MILES FROM CASTLE GIURESCU.
MISS SHERMAN...
SUN UP AND NO VAMPIRES. I'M SORRY, SIDNEY. I KNOW YOU WANTED TO SEE SOME ACTION.
THAT'S OKAY... CAN I ASK YOU SOME-THING?
SHOOT.
I KNOW I'M THE NEW GUY, AND IF I'M OUT OF LINE LET ME KNOW, BUT I HEARD YOU QUIT THE BUREAU AFTER THE CAVENDISH HALL CASE. I READ ABOUT THAT CASE-- HOW THAT OLD GUY LATCHED ON TO YOUR POWERS AND TRIED TO USE THEM...*
THAT MUST HAVE BEEN AWFUL...
YOU WANT TO KNOW WHY I CAME BACK.
I WAS ELEVEN YEARS OLD WHEN MY PSYCHIC "GIFT" ARRIVED. *PYRO-KINESIS.*
THE KID NEXT DOOR WAS MAKING FUN OF MY PONY-TAILS. THEN... HE WAS JUST BURNING. THEN HIS HOUSE. THEN *OUR* HOUSE... JUST KEPT GOING.
I KILLED THIRTY-TWO PEOPLE THAT DAY, INCLUDING MY ENTIRE FAMILY.
THE BUREAU TOOK ME IN, TRAINED ME.
IN TWENTY-THREE YEARS I'VE QUIT THIR-TEEN TIMES, BUT I ALWAYS COME BACK.
WHERE ELSE AM I GOING TO GO?

***HELLBOY: SEED OF DESTRUCTION**

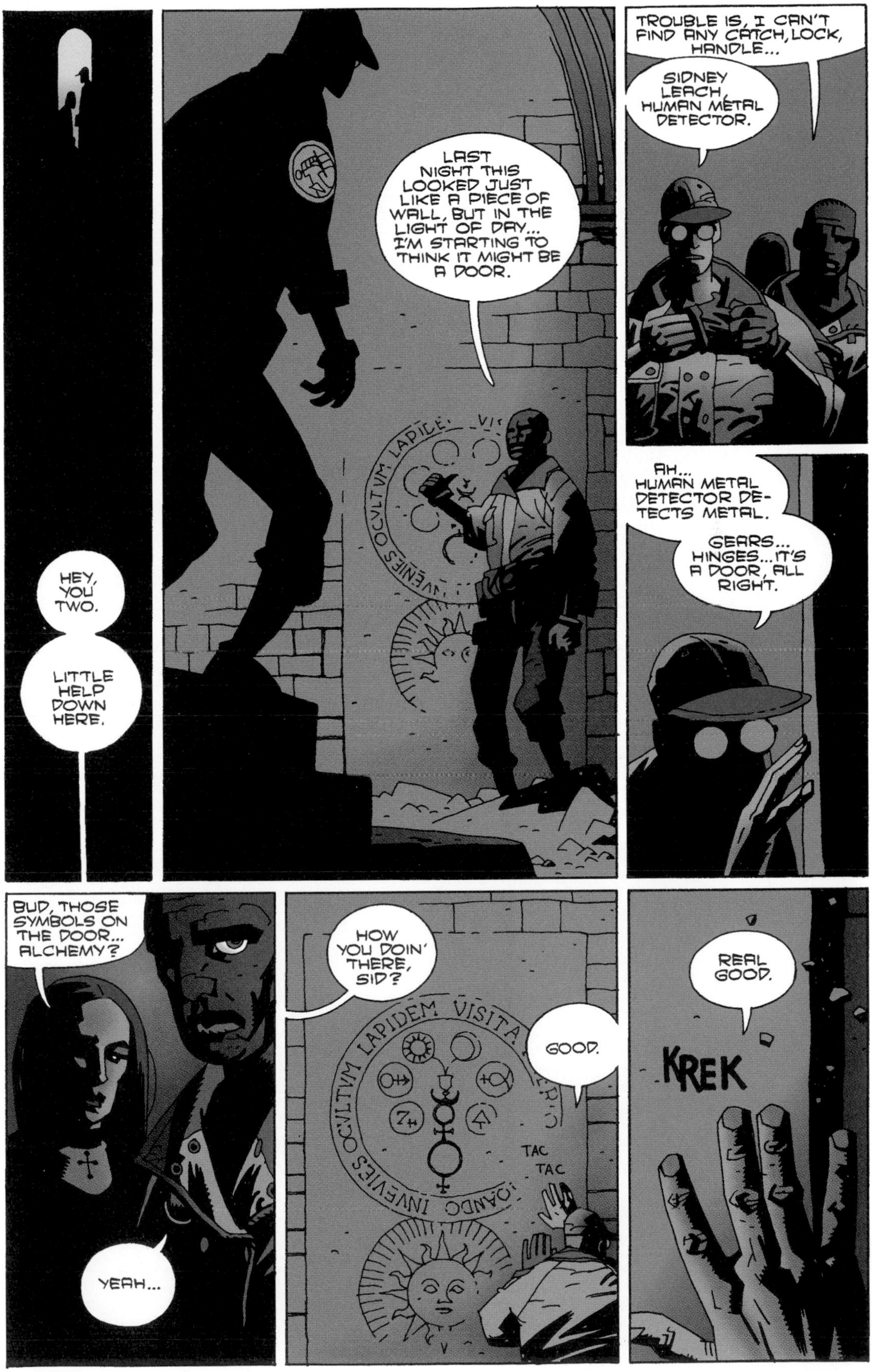

LAST NIGHT THIS LOOKED JUST LIKE A PIECE OF WALL, BUT IN THE LIGHT OF DAY... I'M STARTING TO THINK IT MIGHT BE A DOOR.
TROUBLE IS, I CAN'T FIND ANY CATCH, LOCK, HANDLE...
SIDNEY LEACH, HUMAN METAL DETECTOR.
AH... HUMAN METAL DETECTOR DETECTS METAL.
GEARS... HINGES... IT'S A DOOR, ALL RIGHT.
HEY, YOU TWO.
LITTLE HELP DOWN HERE.
BUD, THOSE SYMBOLS ON THE DOOR... ALCHEMY?
YEAH...
HOW YOU DOIN' THERE, SID?
GOOD.
TAC
TAC
REAL GOOD.
KREK

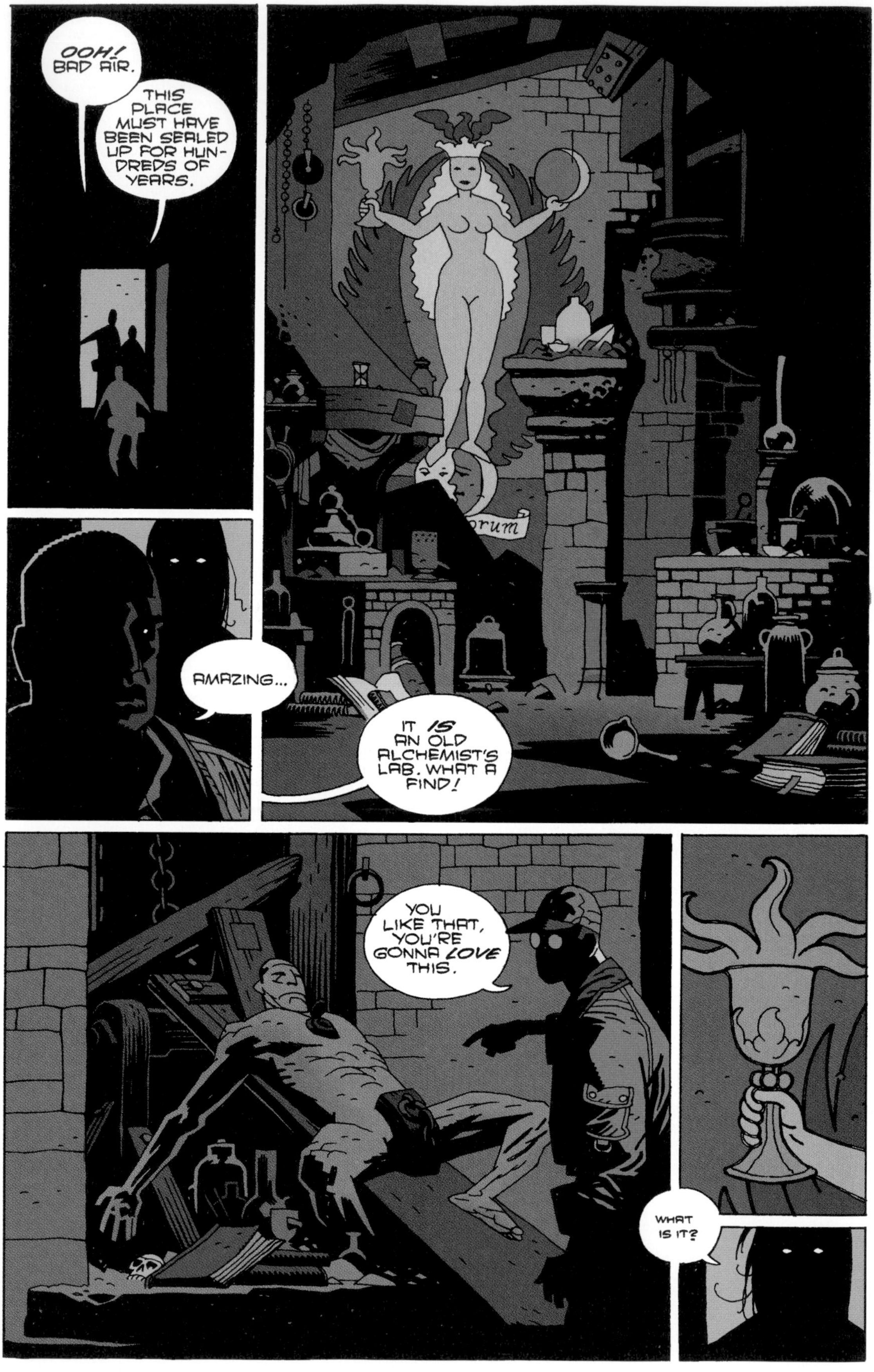
OOH! BAD AIR.
THIS PLACE MUST HAVE BEEN SEALED UP FOR HUNDREDS OF YEARS.
orum
AMAZING...
IT *IS* AN OLD ALCHEMIST'S LAB. WHAT A FIND!
YOU LIKE THAT, YOU'RE GONNA *LOVE* THIS.
WHAT IS IT?

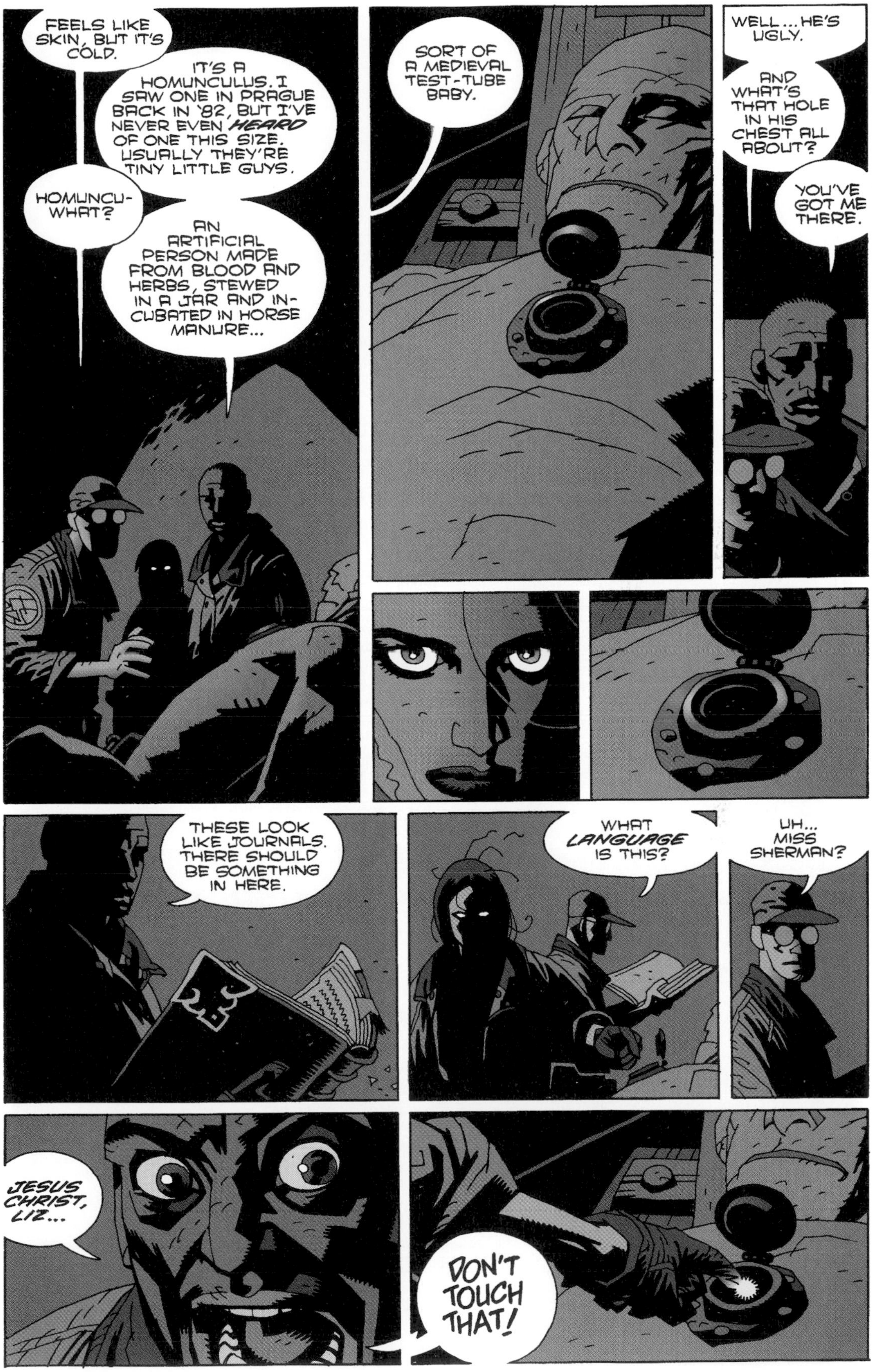
FEELS LIKE SKIN, BUT IT'S COLD.
IT'S A HOMUNCULUS. I SAW ONE IN PRAGUE BACK IN '82, BUT I'VE NEVER EVEN *HEARD* OF ONE THIS SIZE. USUALLY THEY'RE TINY LITTLE GUYS.
HOMUNCU-WHAT?
AN ARTIFICIAL PERSON MADE FROM BLOOD AND HERBS, STEWED IN A JAR AND IN-CUBATED IN HORSE MANURE...
SORT OF A MEDIEVAL TEST-TUBE BABY.
WELL... HE'S UGLY.
AND WHAT'S THAT HOLE IN HIS CHEST ALL ABOUT?
YOU'VE GOT ME THERE.
THESE LOOK LIKE JOURNALS. THERE SHOULD BE SOMETHING IN HERE.
WHAT *LANGUAGE* IS THIS?
UH... MISS SHERMAN?
JESUS CHRIST, LIZ...
DON'T TOUCH THAT!

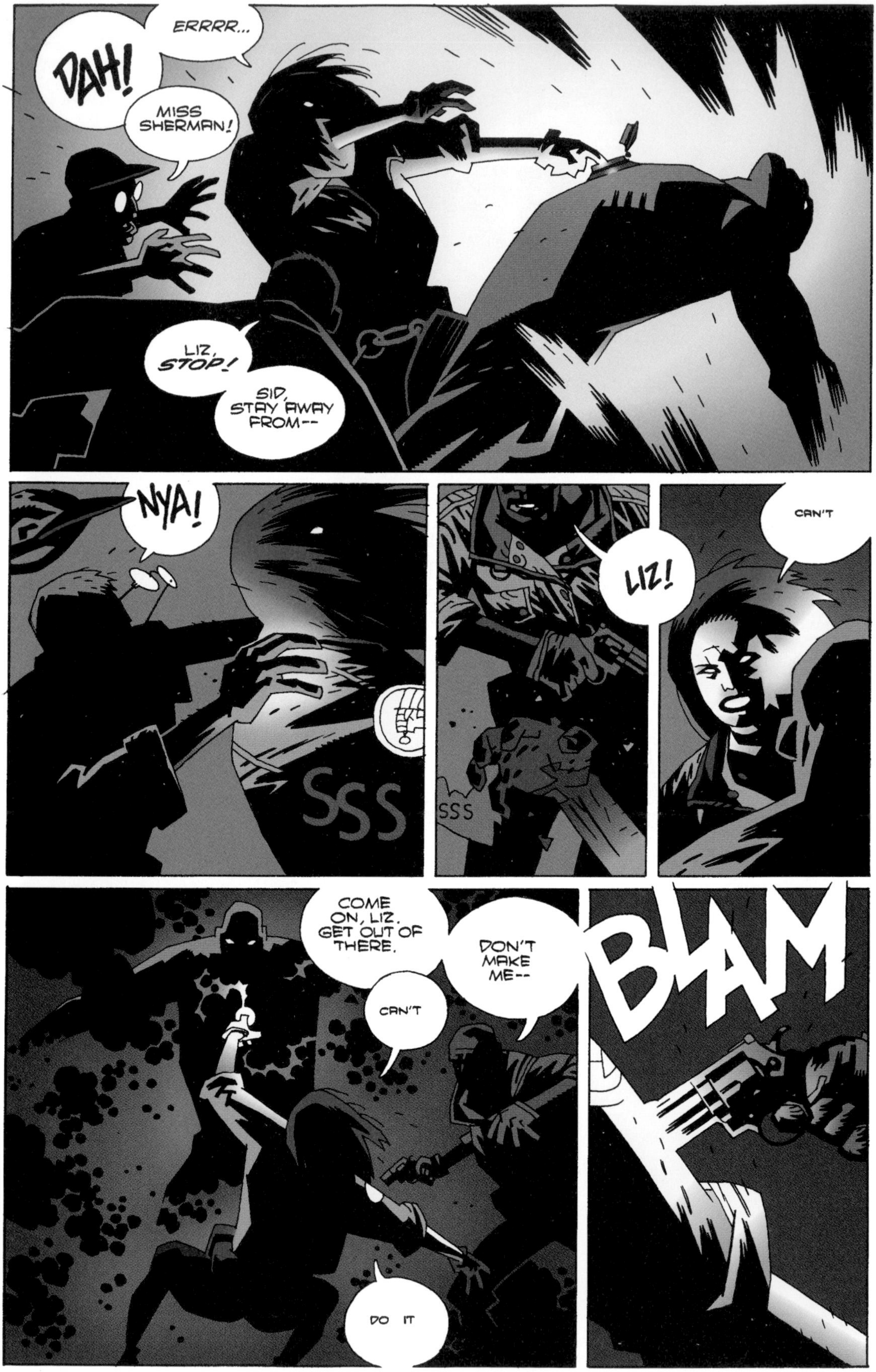
ERRRR...
DAH!
MISS SHERMAN!
LIZ, STOP!
SID, STAY AWAY FROM--
NYA!
SSS
LIZ!
SSS
CAN'T
COME ON, LIZ. GET OUT OF THERE.
DON'T MAKE ME--
CAN'T
DO IT
BLAM

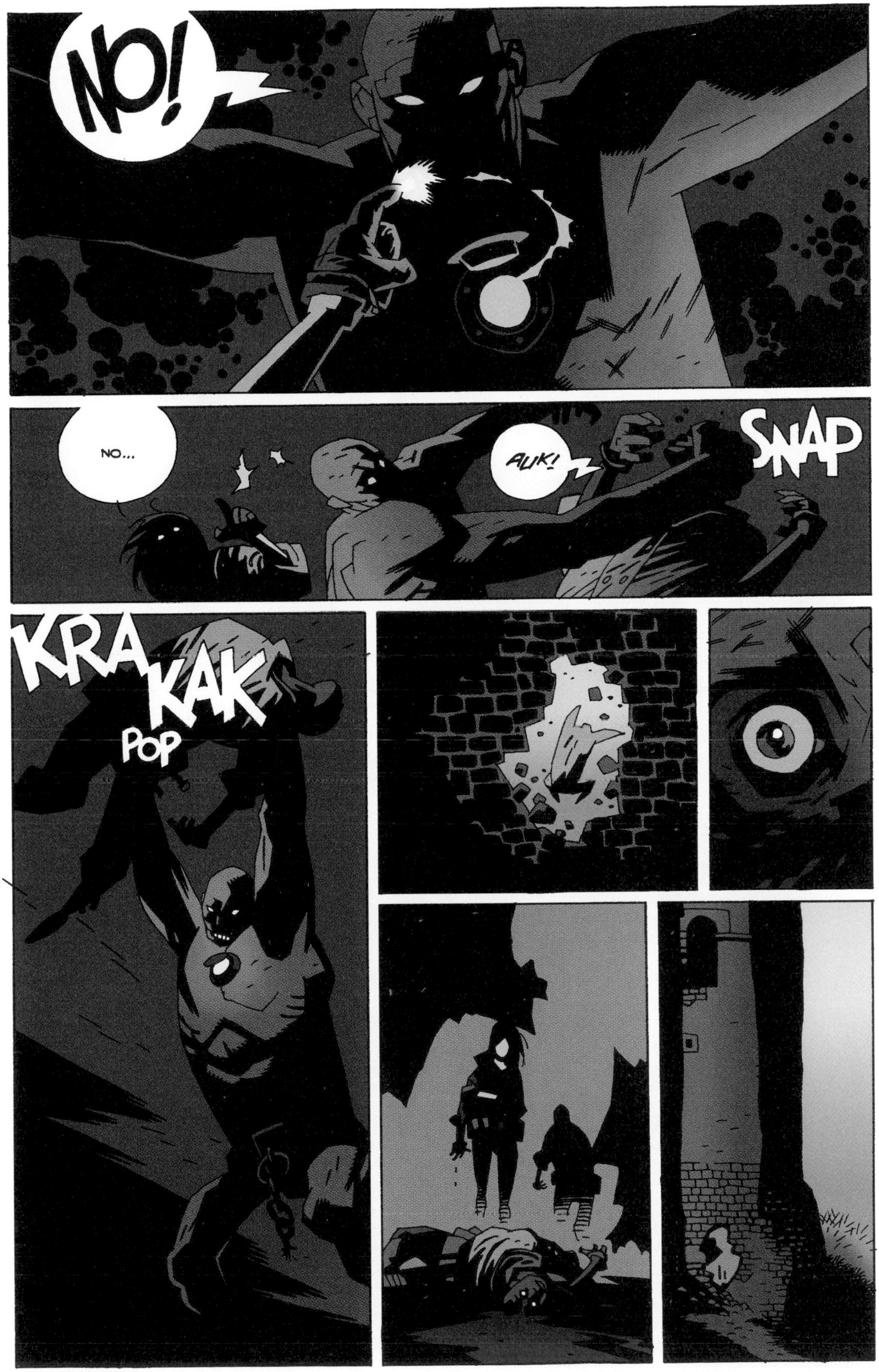
NO!
NO...
AUK!
SNAP
KRA
KAK
POP

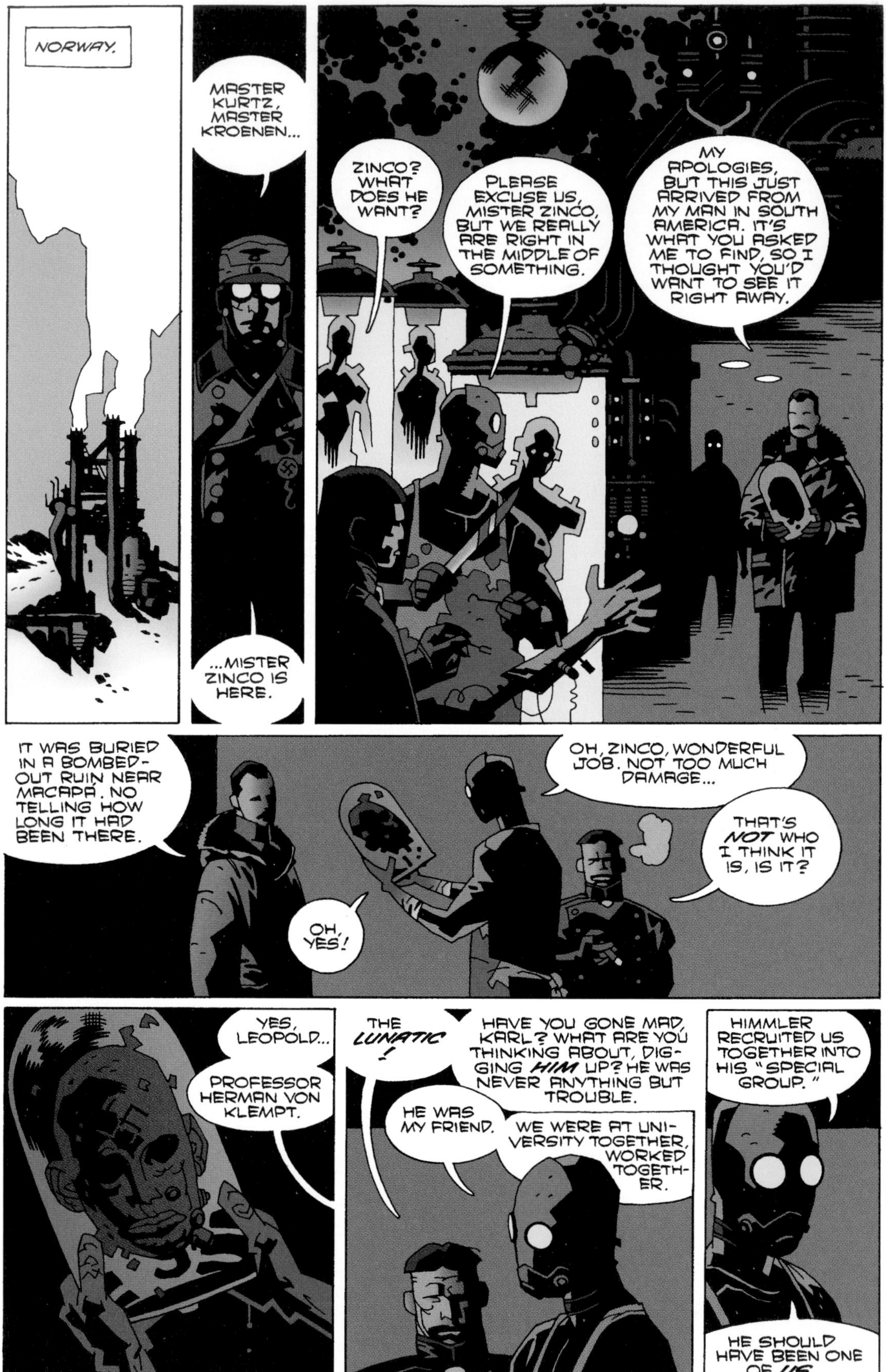
NORWAY.
MASTER KURTZ, MASTER KROENEN...
...MISTER ZINCO IS HERE.
ZINCO? WHAT DOES HE WANT?
PLEASE EXCUSE US, MISTER ZINCO, BUT WE REALLY ARE RIGHT IN THE MIDDLE OF SOMETHING.
MY APOLOGIES, BUT THIS JUST ARRIVED FROM MY MAN IN SOUTH AMERICA. IT'S WHAT YOU ASKED ME TO FIND, SO I THOUGHT YOU'D WANT TO SEE IT RIGHT AWAY.
IT WAS BURIED IN A BOMBED-OUT RUIN NEAR MACAPÁ. NO TELLING HOW LONG IT HAD BEEN THERE.
OH, ZINCO, WONDERFUL JOB. NOT TOO MUCH DAMAGE...
THAT'S NOT WHO I THINK IT IS, IS IT?
OH, YES!
YES, LEOPOLD...
PROFESSOR HERMAN VON KLEMPT.
THE LUNATIC!
HAVE YOU GONE MAD, KARL? WHAT ARE YOU THINKING ABOUT, DIGGING HIM UP? HE WAS NEVER ANYTHING BUT TROUBLE.
HE WAS MY FRIEND.
WE WERE AT UNIVERSITY TOGETHER, WORKED TOGETHER.
HIMMLER RECRUITED US TOGETHER INTO HIS "SPECIAL GROUP."
HE SHOULD HAVE BEEN ONE OF US.

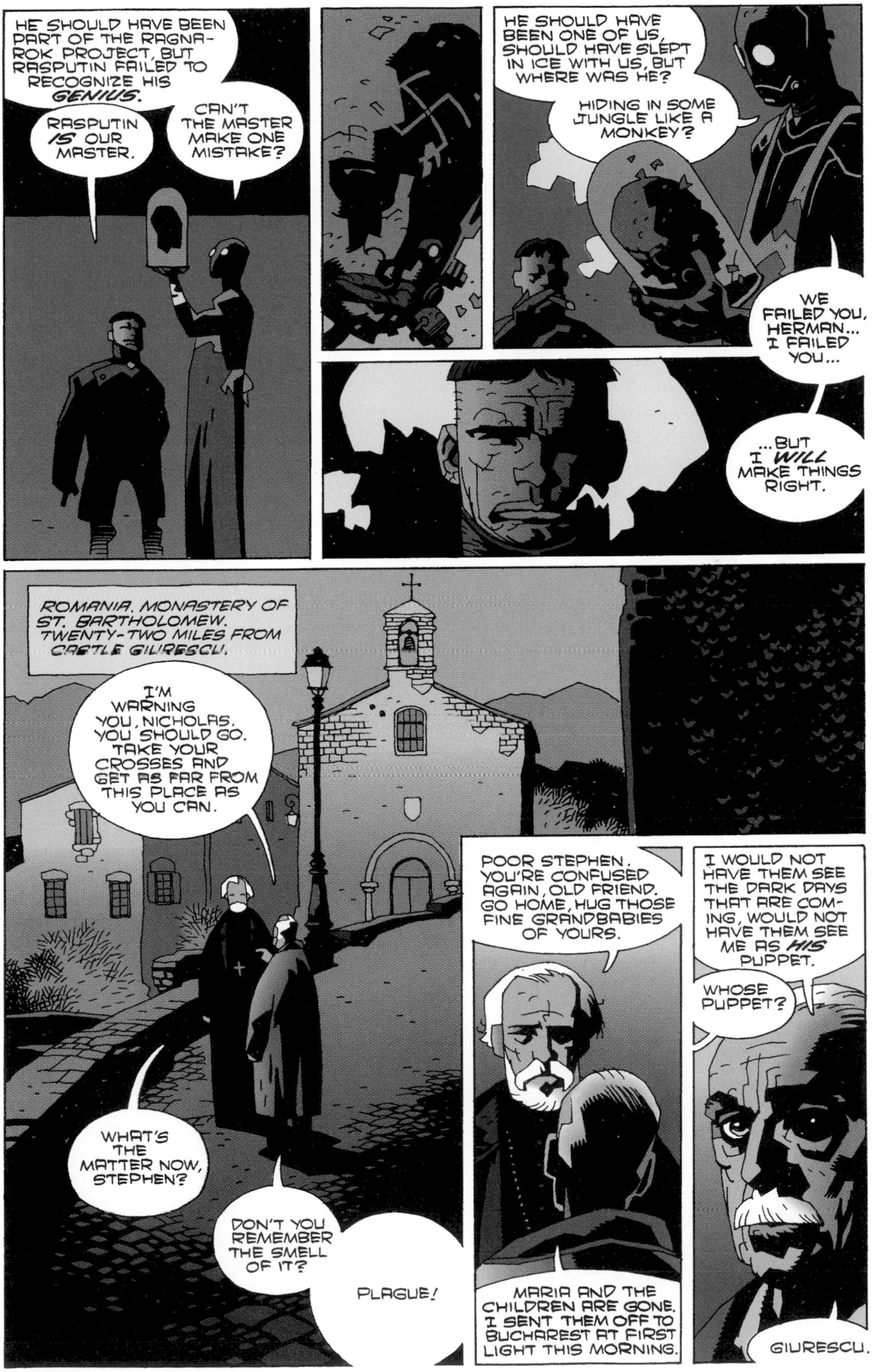
HE SHOULD HAVE BEEN PART OF THE RAGNAROK PROJECT, BUT RASPUTIN FAILED TO RECOGNIZE HIS GENIUS.
RASPUTIN IS OUR MASTER.
CAN'T THE MASTER MAKE ONE MISTAKE?
HE SHOULD HAVE BEEN ONE OF US, SHOULD HAVE SLEPT IN ICE WITH US, BUT WHERE WAS HE?
HIDING IN SOME JUNGLE LIKE A MONKEY?
WE FAILED YOU, HERMAN... I FAILED YOU...
...BUT I WILL MAKE THINGS RIGHT.
ROMANIA. MONASTERY OF ST. BARTHOLOMEW. TWENTY-TWO MILES FROM CASTLE GIURESCU.
I'M WARNING YOU, NICHOLAS. YOU SHOULD GO. TAKE YOUR CROSSES AND GET AS FAR FROM THIS PLACE AS YOU CAN.
WHAT'S THE MATTER NOW, STEPHEN?
DON'T YOU REMEMBER THE SMELL OF IT?
PLAGUE!
POOR STEPHEN. YOU'RE CONFUSED AGAIN, OLD FRIEND. GO HOME, HUG THOSE FINE GRANDBABIES OF YOURS.
MARIA AND THE CHILDREN ARE GONE. I SENT THEM OFF TO BUCHAREST AT FIRST LIGHT THIS MORNING.
I WOULD NOT HAVE THEM SEE THE DARK DAYS THAT ARE COMING, WOULD NOT HAVE THEM SEE ME AS HIS PUPPET.
WHOSE PUPPET?
GIURESCU.

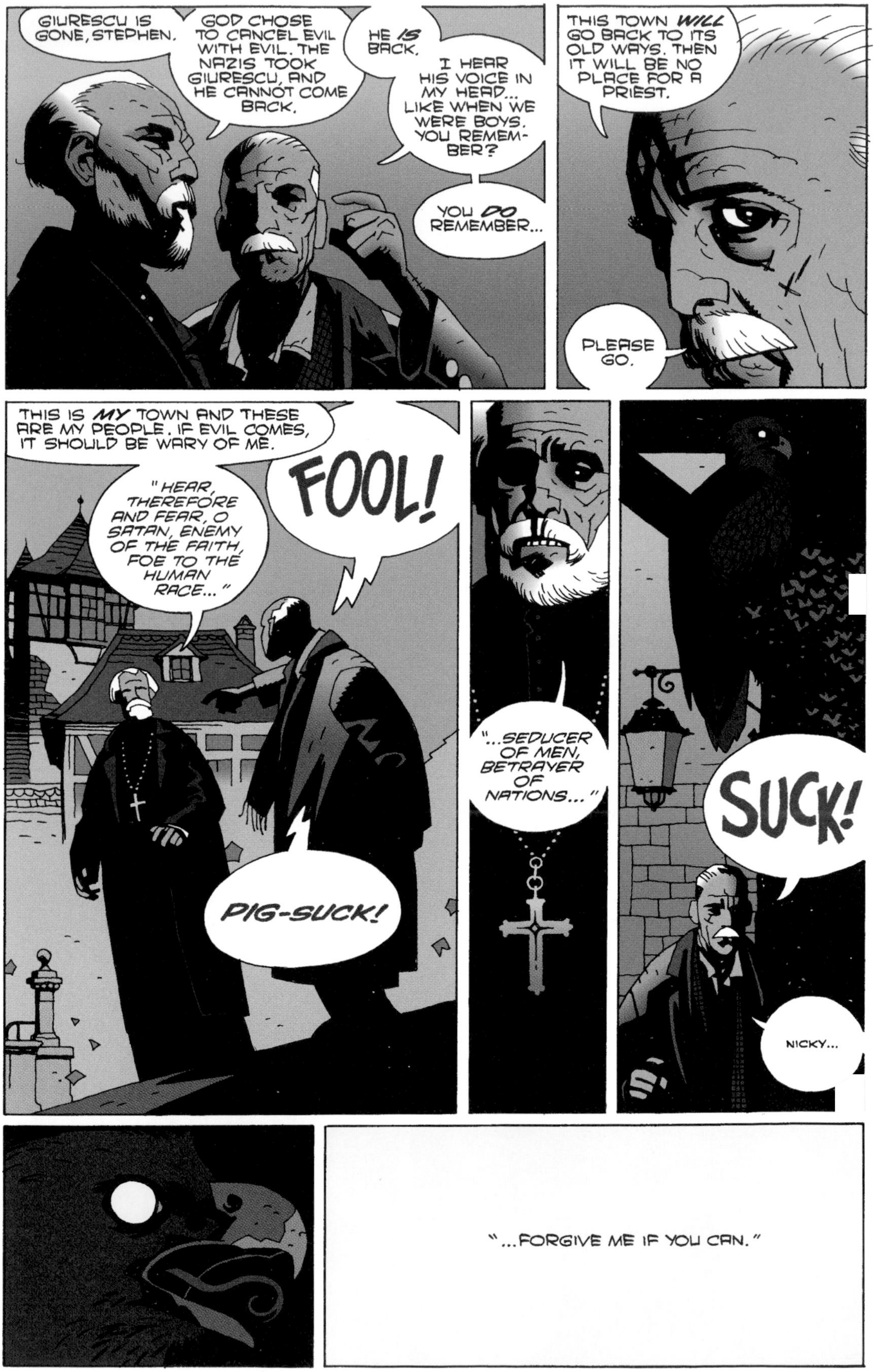
GIURESCU IS GONE, STEPHEN.
GOD CHOSE TO CANCEL EVIL WITH EVIL. THE NAZIS TOOK GIURESCU, AND HE CANNOT COME BACK.
HE *IS* BACK.
I HEAR HIS VOICE IN MY HEAD... LIKE WHEN WE WERE BOYS. YOU REMEMBER?
YOU *DO* REMEMBER...
THIS TOWN *WILL* GO BACK TO ITS OLD WAYS. THEN IT WILL BE NO PLACE FOR A PRIEST.
PLEASE GO.
THIS IS *MY* TOWN AND THESE ARE MY PEOPLE. IF EVIL COMES, IT SHOULD BE WARY OF ME.
"HEAR, THEREFORE AND FEAR, O SATAN, ENEMY OF THE FAITH, FOE TO THE HUMAN RACE..."
FOOL!
PIG-SUCK!
"...SEDUCER OF MEN, BETRAYER OF NATIONS..."
SUCK!
NICKY...
"...FORGIVE ME IF YOU CAN."

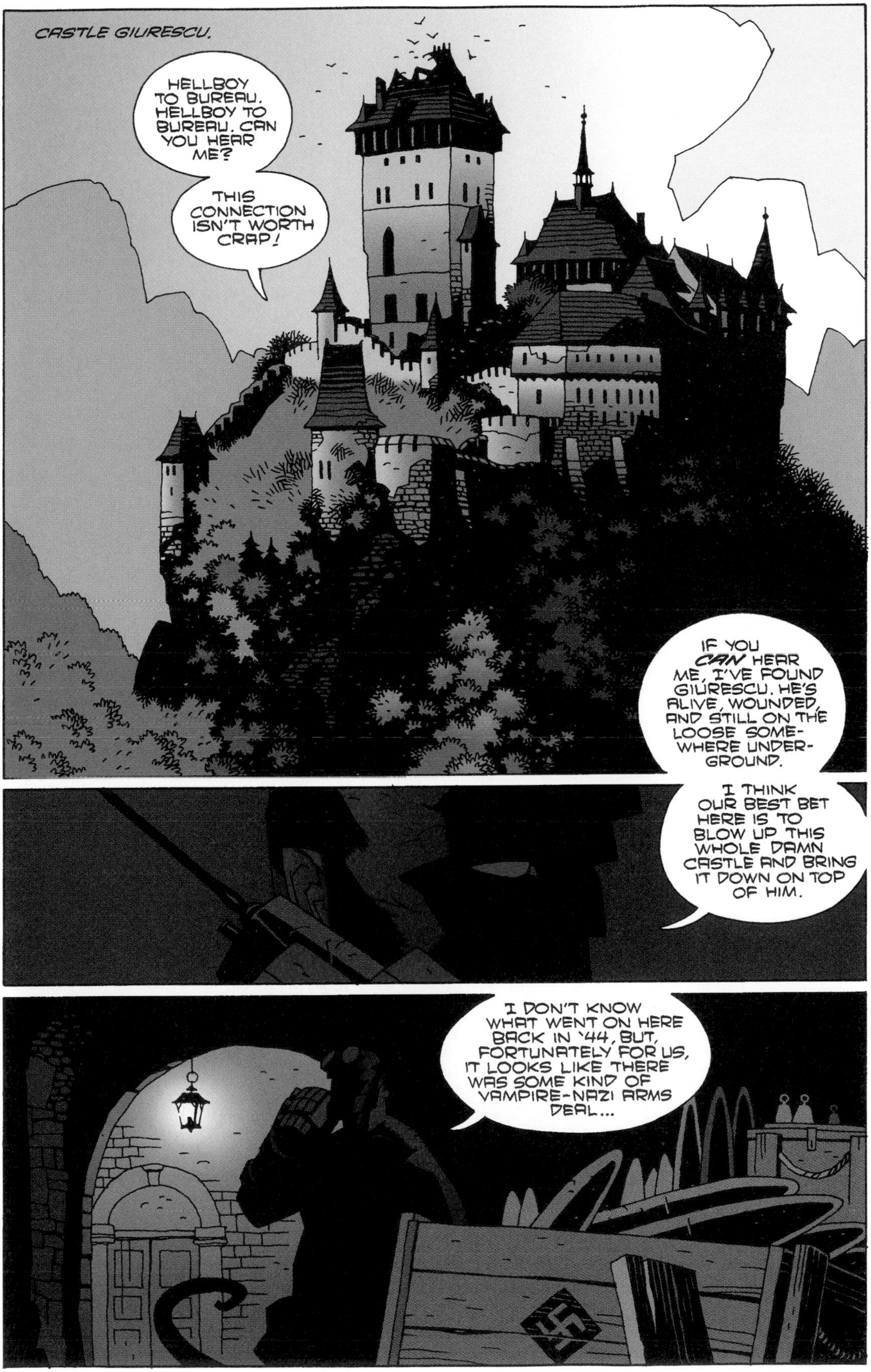
CASTLE GIURESCU.
HELLBOY TO BUREAU. HELLBOY TO BUREAU. CAN YOU HEAR ME?
THIS CONNECTION ISN'T WORTH CRAP!
IF YOU CAN HEAR ME, I'VE FOUND GIURESCU. HE'S ALIVE, WOUNDED, AND STILL ON THE LOOSE SOMEWHERE UNDERGROUND.
I THINK OUR BEST BET HERE IS TO BLOW UP THIS WHOLE DAMN CASTLE AND BRING IT DOWN ON TOP OF HIM.
I DON'T KNOW WHAT WENT ON HERE BACK IN '44, BUT, FORTUNATELY FOR US, IT LOOKS LIKE THERE WAS SOME KIND OF VAMPIRE-NAZI ARMS DEAL...

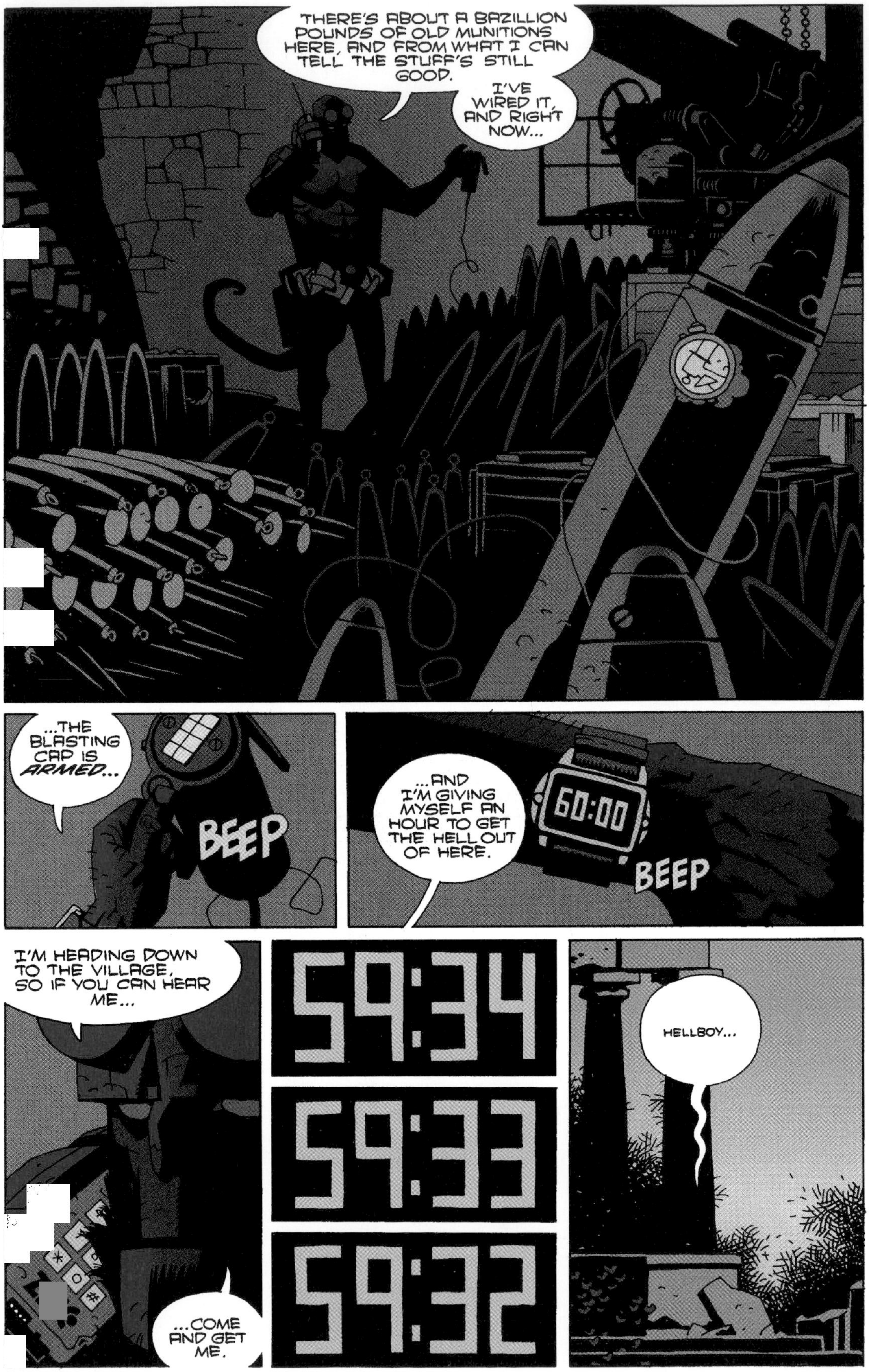
THERE'S ABOUT A BAZILLION POUNDS OF OLD MUNITIONS HERE, AND FROM WHAT I CAN TELL THE STUFF'S STILL GOOD.
I'VE WIRED IT, AND RIGHT NOW...
...THE BLASTING CAP IS *ARMED*...
BEEP
...AND I'M GIVING MYSELF AN HOUR TO GET THE HELL OUT OF HERE.
60:00
BEEP
I'M HEADING DOWN TO THE VILLAGE, SO IF YOU CAN HEAR ME...
...COME AND GET ME.
59:34
59:33
59:32
HELLBOY...

CHAPTER FOUR

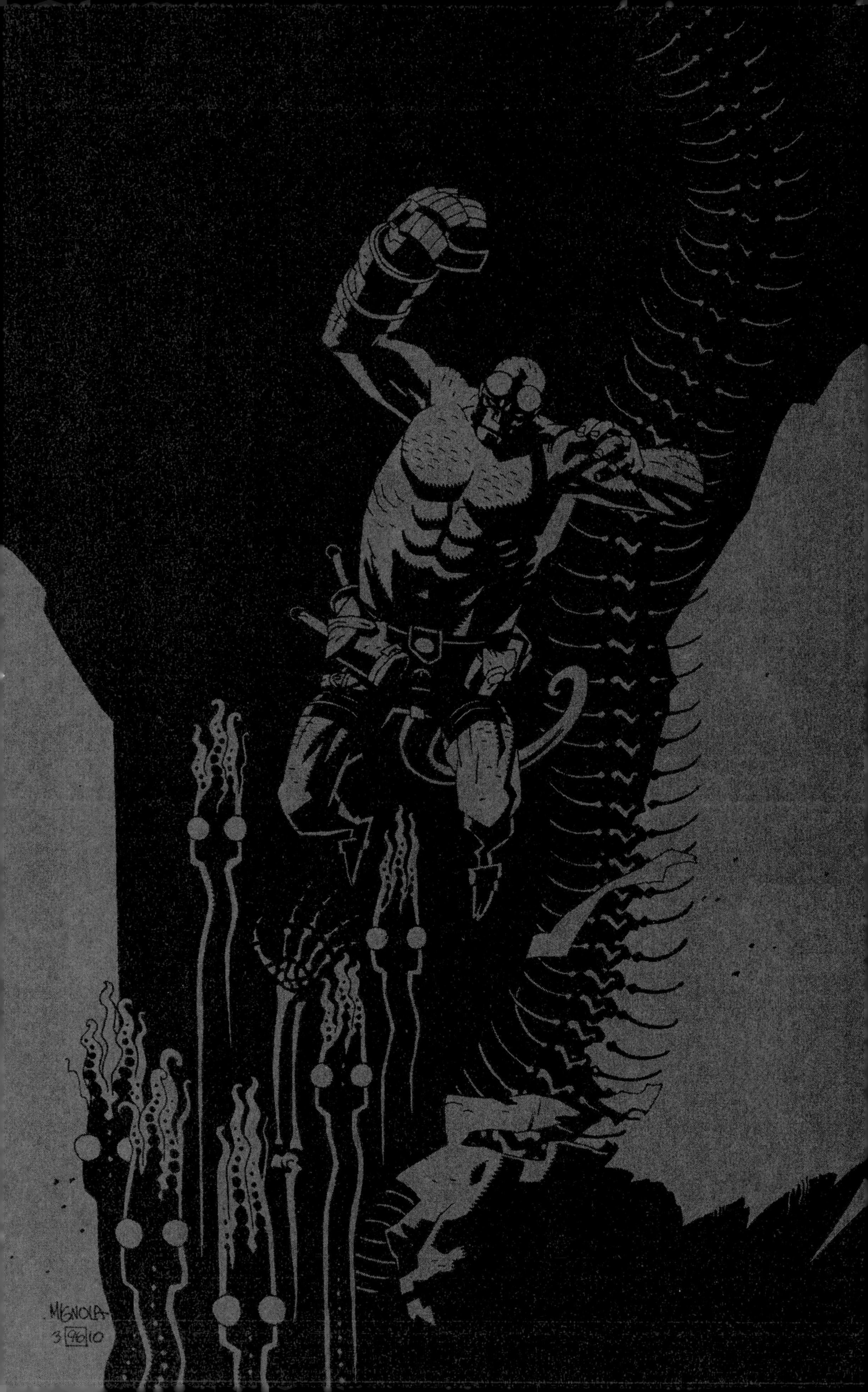
MIGNOLA
3 96 10

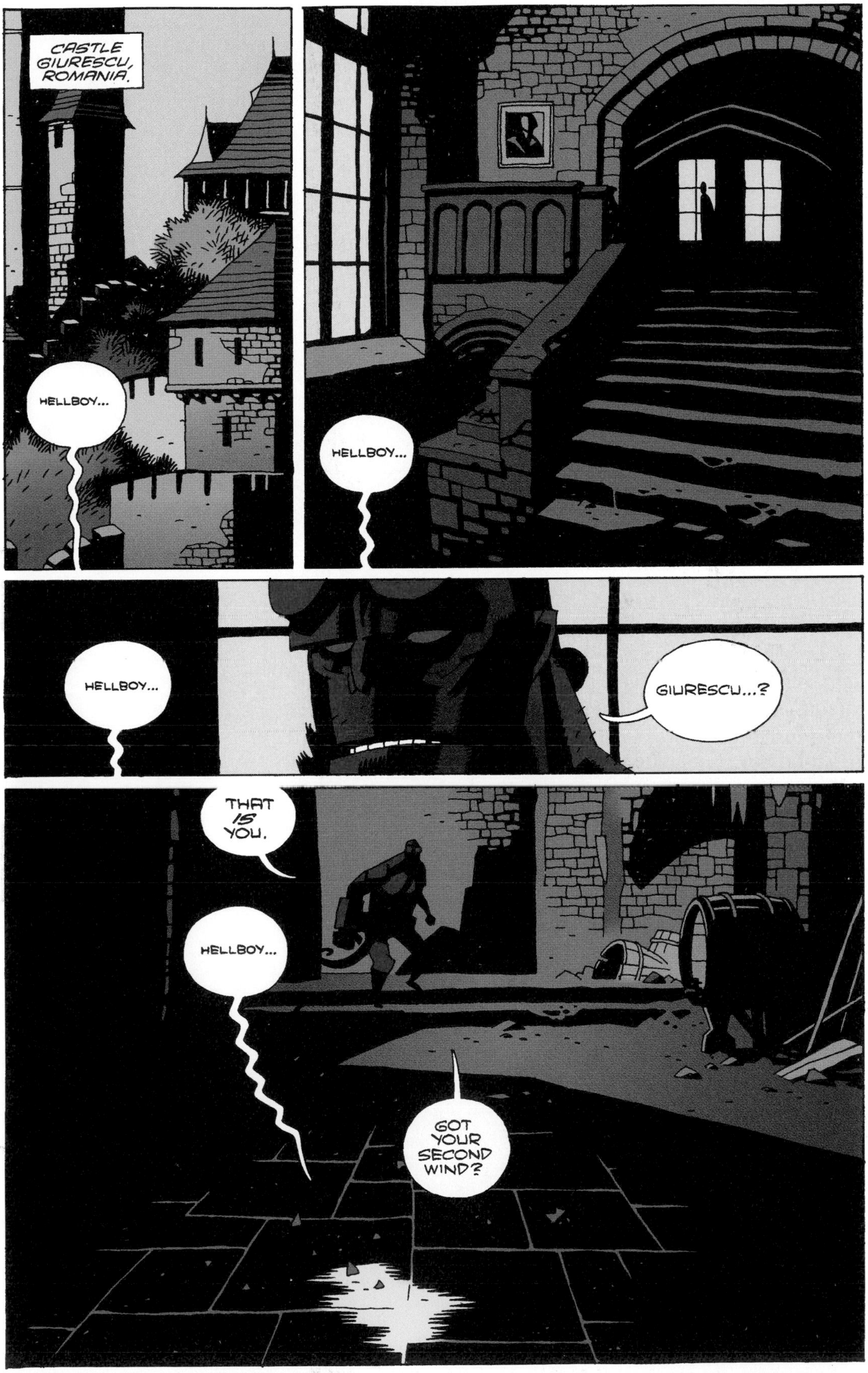
CASTLE GIURESCU, ROMANIA.
HELLBOY...
HELLBOY...
HELLBOY...
GIURESCU...?
THAT IS YOU.
HELLBOY...
GOT YOUR SECOND WIND?

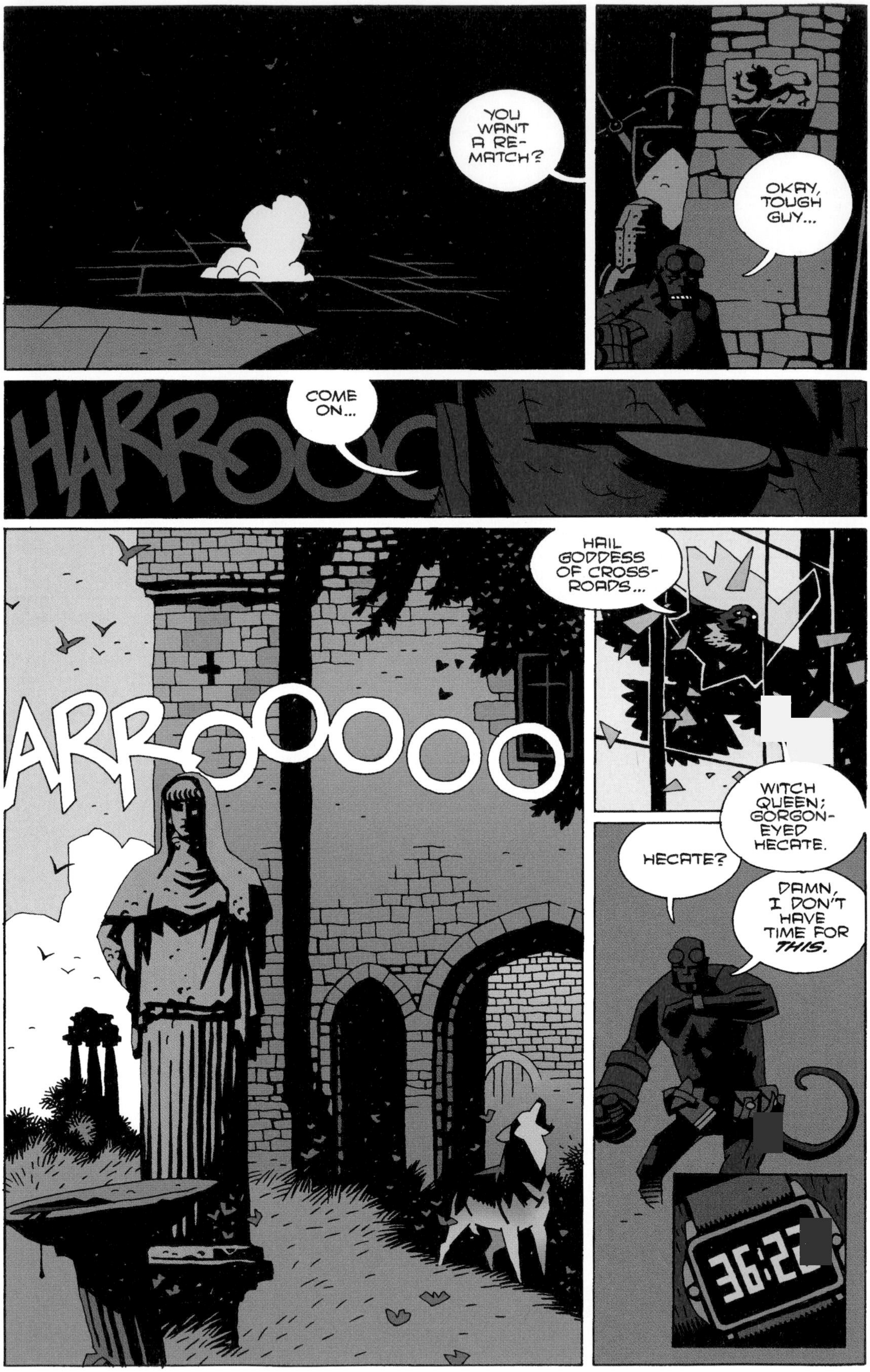
YOU WANT A RE-MATCH?
OKAY, TOUGH GUY...
HARROOO
COME ON...
ARROOOOOO
HAIL GODDESS OF CROSS-ROADS...
WITCH QUEEN; GORGON-EYED HECATE.
HECATE?
DAMN, I DON'T HAVE TIME FOR *THIS.*

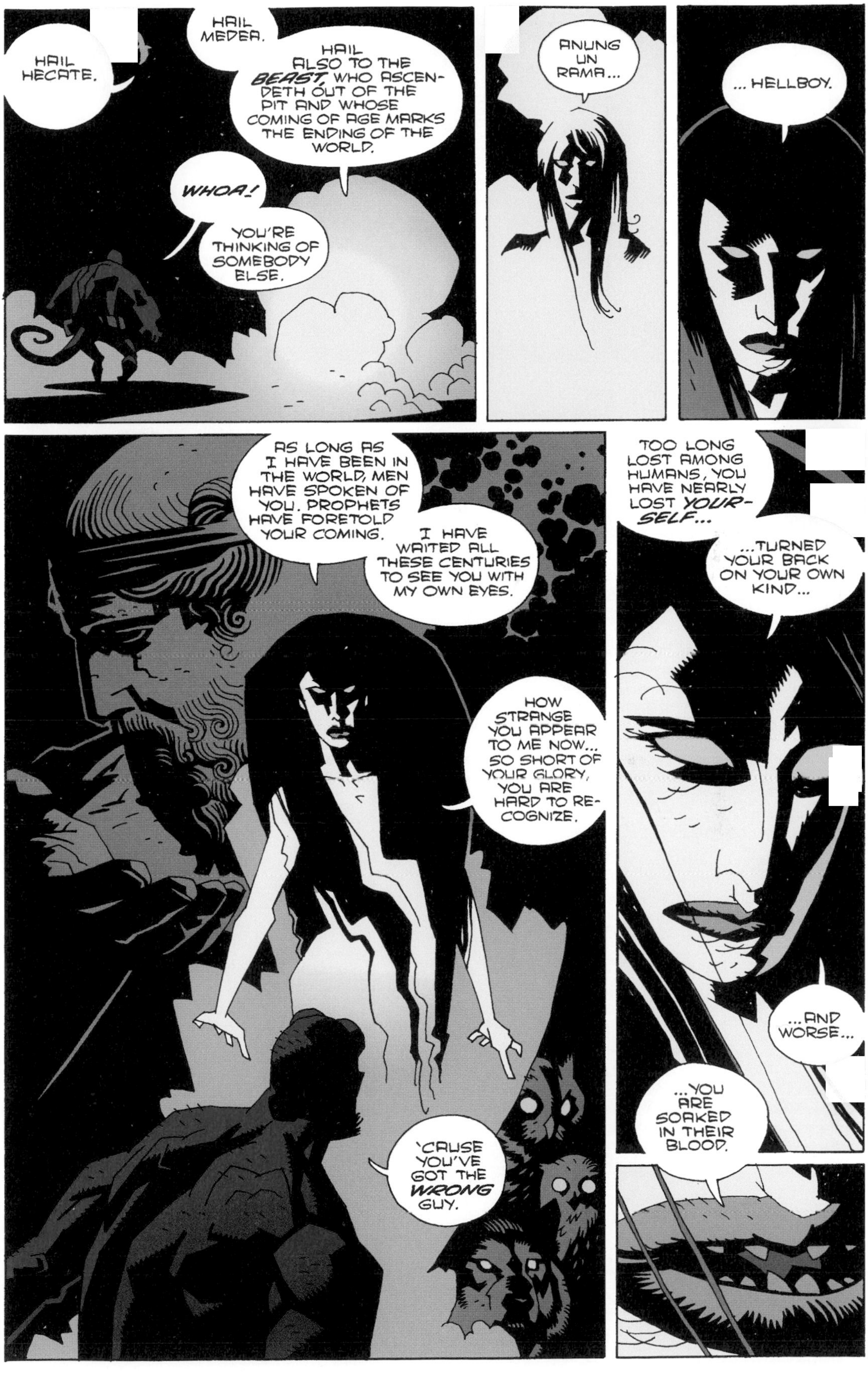
HAIL HECATE.
HAIL MEDEA.
HAIL ALSO TO THE BEAST, WHO ASCENDETH OUT OF THE PIT AND WHOSE COMING OF AGE MARKS THE ENDING OF THE WORLD.
WHOA!
YOU'RE THINKING OF SOMEBODY ELSE.
ANUNG UN RAMA...
... HELLBOY.
AS LONG AS I HAVE BEEN IN THE WORLD, MEN HAVE SPOKEN OF YOU. PROPHETS HAVE FORETOLD YOUR COMING.
I HAVE WAITED ALL THESE CENTURIES TO SEE YOU WITH MY OWN EYES.
HOW STRANGE YOU APPEAR TO ME NOW... SO SHORT OF YOUR GLORY, YOU ARE HARD TO RECOGNIZE.
'CAUSE YOU'VE GOT THE WRONG GUY.
TOO LONG LOST AMONG HUMANS, YOU HAVE NEARLY LOST YOURSELF...
...TURNED YOUR BACK ON YOUR OWN KIND...
...AND WORSE...
...YOU ARE SOAKED IN THEIR BLOOD.

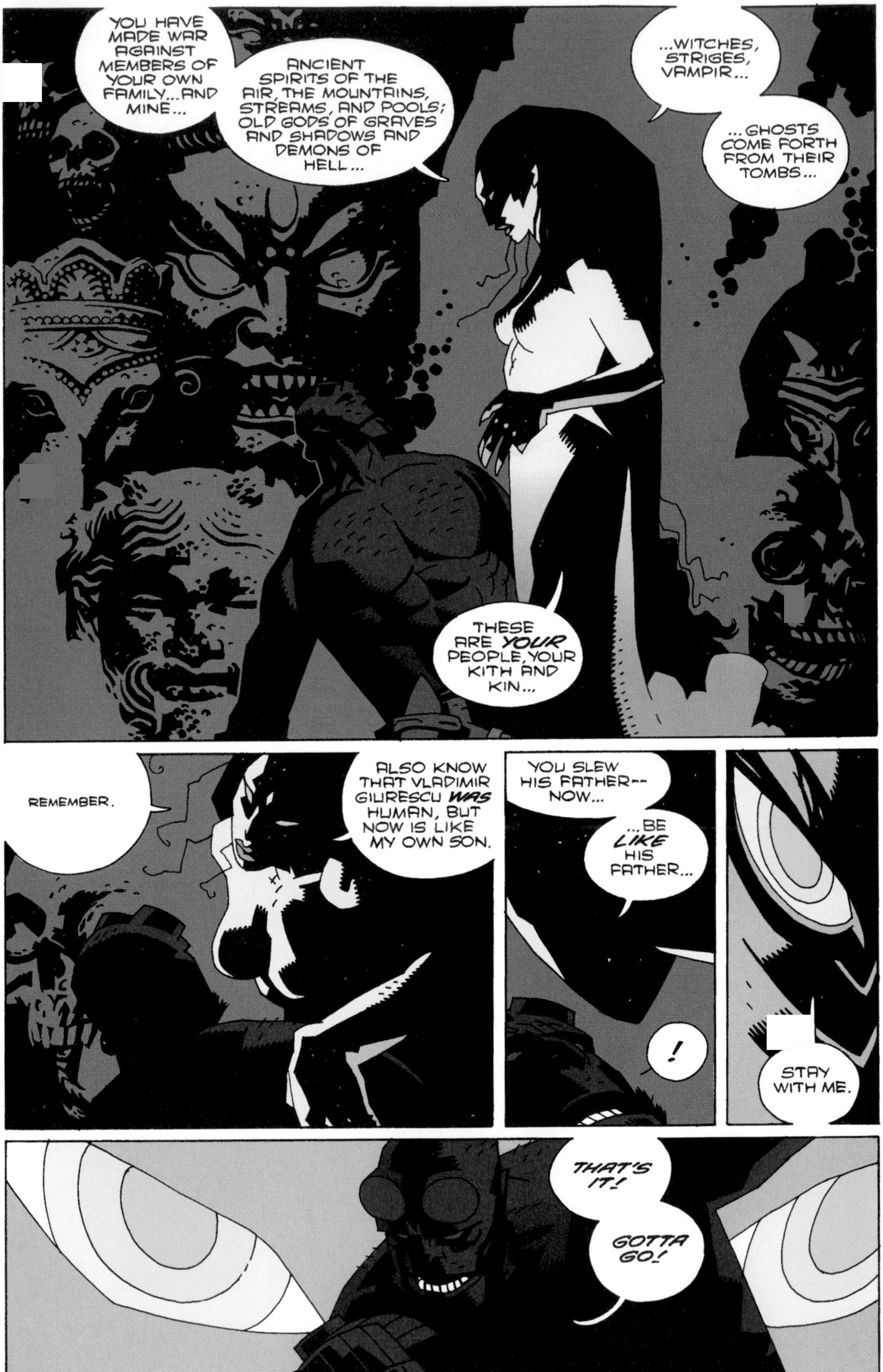
YOU HAVE MADE WAR AGAINST MEMBERS OF YOUR OWN FAMILY...AND MINE...
ANCIENT SPIRITS OF THE AIR, THE MOUNTAINS, STREAMS, AND POOLS; OLD GODS OF GRAVES AND SHADOWS AND DEMONS OF HELL...
...WITCHES, STRIGES, VAMPIR...
...GHOSTS COME FORTH FROM THEIR TOMBS...
THESE ARE YOUR PEOPLE, YOUR KITH AND KIN...
REMEMBER.
ALSO KNOW THAT VLADIMIR GIURESCU WAS HUMAN, BUT NOW IS LIKE MY OWN SON.
YOU SLEW HIS FATHER-- NOW...
...BE LIKE HIS FATHER...
!
STAY WITH ME.
THAT'S IT!
GOTTA GO!

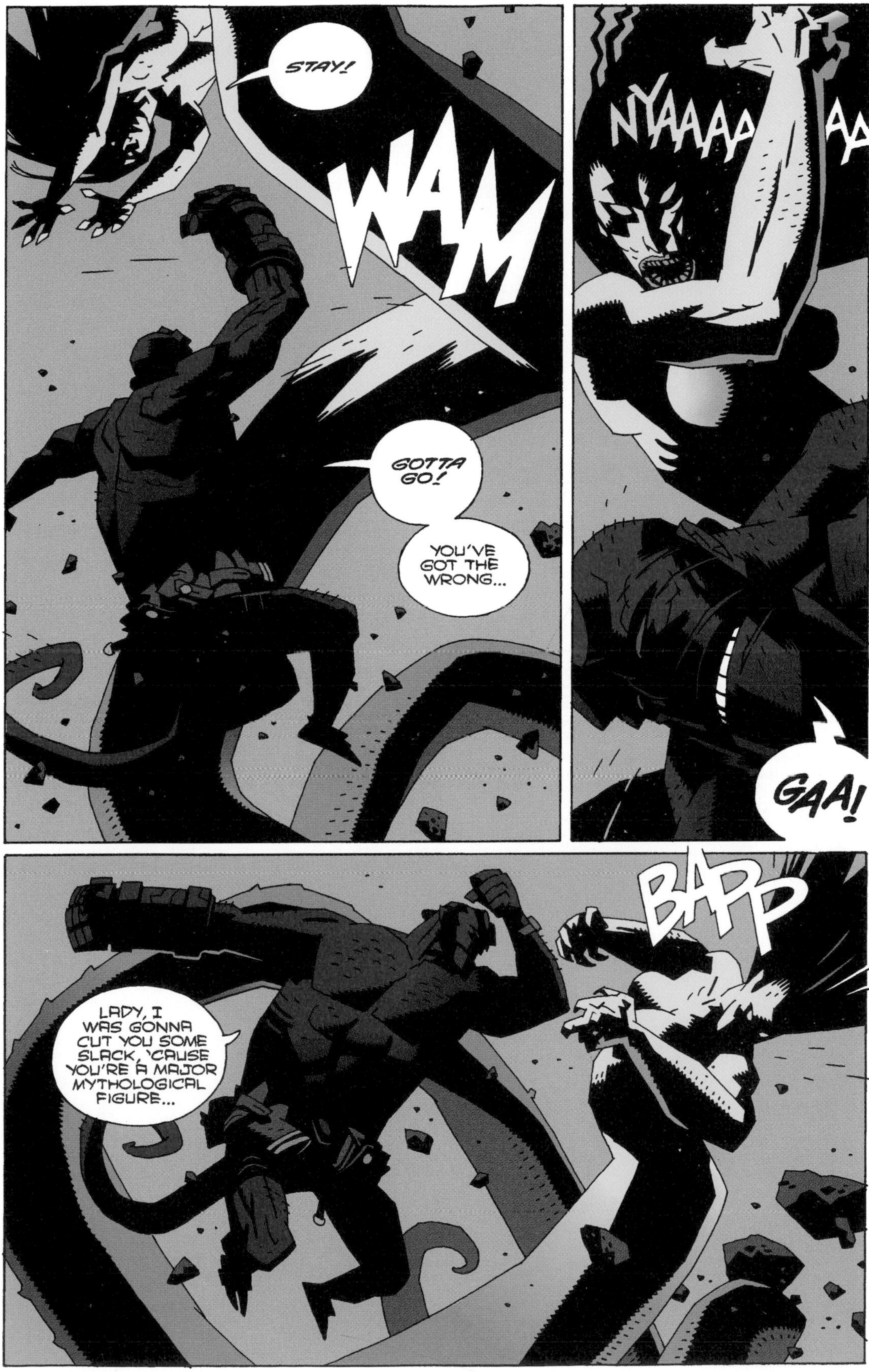

STAY!
WAM
GOTTA GO!
YOU'VE GOT THE WRONG...
NYAAAAAAA
GAA!
BAPP
LADY, I WAS GONNA CUT YOU SOME SLACK, 'CAUSE YOU'RE A MAJOR MYTHOLOGICAL FIGURE...

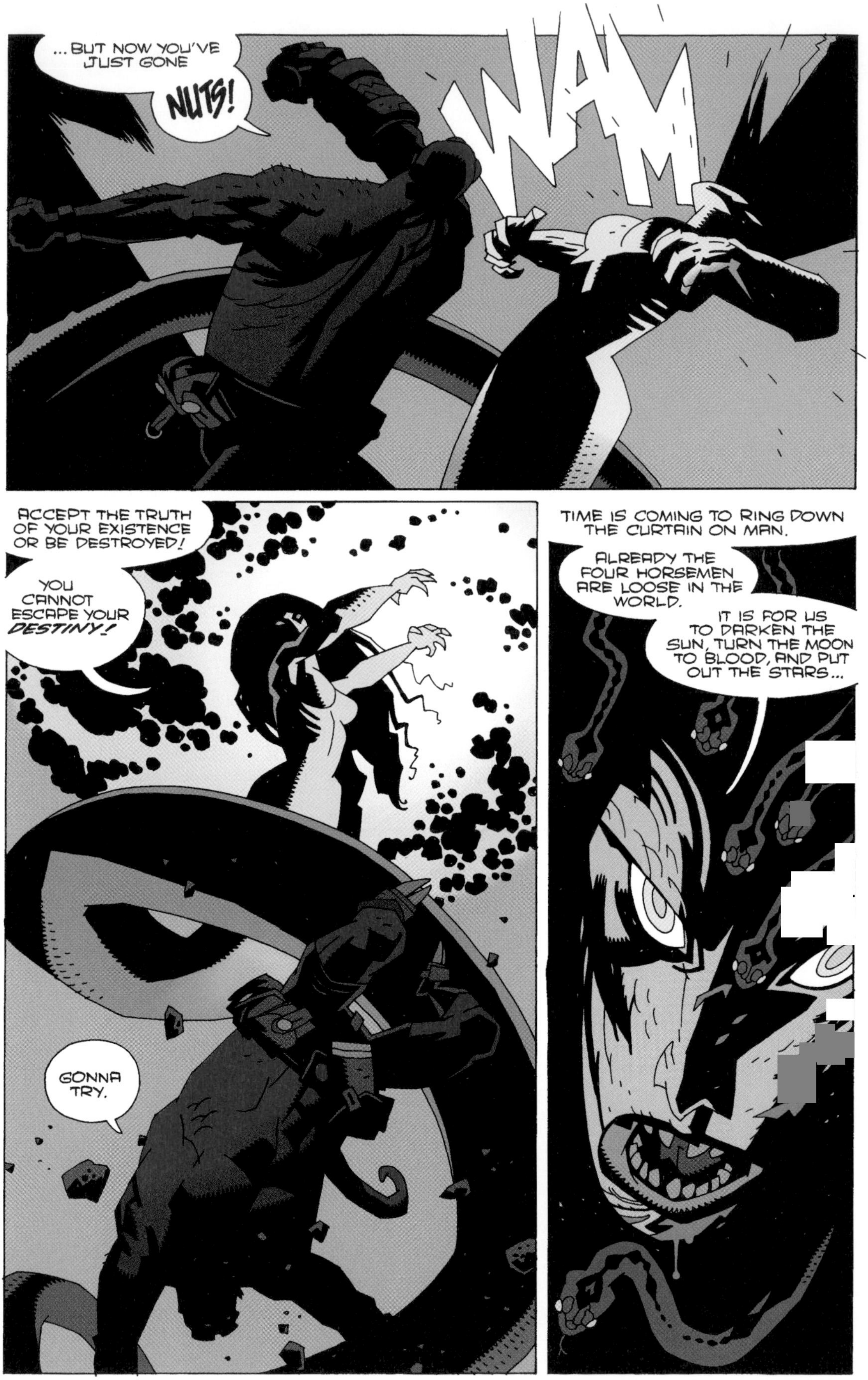
...BUT NOW YOU'VE JUST GONE NUTS!
WAM
ACCEPT THE TRUTH OF YOUR EXISTENCE OR BE DESTROYED!
YOU CANNOT ESCAPE YOUR DESTINY!
GONNA TRY.
TIME IS COMING TO RING DOWN THE CURTAIN ON MAN.
ALREADY THE FOUR HORSEMEN ARE LOOSE IN THE WORLD.
IT IS FOR US TO DARKEN THE SUN, TURN THE MOON TO BLOOD, AND PUT OUT THE STARS...

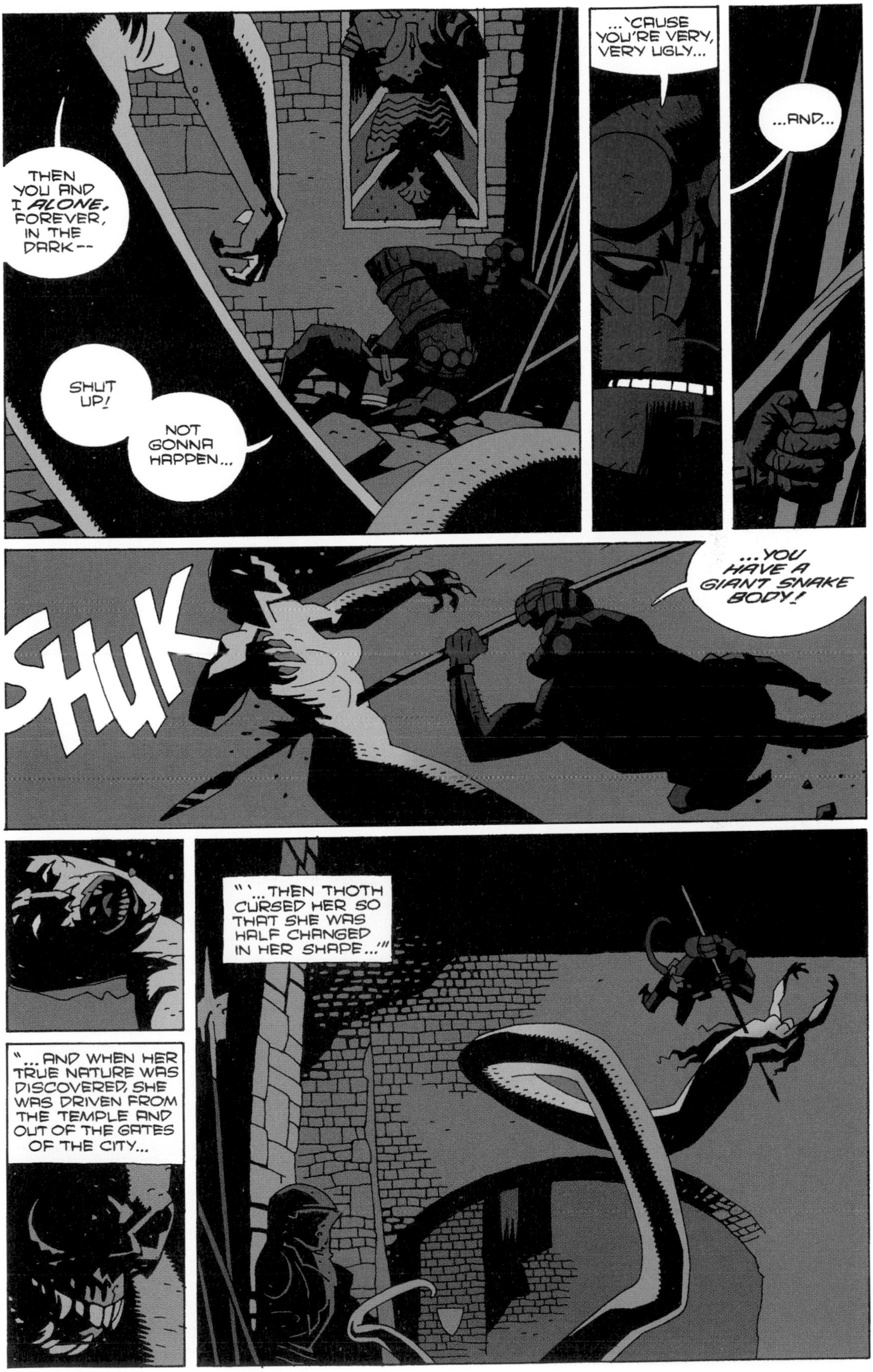
THEN YOU AND I *ALONE,* FOREVER, IN THE DARK--
SHUT UP!
NOT GONNA HAPPEN...
...'CAUSE YOU'RE VERY, VERY UGLY...
...AND...
SHUK
...*YOU HAVE A GIANT SNAKE BODY!*
"'...THEN THOTH CURSED HER SO THAT SHE WAS HALF CHANGED IN HER SHAPE...'"
"...AND WHEN HER TRUE NATURE WAS DISCOVERED, SHE WAS DRIVEN FROM THE TEMPLE AND OUT OF THE GATES OF THE CITY...

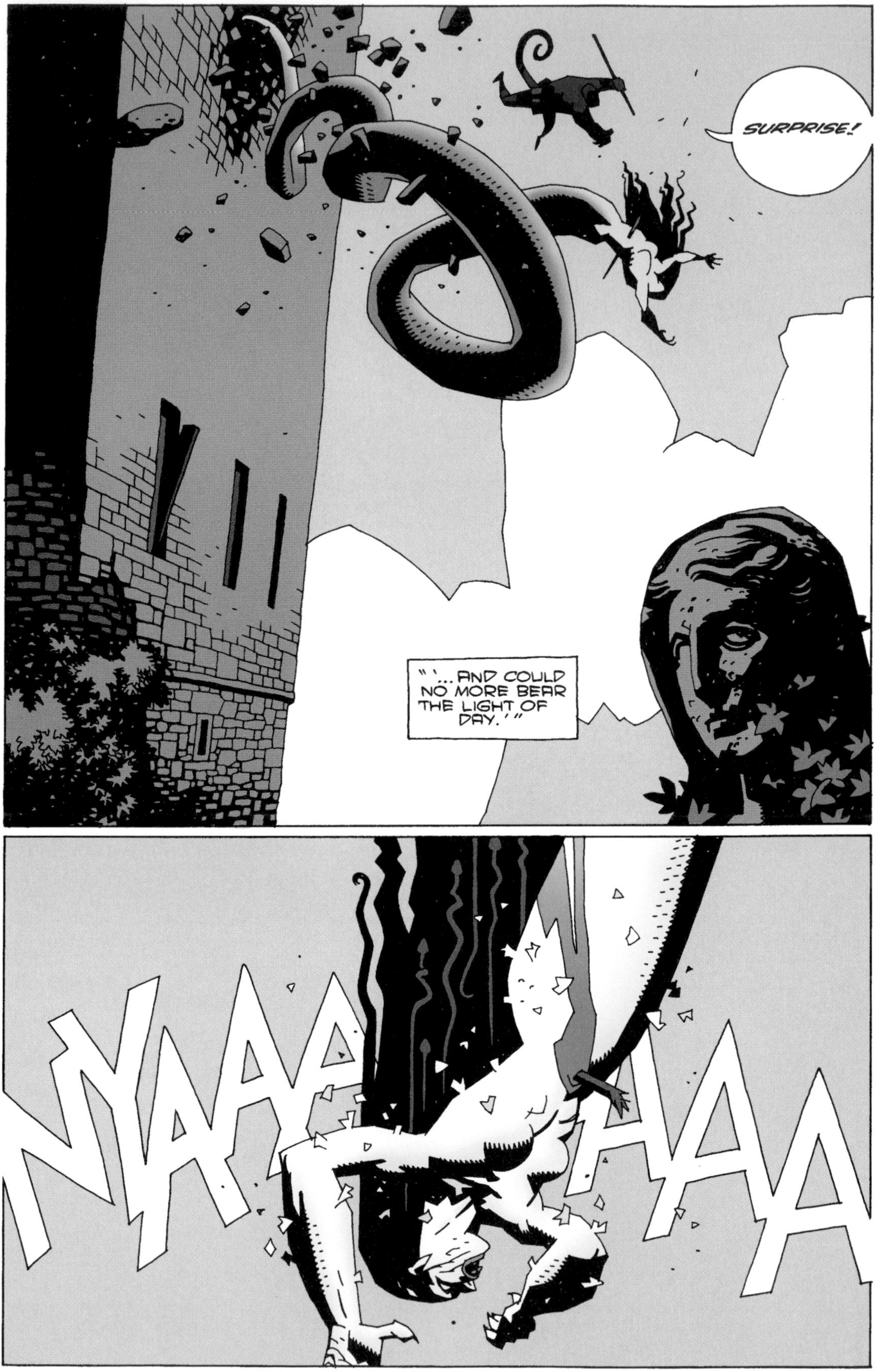
SURPRISE!
"'...AND COULD NO MORE BEAR THE LIGHT OF DAY.'"
NYAAAHAAA

JEEZ!
GODDAMN...
...SON...
...OF...
...A...

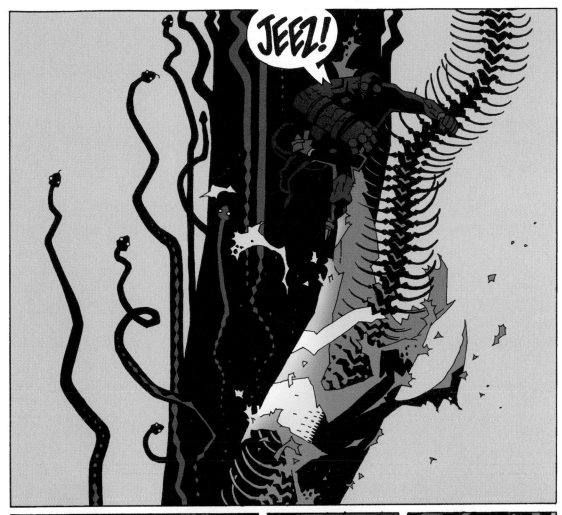

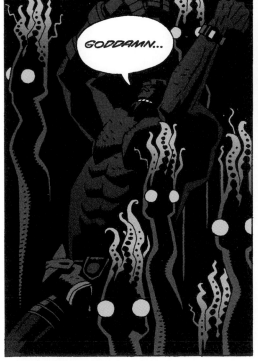

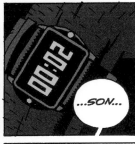

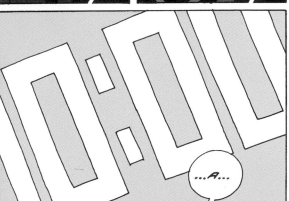

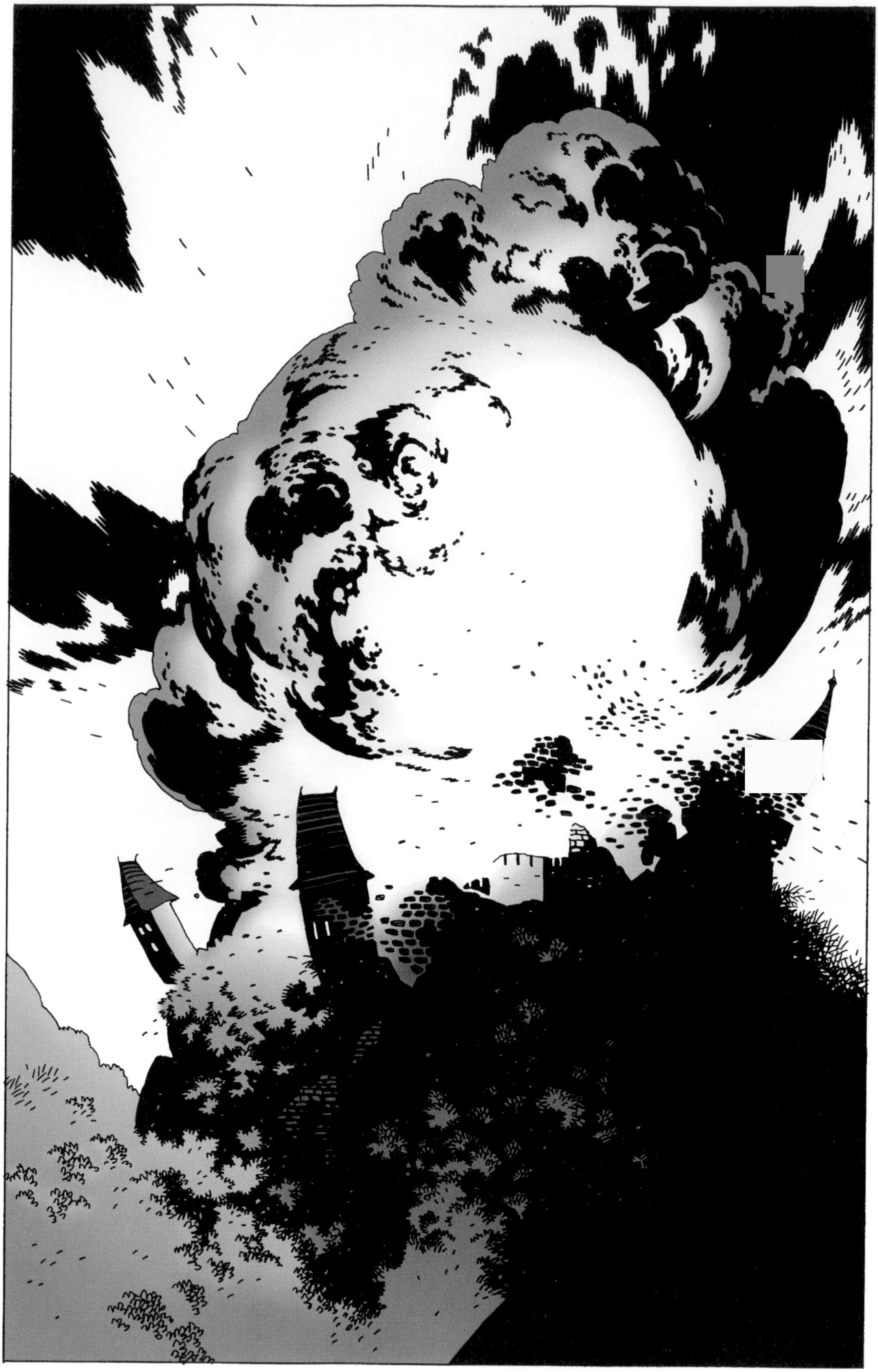

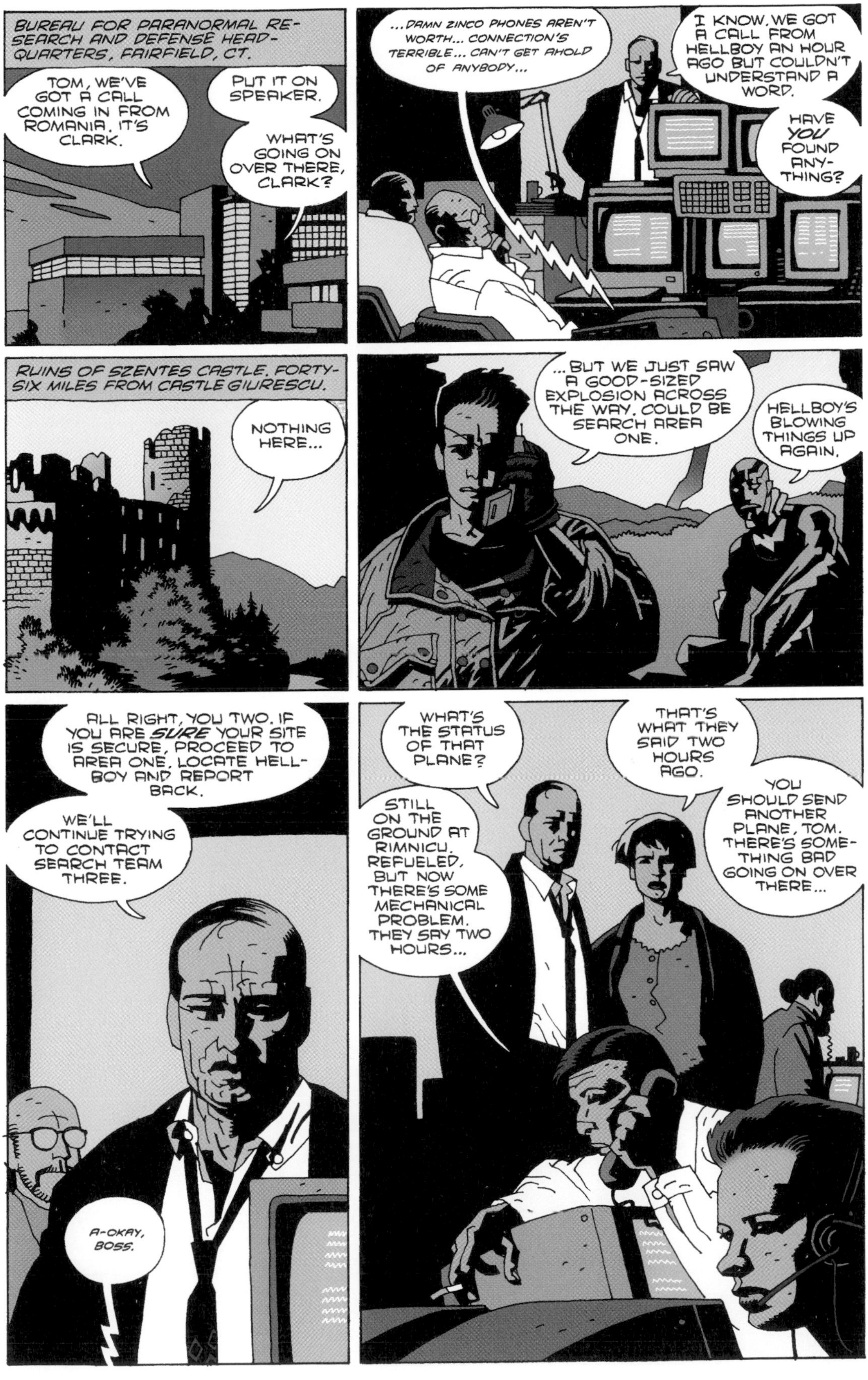
BUREAU FOR PARANORMAL RESEARCH AND DEFENSE HEADQUARTERS, FAIRFIELD, CT.
TOM, WE'VE GOT A CALL COMING IN FROM ROMANIA. IT'S CLARK.
PUT IT ON SPEAKER.
WHAT'S GOING ON OVER THERE, CLARK?
...DAMN ZINCO PHONES AREN'T WORTH... CONNECTION'S TERRIBLE... CAN'T GET AHOLD OF ANYBODY...
I KNOW. WE GOT A CALL FROM HELLBOY AN HOUR AGO BUT COULDN'T UNDERSTAND A WORD.
HAVE YOU FOUND ANYTHING?
RUINS OF SZENTES CASTLE. FORTY-SIX MILES FROM CASTLE GIURESCU.
NOTHING HERE...
...BUT WE JUST SAW A GOOD-SIZED EXPLOSION ACROSS THE WAY. COULD BE SEARCH AREA ONE.
HELLBOY'S BLOWING THINGS UP AGAIN.
ALL RIGHT, YOU TWO. IF YOU ARE SURE YOUR SITE IS SECURE, PROCEED TO AREA ONE, LOCATE HELLBOY AND REPORT BACK.
WE'LL CONTINUE TRYING TO CONTACT SEARCH TEAM THREE.
A-OKAY, BOSS.
WHAT'S THE STATUS OF THAT PLANE?
STILL ON THE GROUND AT RIMNICU. REFUELED, BUT NOW THERE'S SOME MECHANICAL PROBLEM. THEY SAY TWO HOURS...
THAT'S WHAT THEY SAID TWO HOURS AGO.
YOU SHOULD SEND ANOTHER PLANE, TOM. THERE'S SOMETHING BAD GOING ON OVER THERE...

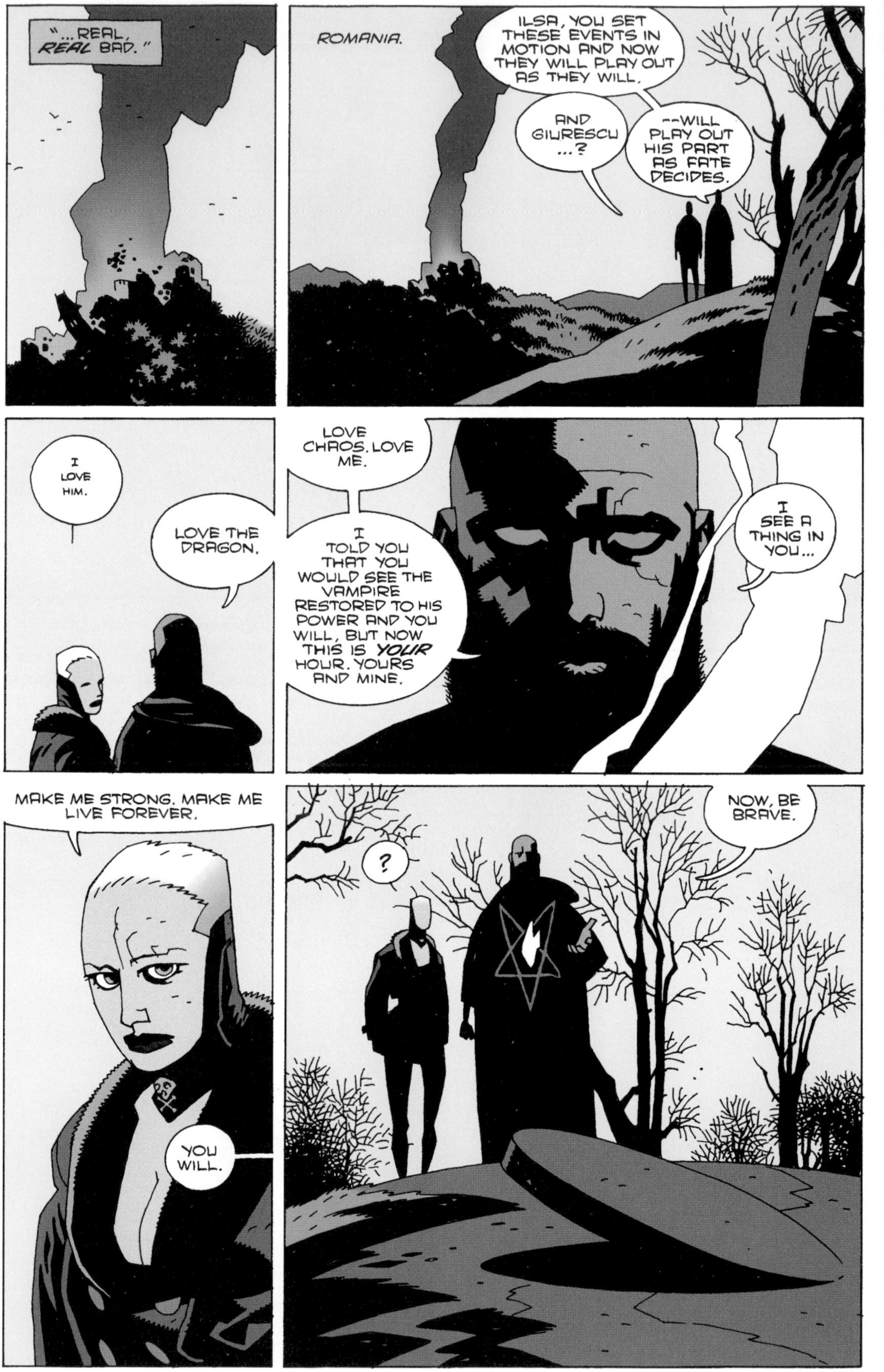
"...REAL, *REAL* BAD."
ROMANIA.
ILSA, YOU SET THESE EVENTS IN MOTION AND NOW THEY WILL PLAY OUT AS THEY WILL.
AND GIURESCU ...?
--WILL PLAY OUT HIS PART AS FATE DECIDES.
I LOVE HIM.
LOVE THE DRAGON.
LOVE CHAOS. LOVE ME.
I TOLD YOU THAT YOU WOULD SEE THE VAMPIRE RESTORED TO HIS POWER AND YOU WILL, BUT NOW THIS IS *YOUR* HOUR. YOURS AND MINE.
I SEE A THING IN YOU...
MAKE ME STRONG. MAKE ME LIVE FOREVER.
YOU WILL.
?
NOW, BE BRAVE.

WHAT IS THIS?

BEHOLD... YOURSELF.

WHAT?

HELLO, GRIGORI, AND HELLO ALSO TO YOU, ILSA HAUPSTEIN. I HAVE FOR YOU THIS GIFT FROM THE BABA YAGA.

AN IRON MAIDEN?

THE TERRIBLE "MAIDEN OF JOO," FAVORITE TORTURE MACHINE OF THAT LONG-AGO COUNTESS, ELIZABETH BATHORY.

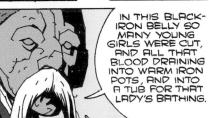

IN THIS BLACK-IRON BELLY SO MANY YOUNG GIRLS WERE CUT, AND ALL THAT BLOOD DRAINING INTO WARM IRON POTS, AND INTO A TUB FOR THAT LADY'S BATHING.

ALL THAT BLOOD DID THAT LADY MUCH GOOD AND KEPT HER IN YOUTHFUL COLOR... EVEN THROUGH HER ARREST AND TRIAL, AND FINALLY SHE IS BRICKED-UP ALIVE INSIDE HER OWN CASTLE WALL...

...AND FINALLY SHE IS DYING THERE...

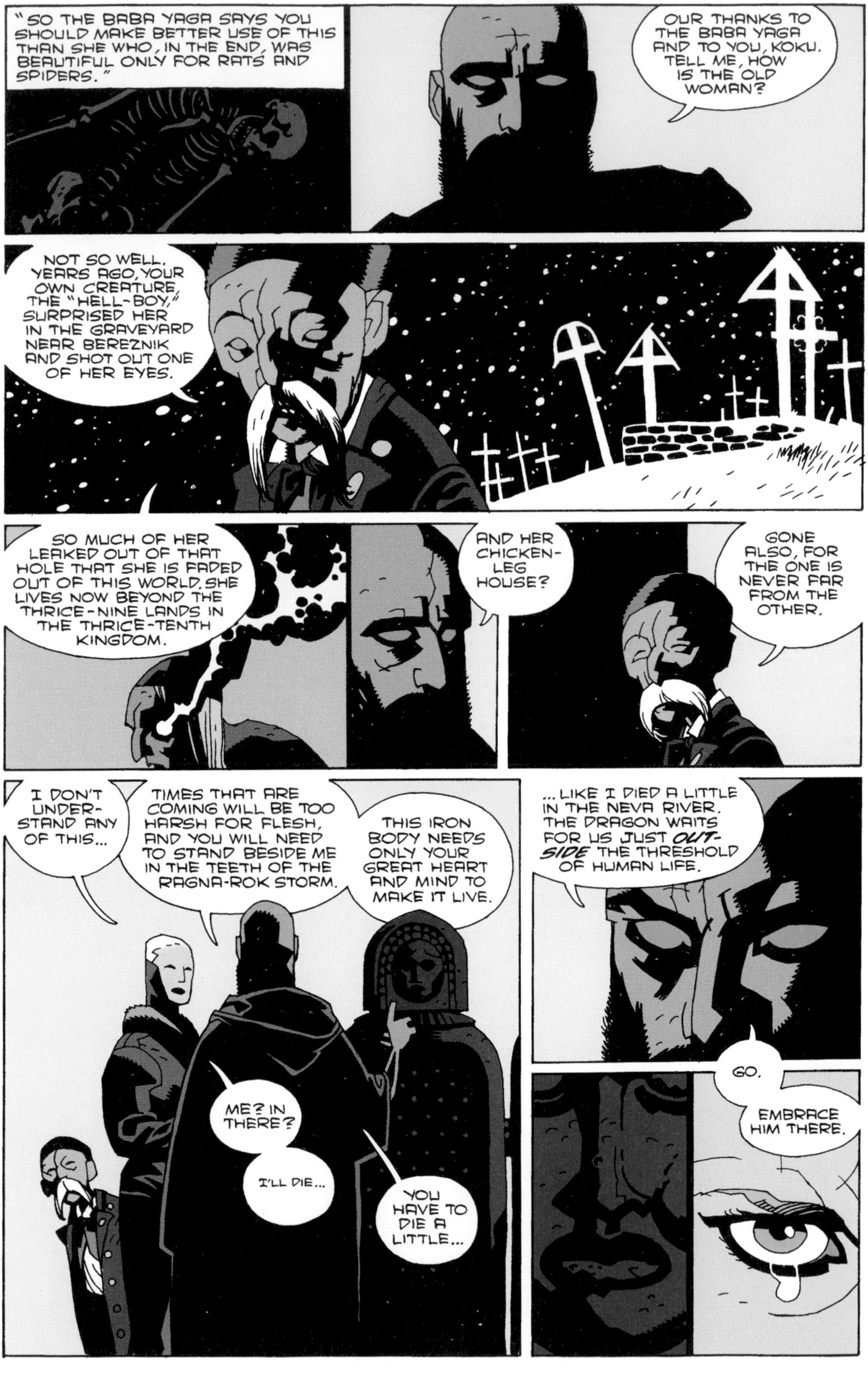
"SO THE BABA YAGA SAYS YOU SHOULD MAKE BETTER USE OF THIS THAN SHE WHO, IN THE END, WAS BEAUTIFUL ONLY FOR RATS AND SPIDERS."
OUR THANKS TO THE BABA YAGA AND TO YOU, KOKU. TELL ME, HOW IS THE OLD WOMAN?
NOT SO WELL. YEARS AGO, YOUR OWN CREATURE, THE "HELL-BOY," SURPRISED HER IN THE GRAVEYARD NEAR BEREZNIK AND SHOT OUT ONE OF HER EYES.
SO MUCH OF HER LEAKED OUT OF THAT HOLE THAT SHE IS FADED OUT OF THIS WORLD. SHE LIVES NOW BEYOND THE THRICE-NINE LANDS IN THE THRICE-TENTH KINGDOM.
AND HER CHICKEN-LEG HOUSE?
GONE ALSO, FOR THE ONE IS NEVER FAR FROM THE OTHER.
I DON'T UNDER-STAND ANY OF THIS...
TIMES THAT ARE COMING WILL BE TOO HARSH FOR FLESH, AND YOU WILL NEED TO STAND BESIDE ME IN THE TEETH OF THE RAGNA-ROK STORM.
THIS IRON BODY NEEDS ONLY YOUR GREAT HEART AND MIND TO MAKE IT LIVE.
ME? IN THERE?
I'LL DIE...
YOU HAVE TO DIE A LITTLE...
...LIKE I DIED A LITTLE IN THE NEVA RIVER. THE DRAGON WAITS FOR US JUST OUT-SIDE THE THRESHOLD OF HUMAN LIFE.
GO.
EMBRACE HIM THERE.

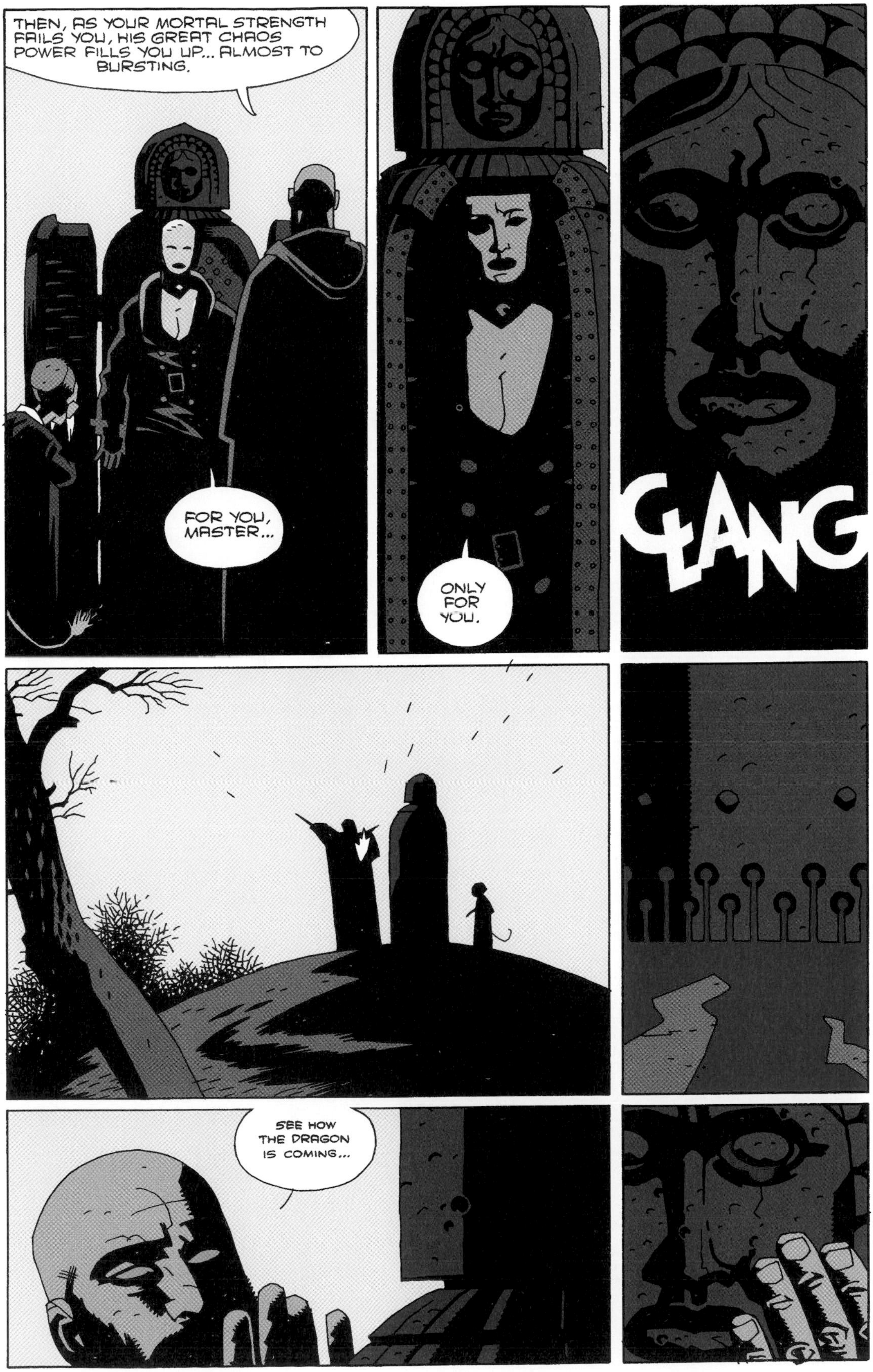
THEN, AS YOUR MORTAL STRENGTH FAILS YOU, HIS GREAT CHAOS POWER FILLS YOU UP... ALMOST TO BURSTING.
FOR YOU, MASTER...
ONLY FOR YOU.
CLANG
SEE HOW THE DRAGON IS COMING...

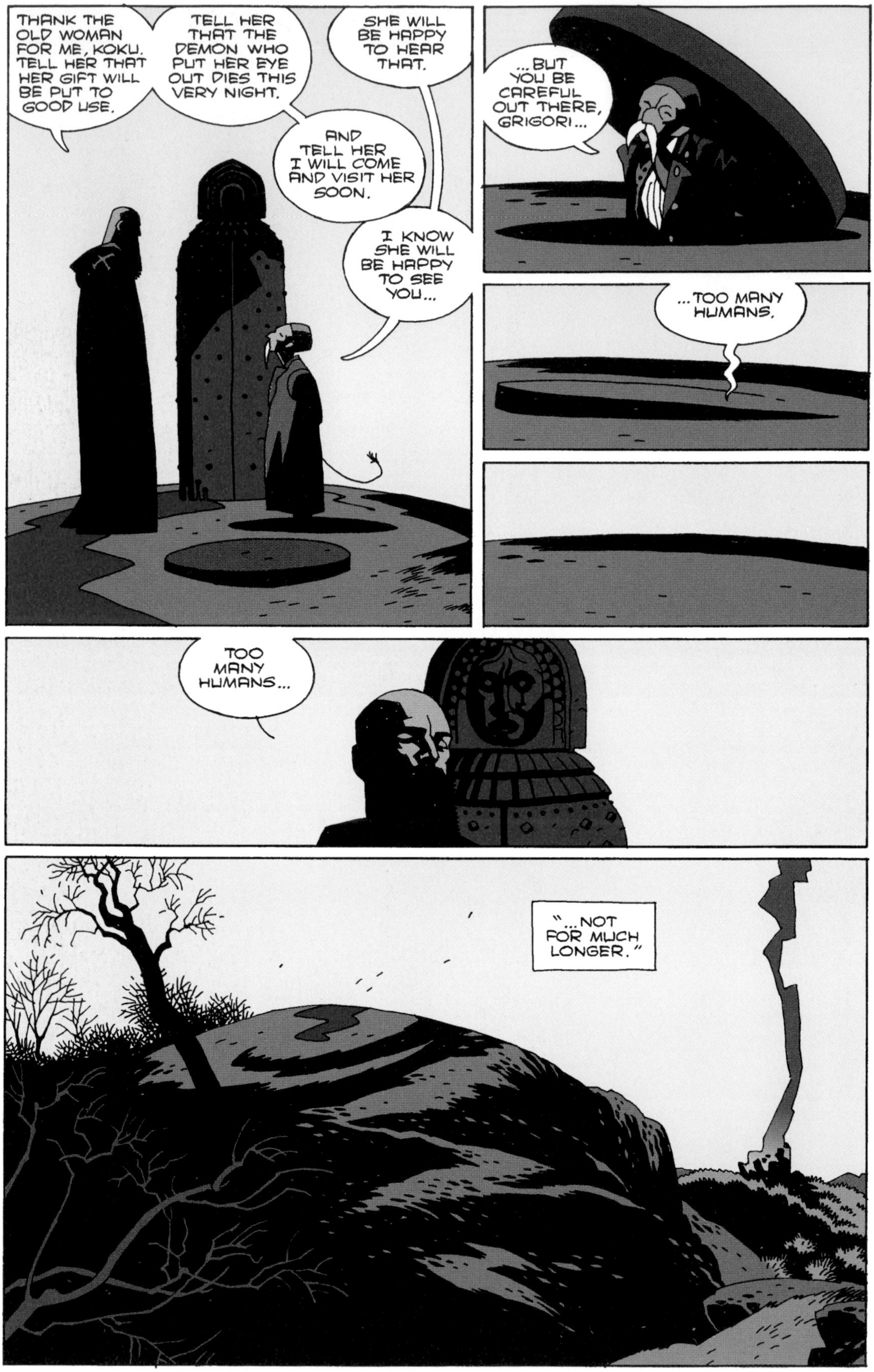
THANK THE OLD WOMAN FOR ME, KOKU. TELL HER THAT HER GIFT WILL BE PUT TO GOOD USE.
TELL HER THAT THE DEMON WHO PUT HER EYE OUT DIES THIS VERY NIGHT.
SHE WILL BE HAPPY TO HEAR THAT.
AND TELL HER I WILL COME AND VISIT HER SOON.
I KNOW SHE WILL BE HAPPY TO SEE YOU...
...BUT YOU BE CAREFUL OUT THERE, GRIGORI...
...TOO MANY HUMANS.
TOO MANY HUMANS...
"...NOT FOR MUCH LONGER."

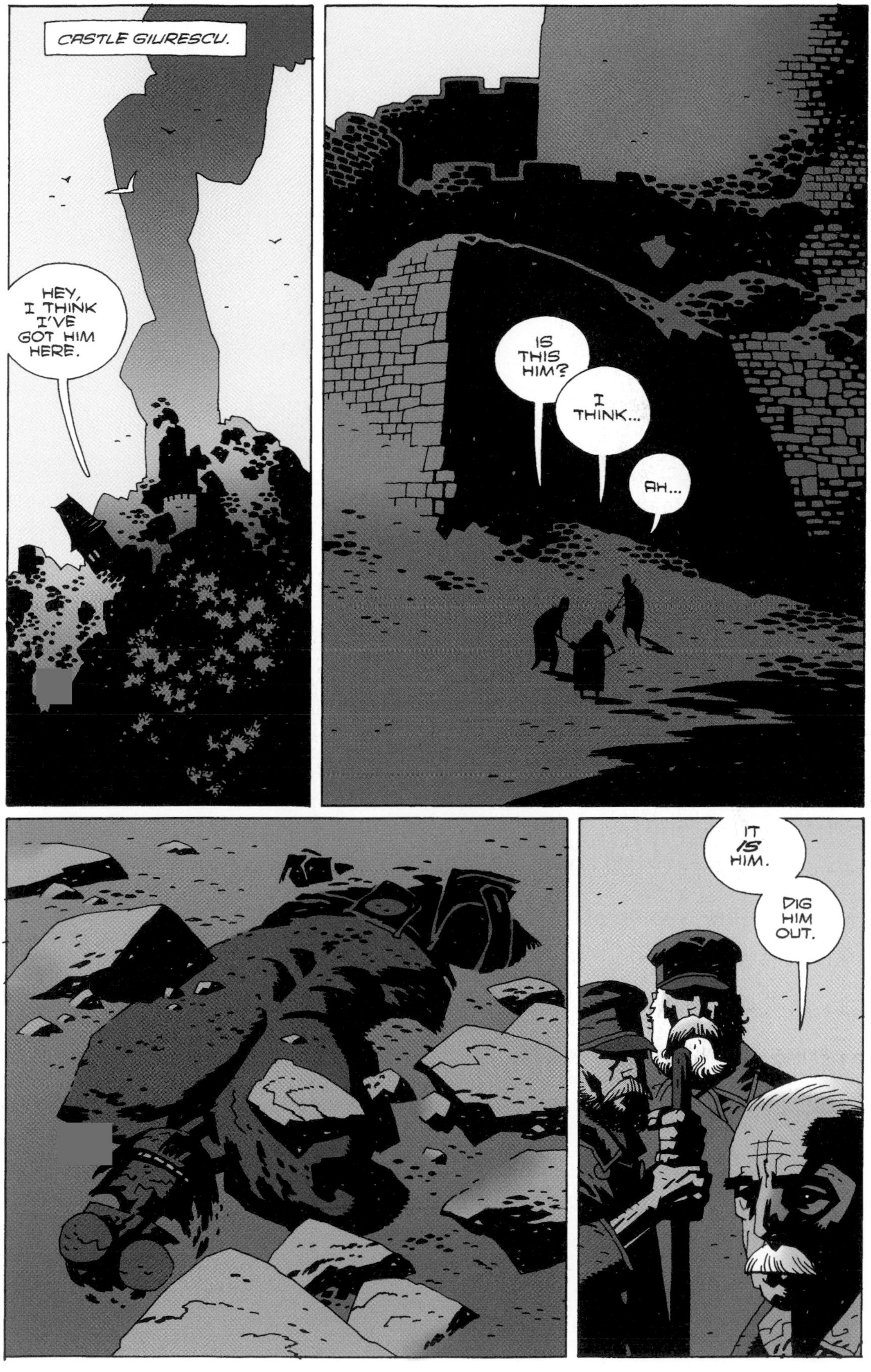
CASTLE GIURESCU.
HEY, I THINK I'VE GOT HIM HERE.
IS THIS HIM?
I THINK...
AH...
IT IS HIM.
DIG HIM OUT.

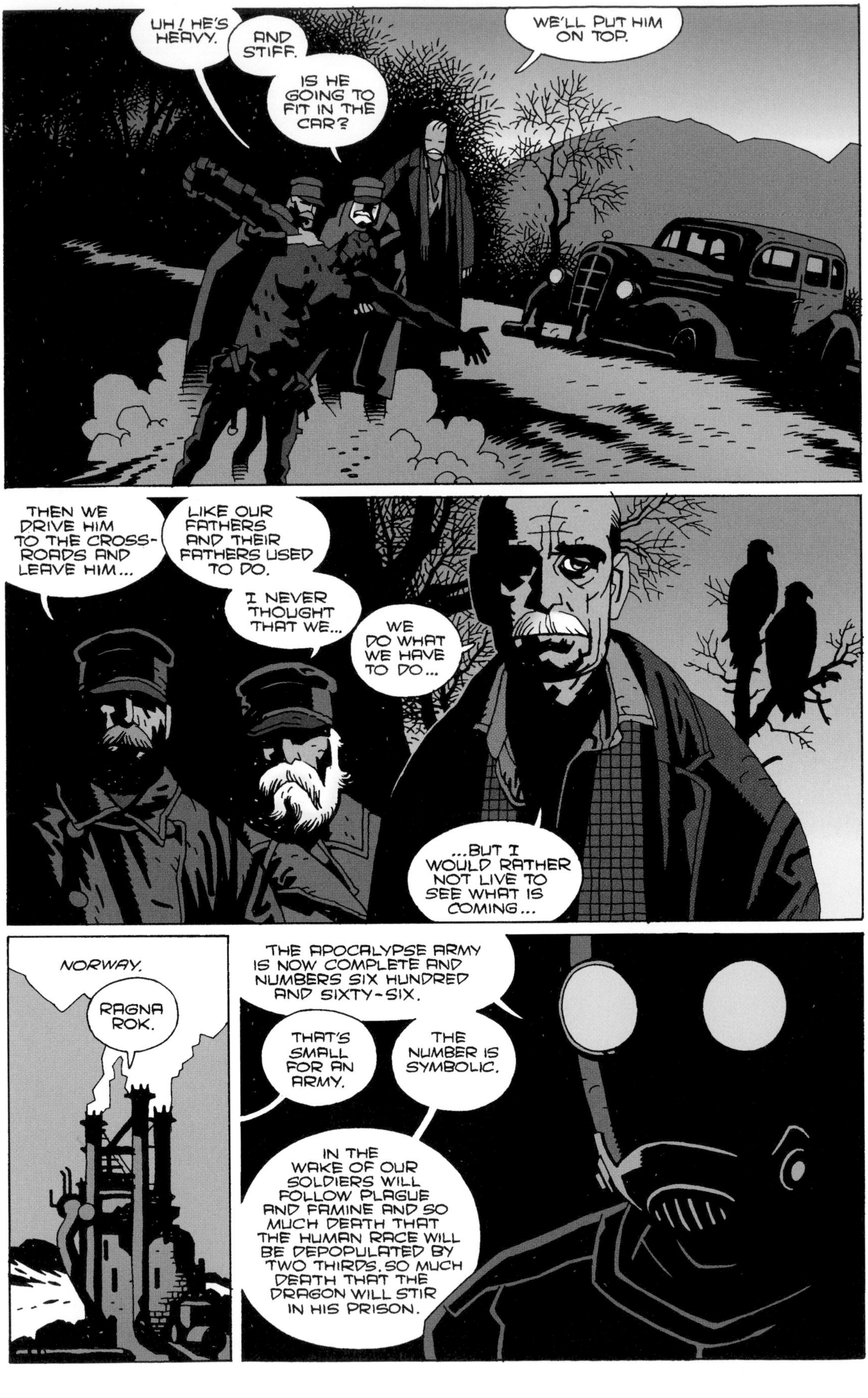
UH! HE'S HEAVY.
AND STIFF.
IS HE GOING TO FIT IN THE CAR?
WE'LL PUT HIM ON TOP.
THEN WE DRIVE HIM TO THE CROSS-ROADS AND LEAVE HIM...
LIKE OUR FATHERS AND THEIR FATHERS USED TO DO.
I NEVER THOUGHT THAT WE...
WE DO WHAT WE HAVE TO DO...
...BUT I WOULD RATHER NOT LIVE TO SEE WHAT IS COMING...
NORWAY.
RAGNA ROK.
THE APOCALYPSE ARMY IS NOW COMPLETE AND NUMBERS SIX HUNDRED AND SIXTY-SIX.
THAT'S SMALL FOR AN ARMY.
THE NUMBER IS SYMBOLIC.
IN THE WAKE OF OUR SOLDIERS WILL FOLLOW PLAGUE AND FAMINE AND SO MUCH DEATH THAT THE HUMAN RACE WILL BE DEPOPULATED BY TWO THIRDS. SO MUCH DEATH THAT THE DRAGON WILL STIR IN HIS PRISON.

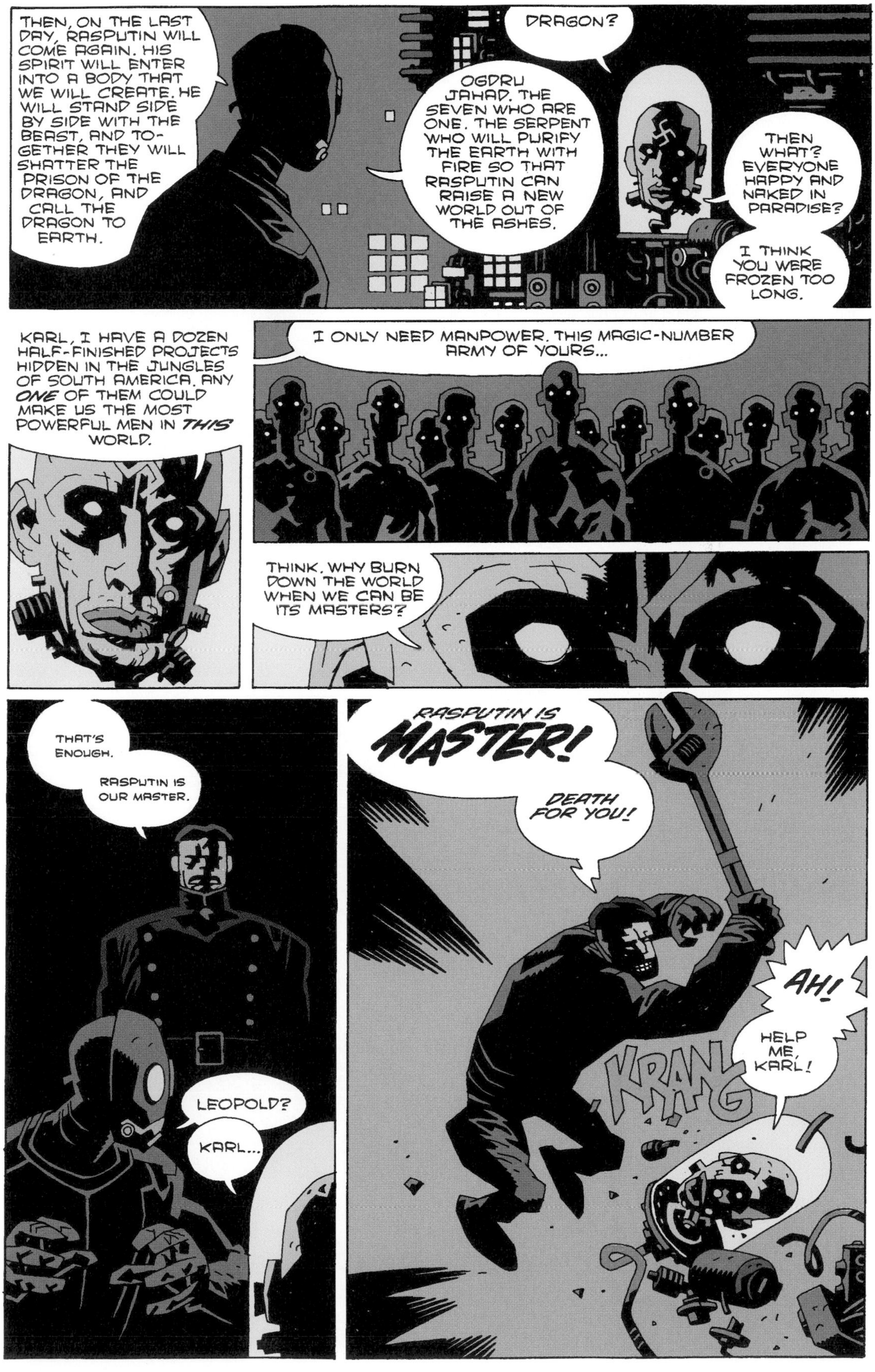
THEN, ON THE LAST DAY, RASPUTIN WILL COME AGAIN. HIS SPIRIT WILL ENTER INTO A BODY THAT WE WILL CREATE. HE WILL STAND SIDE BY SIDE WITH THE BEAST, AND TOGETHER THEY WILL SHATTER THE PRISON OF THE DRAGON, AND CALL THE DRAGON TO EARTH.
DRAGON?
OGDRU JAHAD. THE SEVEN WHO ARE ONE. THE SERPENT WHO WILL PURIFY THE EARTH WITH FIRE SO THAT RASPUTIN CAN RAISE A NEW WORLD OUT OF THE ASHES.
THEN WHAT? EVERYONE HAPPY AND NAKED IN PARADISE?
I THINK YOU WERE FROZEN TOO LONG.
KARL, I HAVE A DOZEN HALF-FINISHED PROJECTS HIDDEN IN THE JUNGLES OF SOUTH AMERICA. ANY ONE OF THEM COULD MAKE US THE MOST POWERFUL MEN IN THIS WORLD.
I ONLY NEED MANPOWER. THIS MAGIC-NUMBER ARMY OF YOURS...
THINK. WHY BURN DOWN THE WORLD WHEN WE CAN BE ITS MASTERS?
THAT'S ENOUGH.
RASPUTIN IS OUR MASTER.
LEOPOLD?
KARL...
RASPUTIN IS MASTER!
DEATH FOR YOU!
KRANG
AH!
HELP ME, KARL!

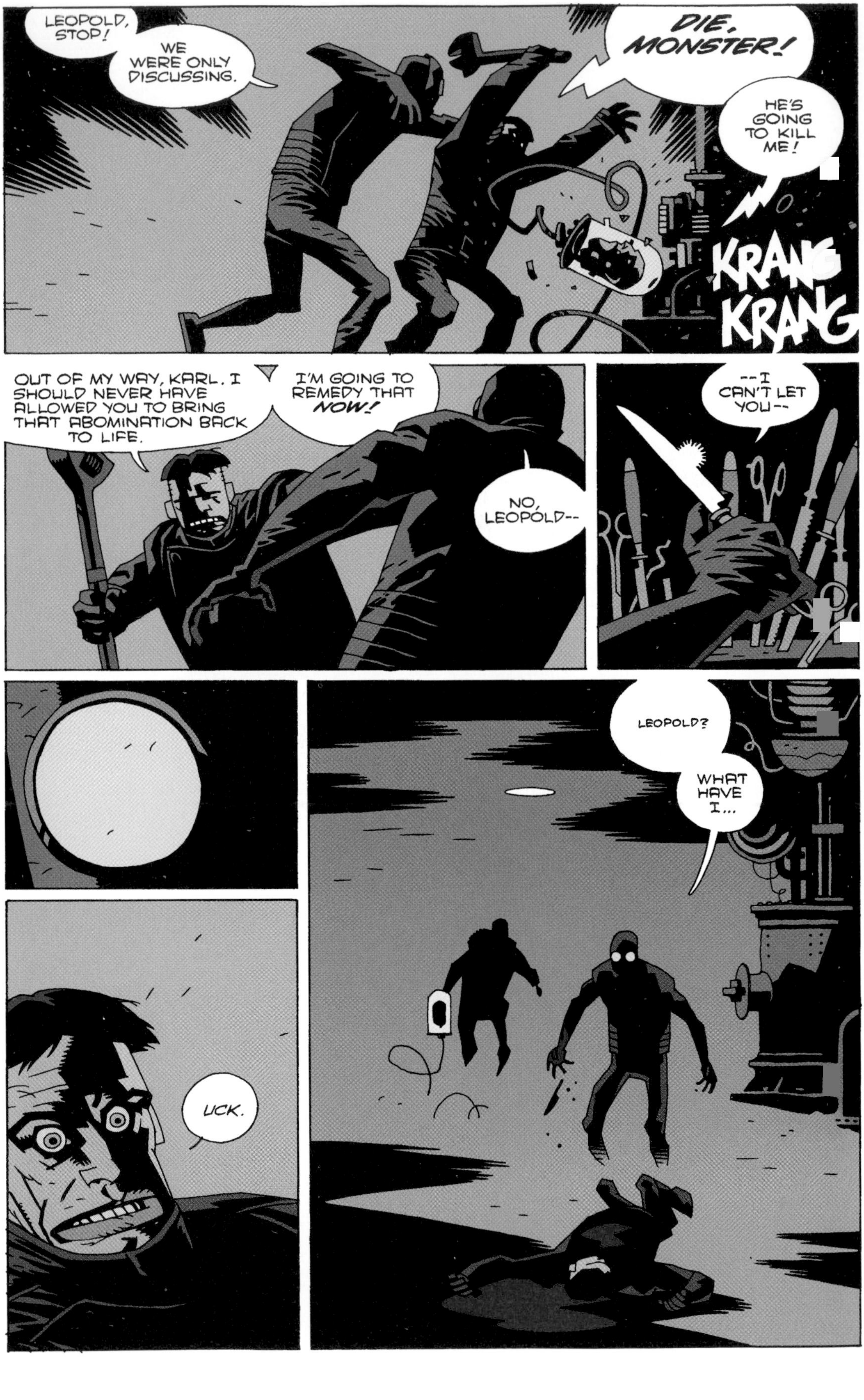

LEOPOLD, STOP!
WE WERE ONLY DISCUSSING.
DIE, MONSTER!
HE'S GOING TO KILL ME!
KRANG KRANG
OUT OF MY WAY, KARL. I SHOULD NEVER HAVE ALLOWED YOU TO BRING THAT ABOMINATION BACK TO LIFE.
I'M GOING TO REMEDY THAT NOW!
NO, LEOPOLD--
--I CAN'T LET YOU--
UCK.
LEOPOLD?
WHAT HAVE I...

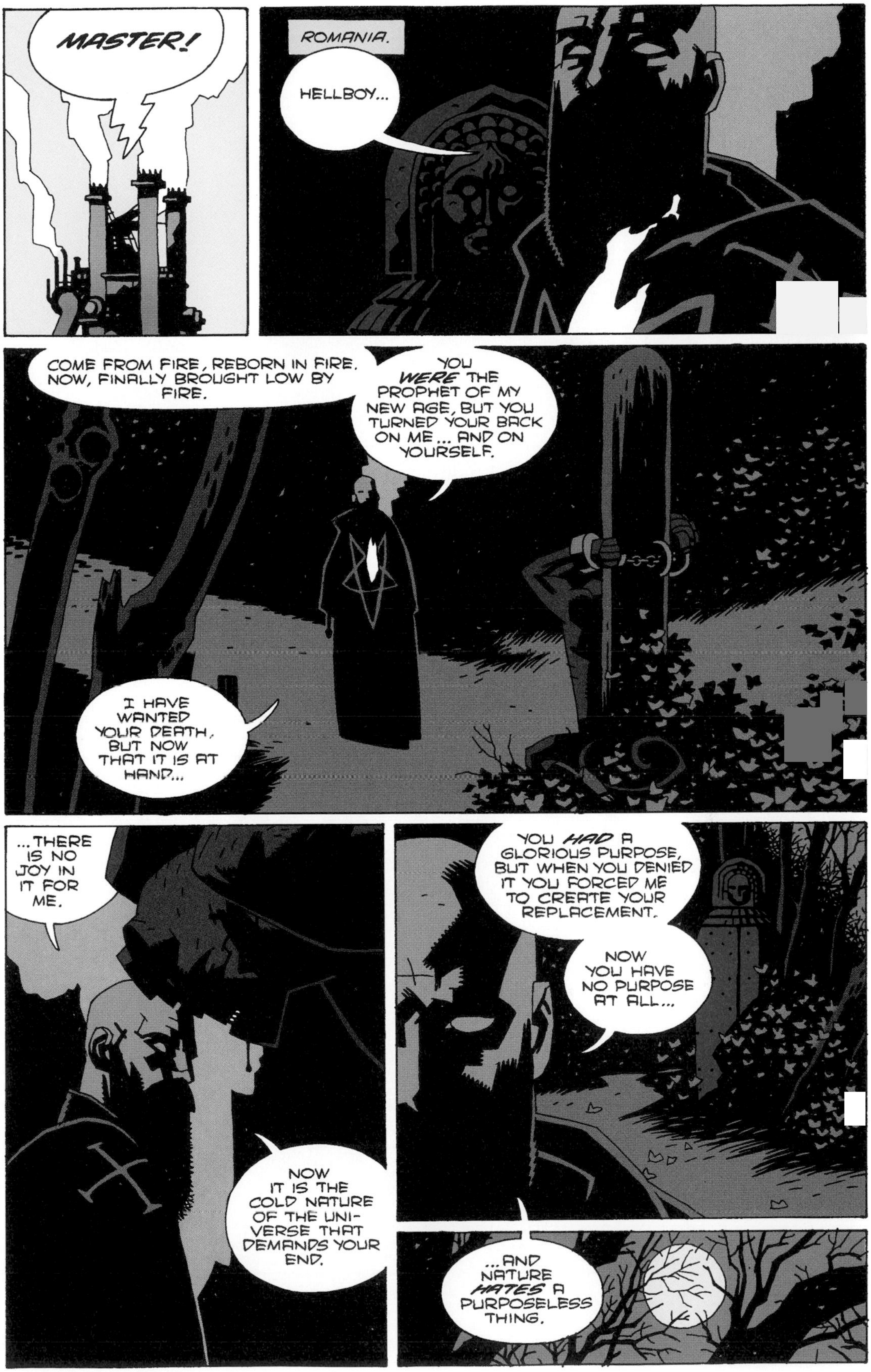
MASTER!
ROMANIA.
HELLBOY...
COME FROM FIRE, REBORN IN FIRE. NOW, FINALLY BROUGHT LOW BY FIRE.
YOU WERE THE PROPHET OF MY NEW AGE, BUT YOU TURNED YOUR BACK ON ME... AND ON YOURSELF.
I HAVE WANTED YOUR DEATH, BUT NOW THAT IT IS AT HAND...
...THERE IS NO JOY IN IT FOR ME.
NOW IT IS THE COLD NATURE OF THE UNI-VERSE THAT DEMANDS YOUR END.
YOU HAD A GLORIOUS PURPOSE, BUT WHEN YOU DENIED IT YOU FORCED ME TO CREATE YOUR REPLACEMENT.
NOW YOU HAVE NO PURPOSE AT ALL...
...AND NATURE HATES A PURPOSELESS THING.

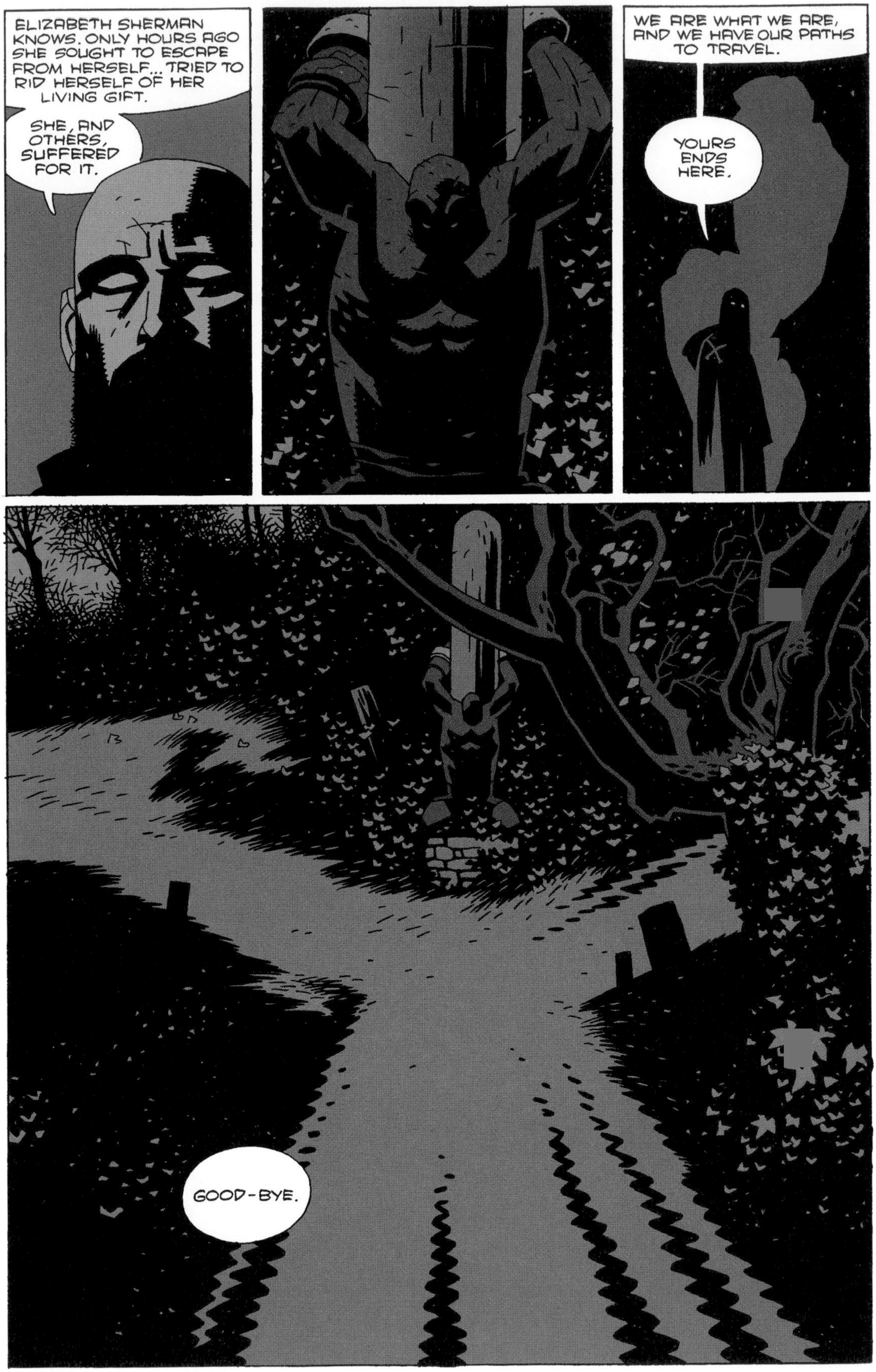
ELIZABETH SHERMAN KNOWS. ONLY HOURS AGO SHE SOUGHT TO ESCAPE FROM HERSELF... TRIED TO RID HERSELF OF HER LIVING GIFT.
SHE, AND OTHERS, SUFFERED FOR IT.
WE ARE WHAT WE ARE, AND WE HAVE OUR PATHS TO TRAVEL.
YOURS ENDS HERE.
GOOD-BYE.

CHAPTER FIVE

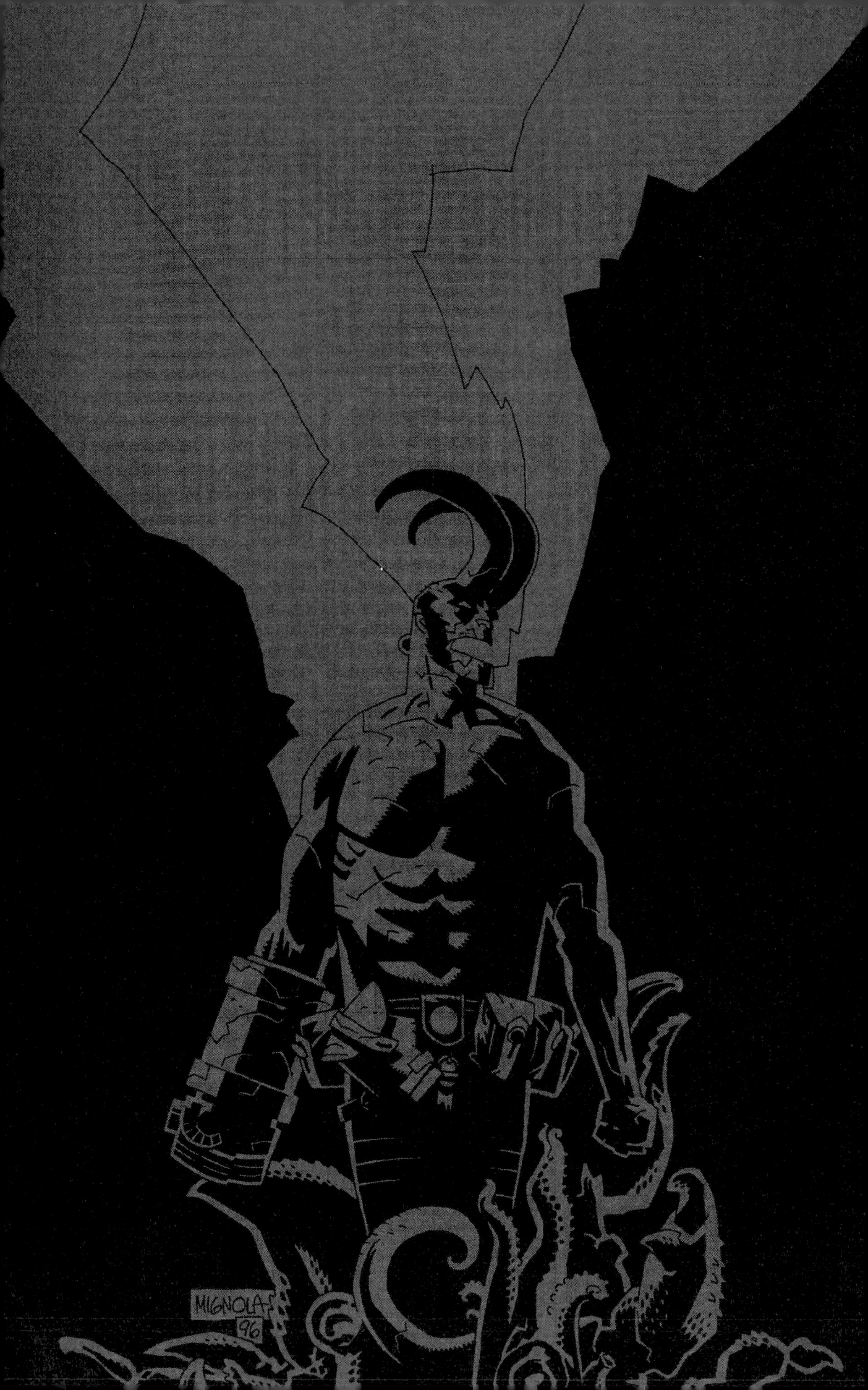
MIGNOLA
96

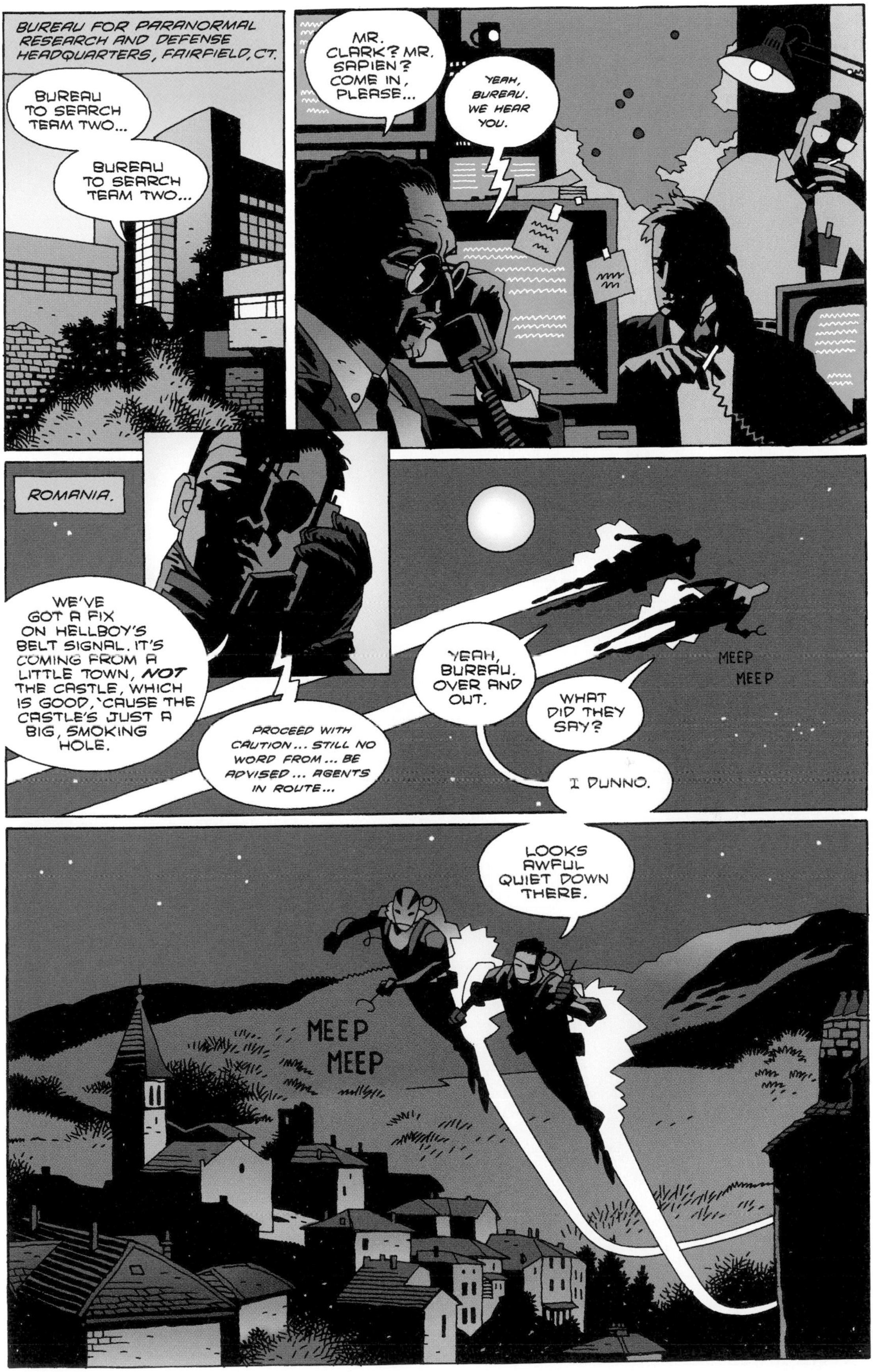
BUREAU FOR PARANORMAL RESEARCH AND DEFENSE HEADQUARTERS, FAIRFIELD, CT.
BUREAU TO SEARCH TEAM TWO...
BUREAU TO SEARCH TEAM TWO...
MR. CLARK? MR. SAPIEN? COME IN, PLEASE...
YEAH, BUREAU. WE HEAR YOU.
ROMANIA.
WE'VE GOT A FIX ON HELLBOY'S BELT SIGNAL. IT'S COMING FROM A LITTLE TOWN, NOT THE CASTLE, WHICH IS GOOD, 'CAUSE THE CASTLE'S JUST A BIG, SMOKING HOLE.
PROCEED WITH CAUTION... STILL NO WORD FROM... BE ADVISED... AGENTS IN ROUTE...
YEAH, BUREAU. OVER AND OUT.
MEEP MEEP
WHAT DID THEY SAY?
I DUNNO.
LOOKS AWFUL QUIET DOWN THERE.
MEEP MEEP

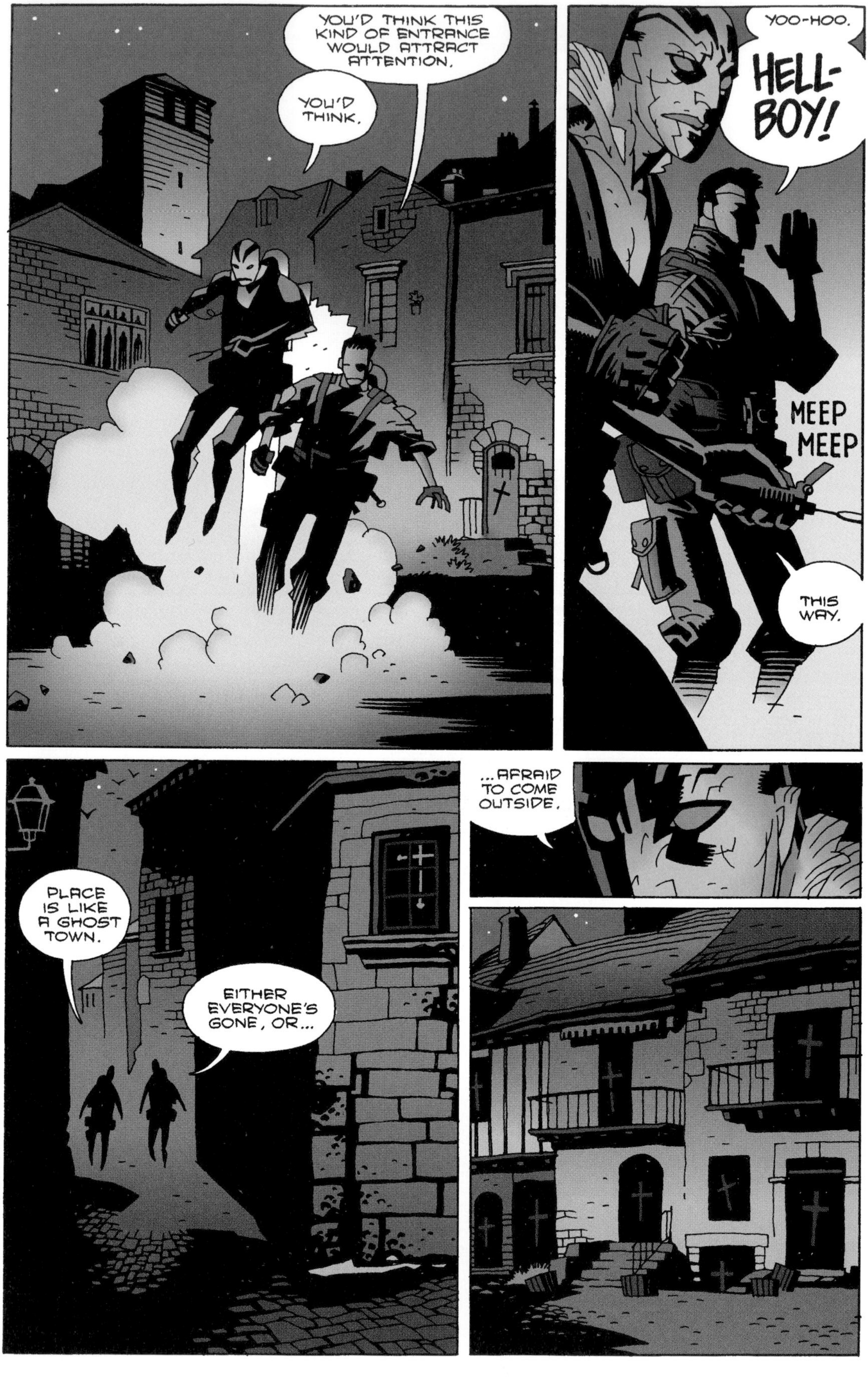
YOU'D THINK THIS KIND OF ENTRANCE WOULD ATTRACT ATTENTION.
YOU'D THINK.
YOO-HOO.
HELL-BOY!
MEEP MEEP
THIS WAY.
PLACE IS LIKE A GHOST TOWN.
EITHER EVERYONE'S GONE, OR...
...AFRAID TO COME OUTSIDE.

62
VAMPIRE TOWN.
THIS WAY.
MEEP MEEP
MEEEP
CLICK

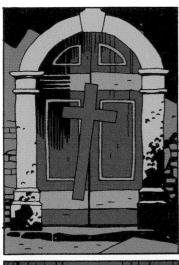

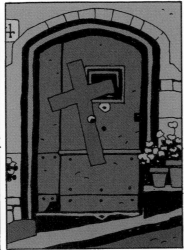

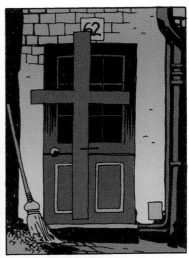

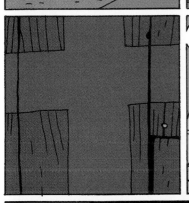

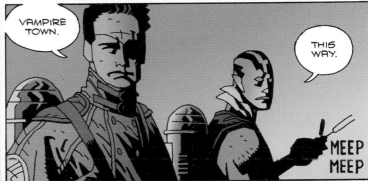

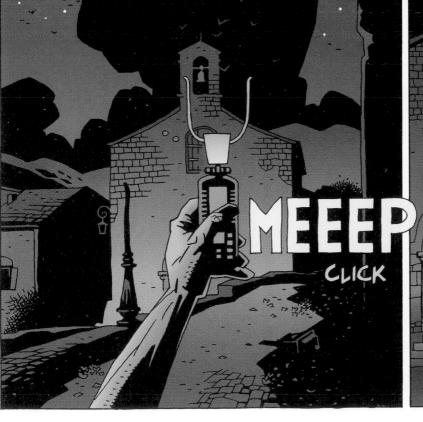

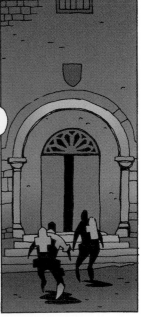

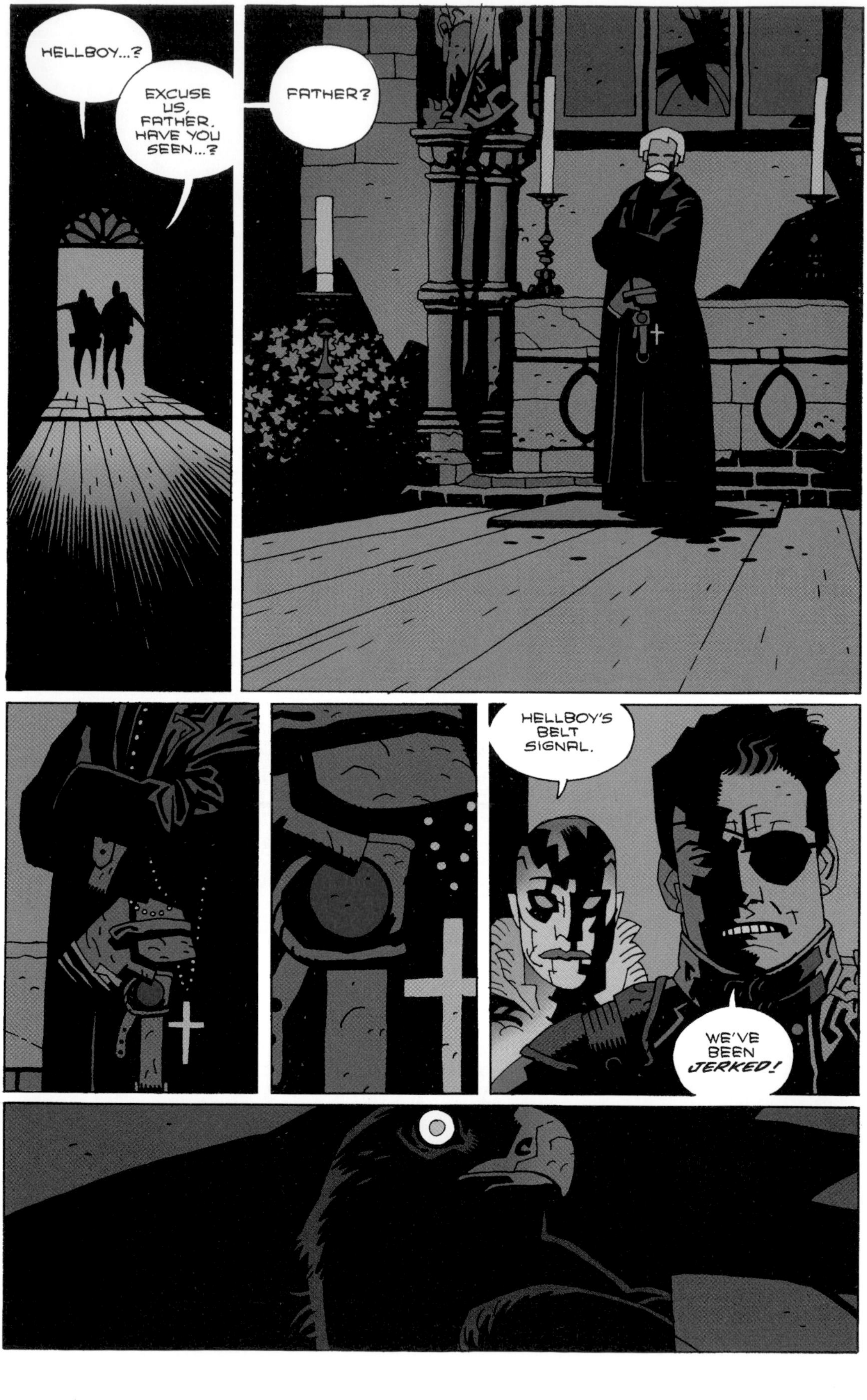
HELLBOY...?
EXCUSE US, FATHER. HAVE YOU SEEN...?
FATHER?
HELLBOY'S BELT SIGNAL.
WE'VE BEEN JERKED!

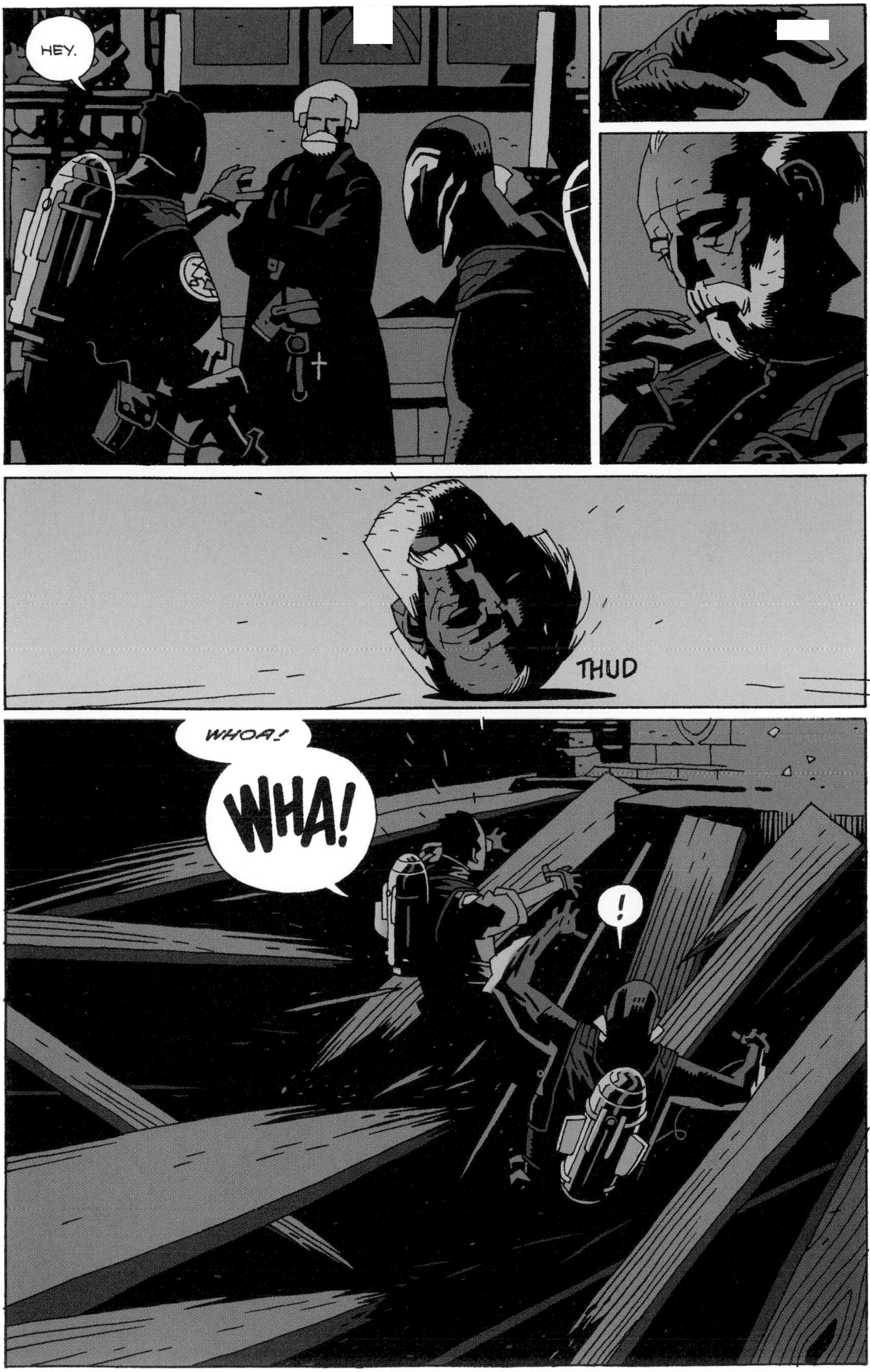
HEY.
THUD
WHOA!
WHA!
!

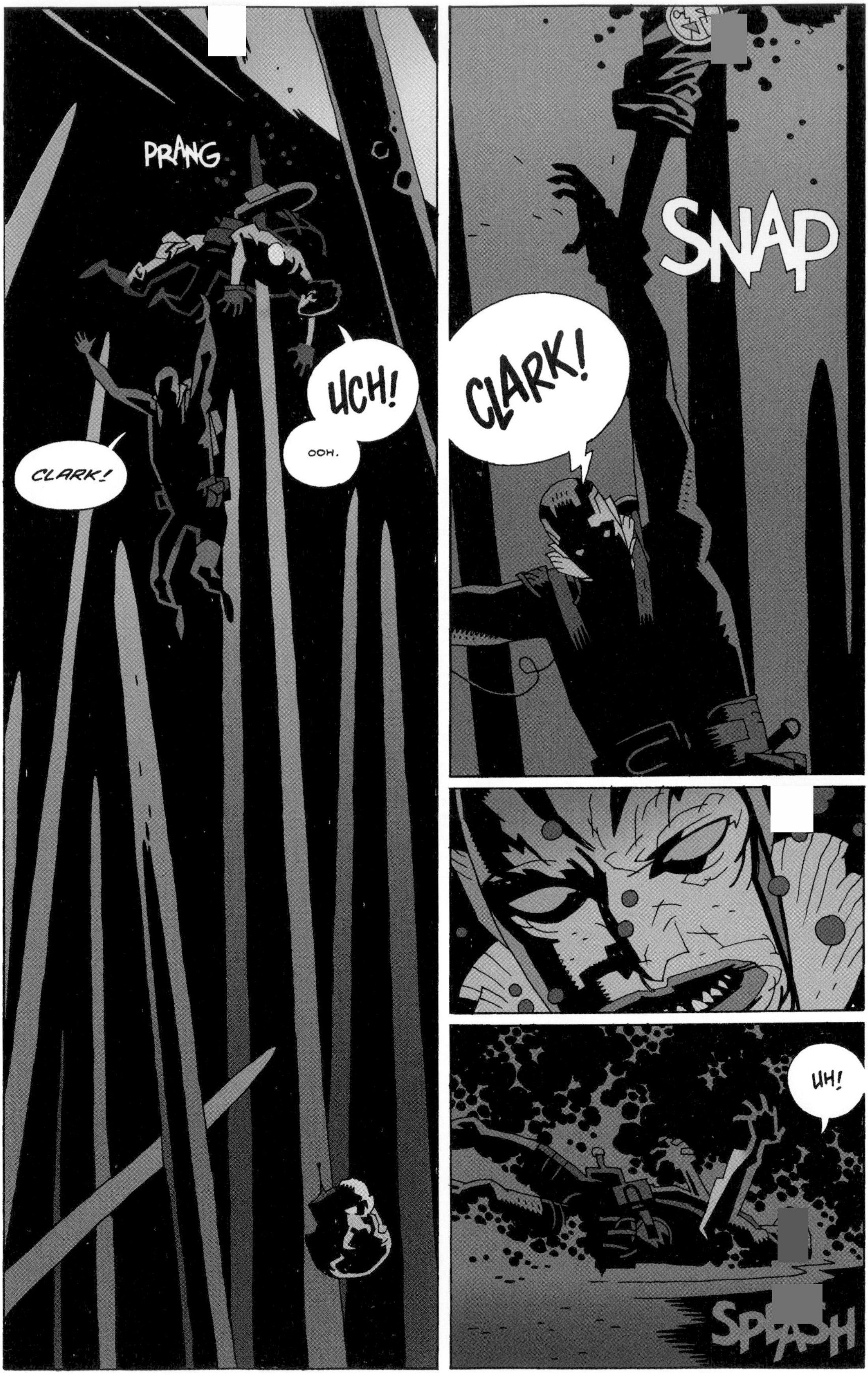
PRANG
CLARK!
UCH!
OOH.
SNAP
CLARK!
UH!
SPLASH

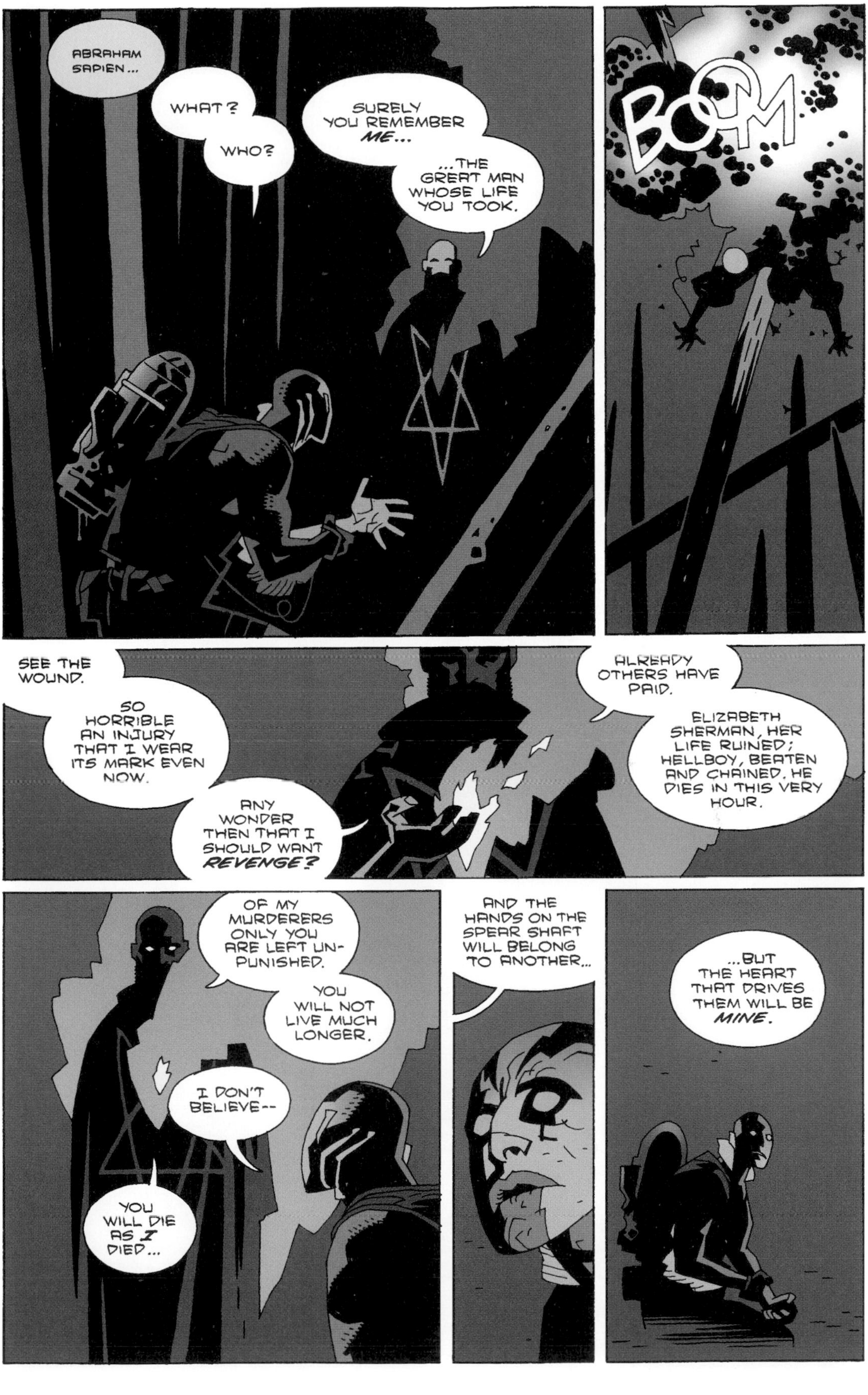
ABRAHAM SAPIEN...
WHAT? WHO?
SURELY YOU REMEMBER *ME*...
...THE GREAT MAN WHOSE LIFE YOU TOOK.
BOOM
SEE THE WOUND.
SO HORRIBLE AN INJURY THAT I WEAR ITS MARK EVEN NOW.
ANY WONDER THEN THAT I SHOULD WANT *REVENGE?*
ALREADY OTHERS HAVE PAID.
ELIZABETH SHERMAN, HER LIFE RUINED; HELLBOY, BEATEN AND CHAINED. HE DIES IN THIS VERY HOUR.
OF MY MURDERERS ONLY YOU ARE LEFT UN-PUNISHED.
YOU WILL NOT LIVE MUCH LONGER.
I DON'T BELIEVE--
YOU WILL DIE AS *I* DIED...
AND THE HANDS ON THE SPEAR SHAFT WILL BELONG TO ANOTHER...
...BUT THE HEART THAT DRIVES THEM WILL BE *MINE*.

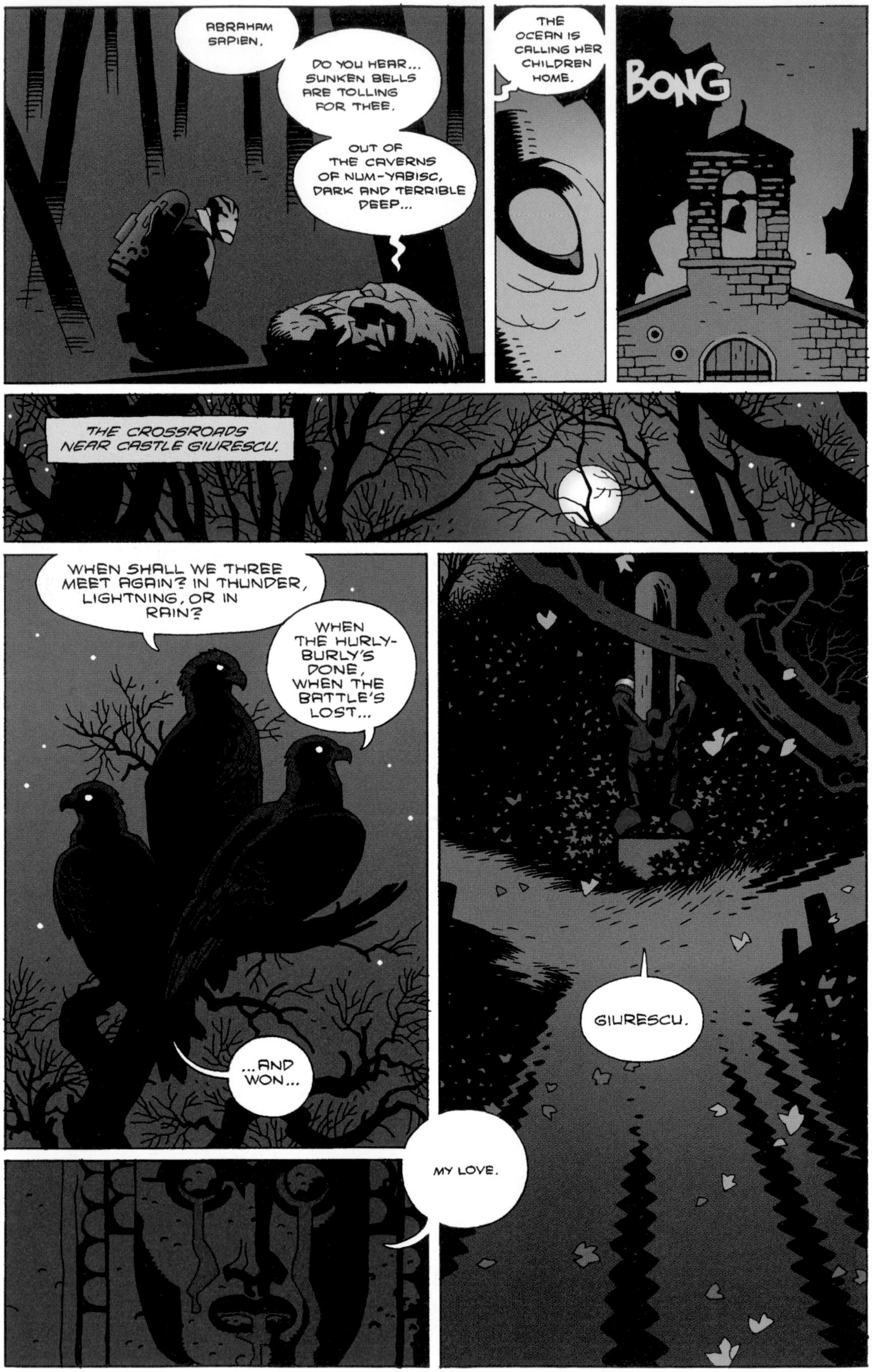
ABRAHAM SAPIEN.
DO YOU HEAR... SUNKEN BELLS ARE TOLLING FOR THEE.
OUT OF THE CAVERNS OF NUM-YABISC, DARK AND TERRIBLE DEEP...
THE OCEAN IS CALLING HER CHILDREN HOME.
BONG
THE CROSSROADS NEAR CASTLE GIURESCU.
WHEN SHALL WE THREE MEET AGAIN? IN THUNDER, LIGHTNING, OR IN RAIN?
WHEN THE HURLY-BURLY'S DONE, WHEN THE BATTLE'S LOST...
...AND WON...
GIURESCU.
MY LOVE.

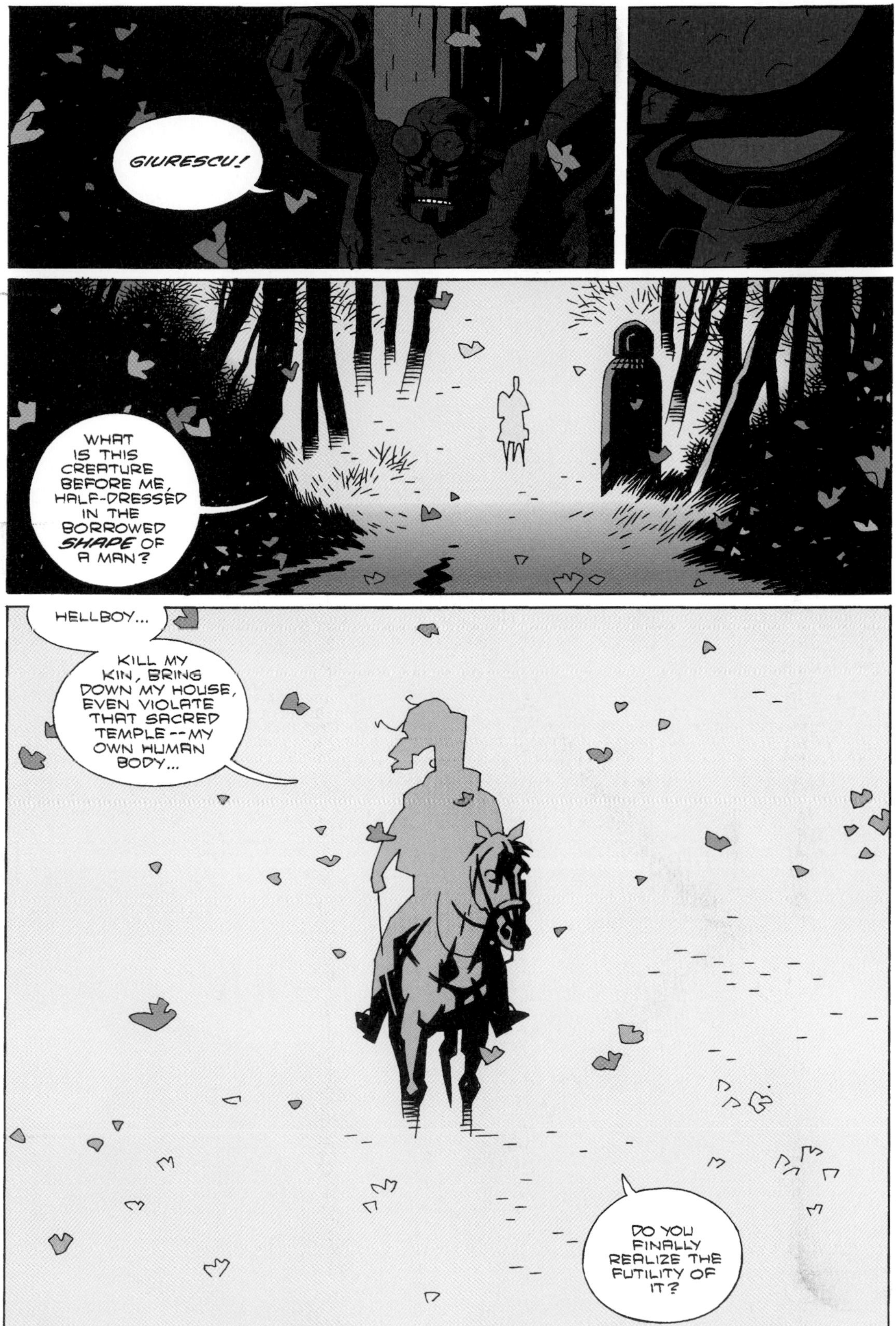
GIURESCU!
WHAT IS THIS CREATURE BEFORE ME, HALF-DRESSED IN THE BORROWED *SHAPE* OF A MAN?
HELLBOY...
KILL MY KIN, BRING DOWN MY HOUSE, EVEN VIOLATE THAT SACRED TEMPLE--MY OWN HUMAN BODY...
DO YOU FINALLY REALIZE THE FUTILITY OF IT?

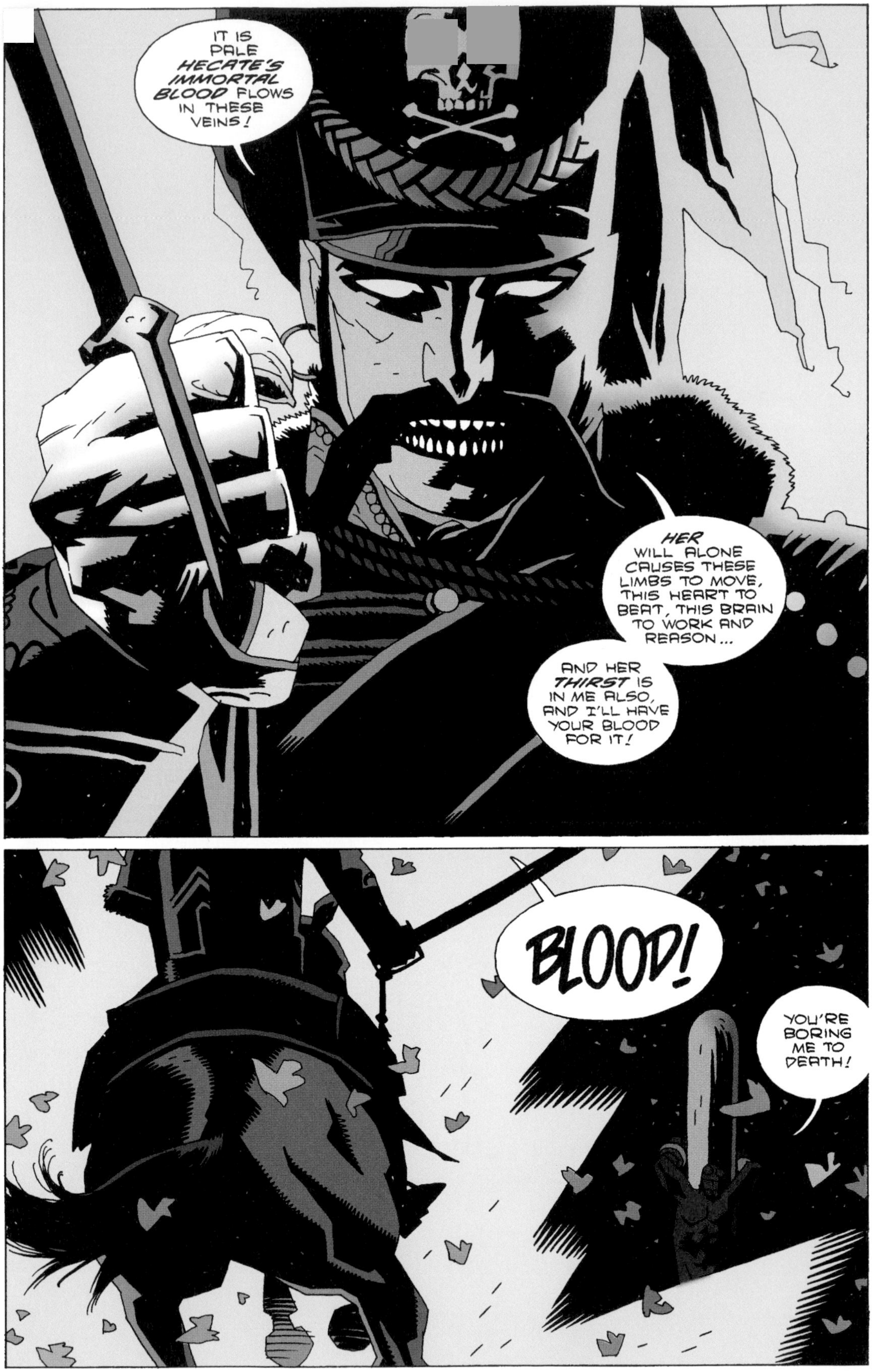
IT IS PALE HECATE'S IMMORTAL BLOOD FLOWS IN THESE VEINS!
HER WILL ALONE CAUSES THESE LIMBS TO MOVE, THIS HEART TO BEAT, THIS BRAIN TO WORK AND REASON...
AND HER THIRST IS IN ME ALSO, AND I'LL HAVE YOUR BLOOD FOR IT!
BLOOD!
YOU'RE BORING ME TO DEATH!

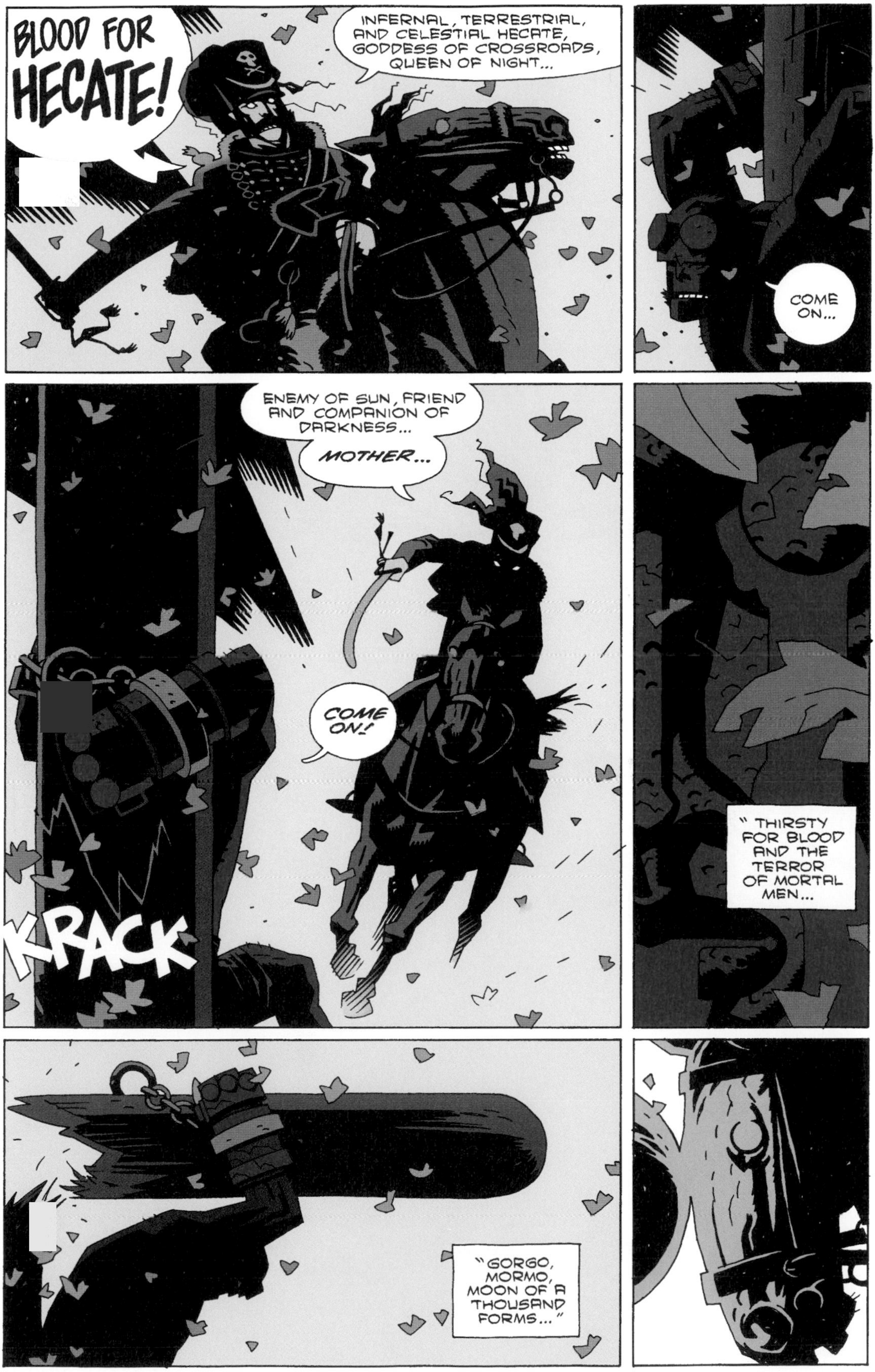
BLOOD FOR HECATE!
INFERNAL, TERRESTRIAL, AND CELESTIAL HECATE, GODDESS OF CROSSROADS, QUEEN OF NIGHT...
COME ON...
ENEMY OF SUN, FRIEND AND COMPANION OF DARKNESS...
MOTHER...
COME ON!
KRACK
"THIRSTY FOR BLOOD AND THE TERROR OF MORTAL MEN...
"GORGO, MORMO, MOON OF A THOUSAND FORMS..."

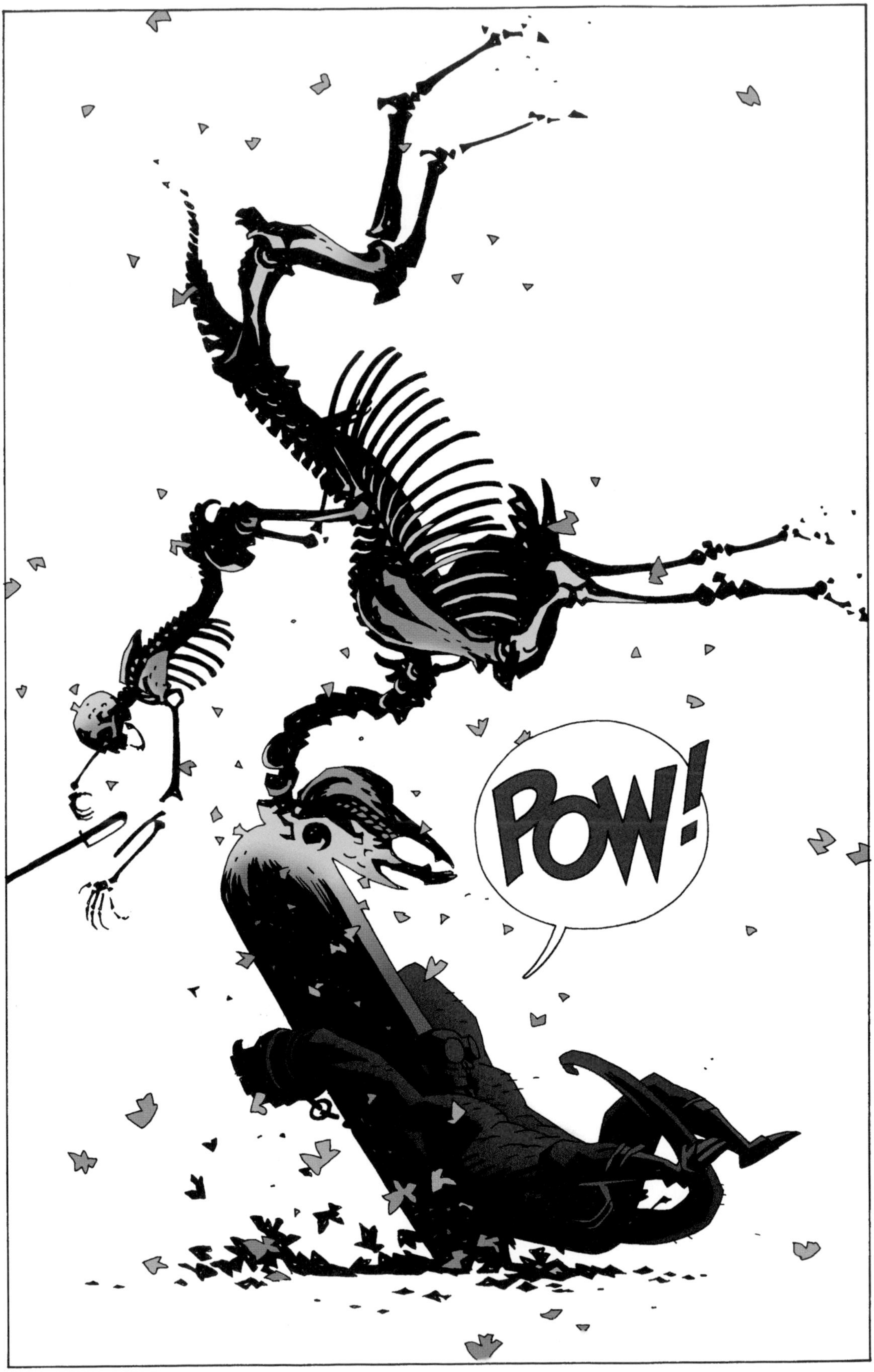
POW!

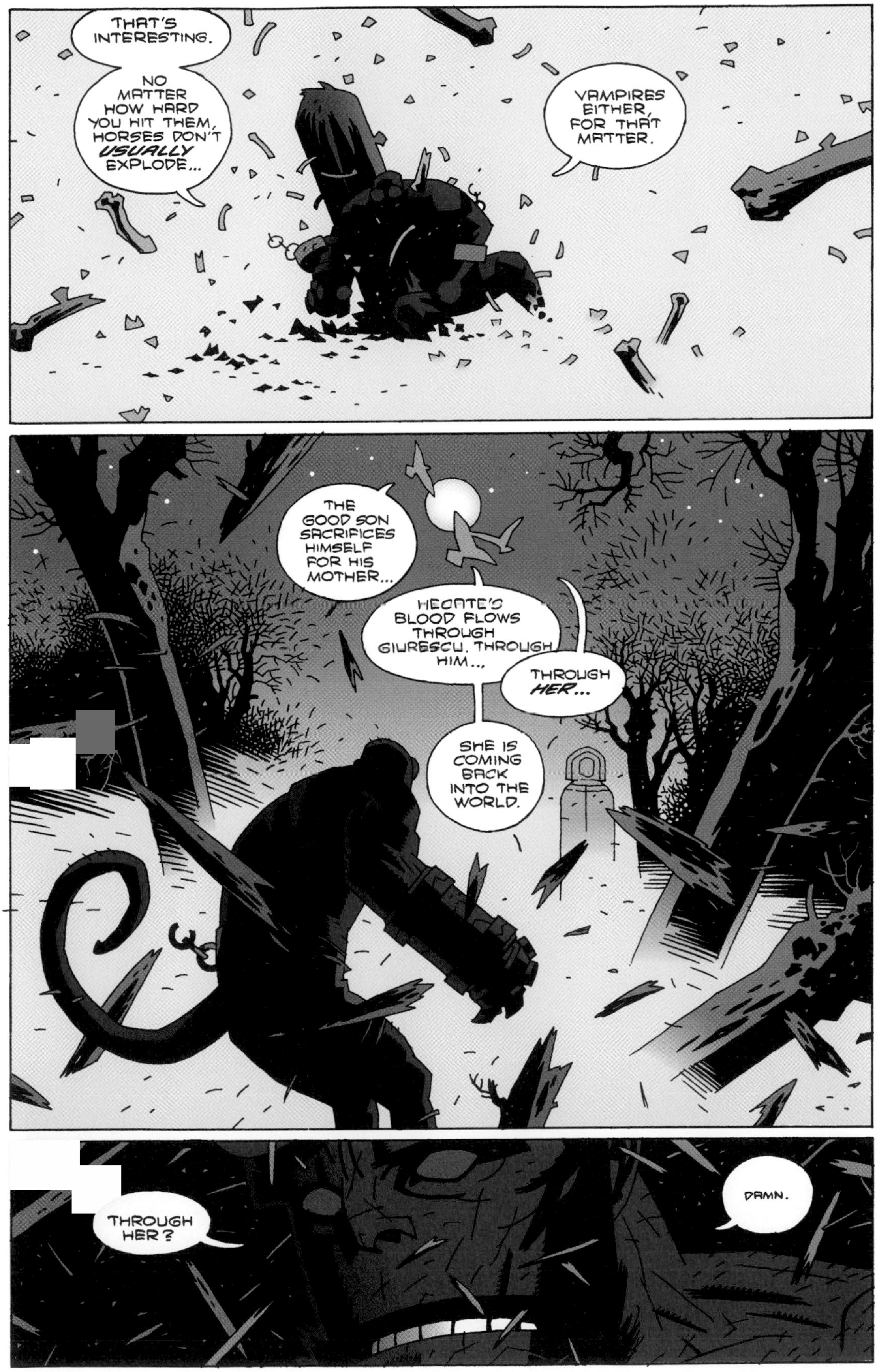
THAT'S INTERESTING.
NO MATTER HOW HARD YOU HIT THEM, HORSES DON'T USUALLY EXPLODE...
VAMPIRES EITHER, FOR THAT MATTER.
THE GOOD SON SACRIFICES HIMSELF FOR HIS MOTHER...
HECATE'S BLOOD FLOWS THROUGH GIURESCU. THROUGH HIM...
THROUGH HER...
SHE IS COMING BACK INTO THE WORLD.
THROUGH HER?
DAMN.

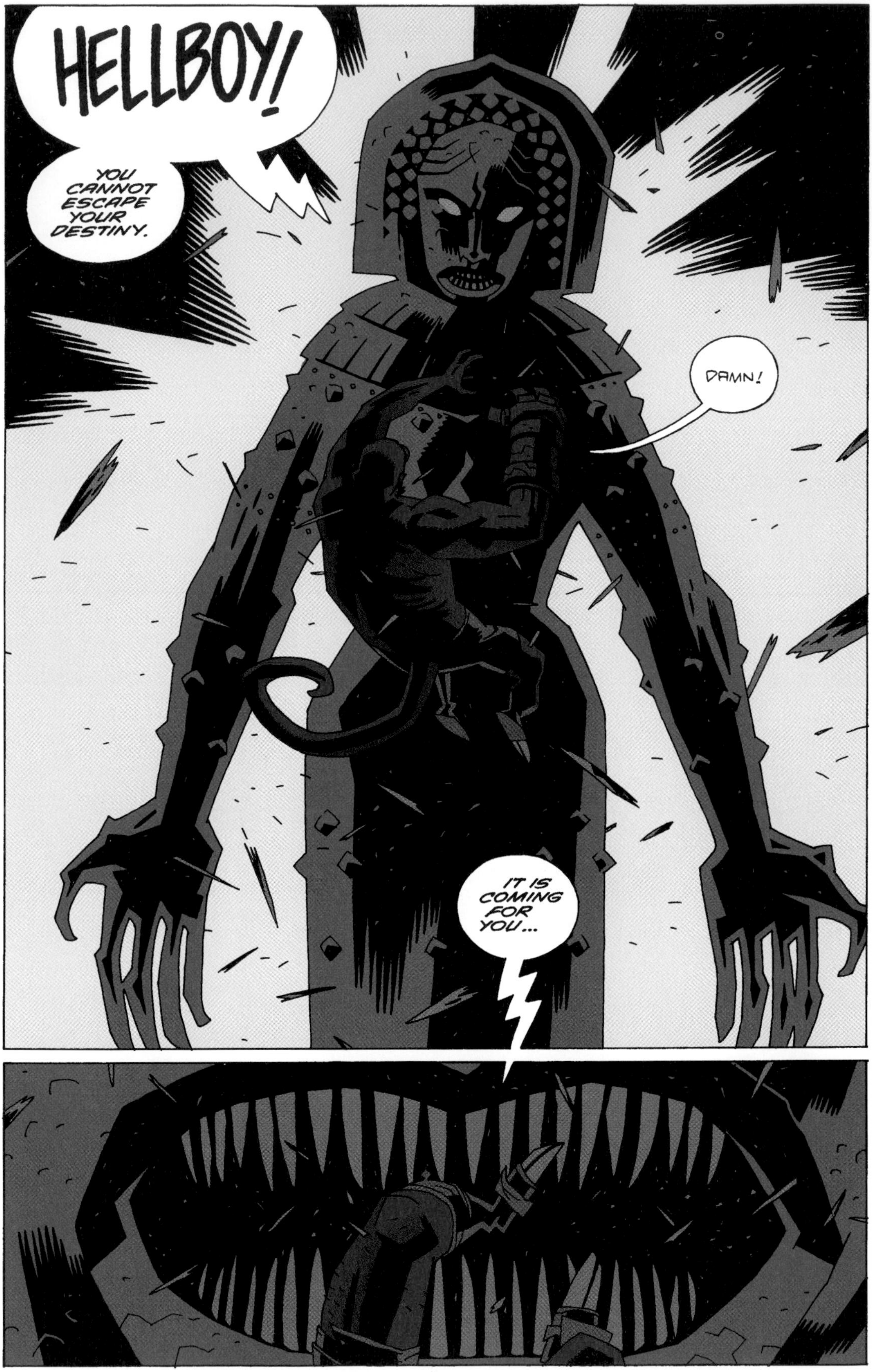
HELLBOY!
YOU CANNOT ESCAPE YOUR DESTINY.
DAMN!
IT IS COMING FOR YOU...

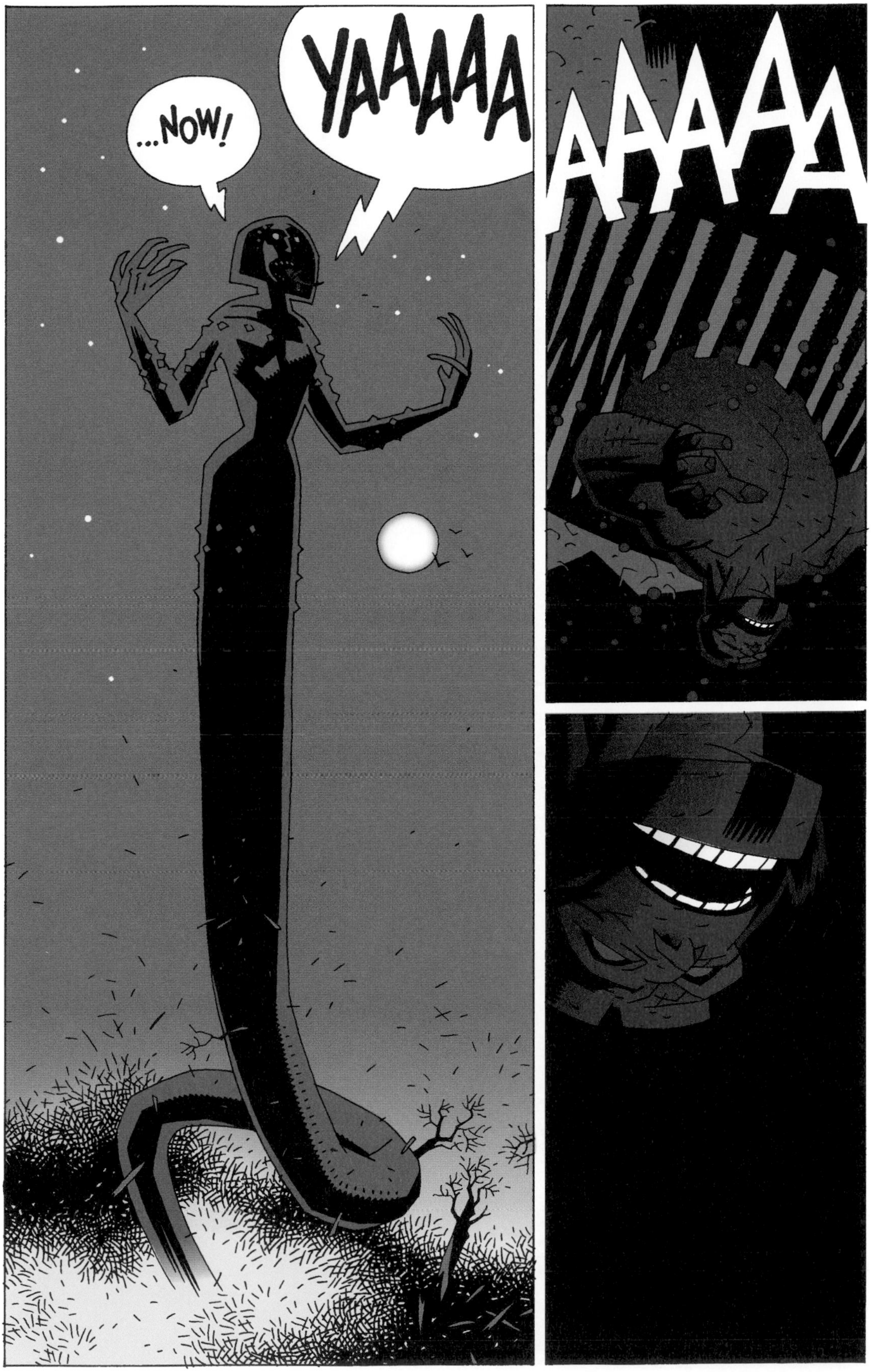
...NOW!
YAAAAA
AAAAAA

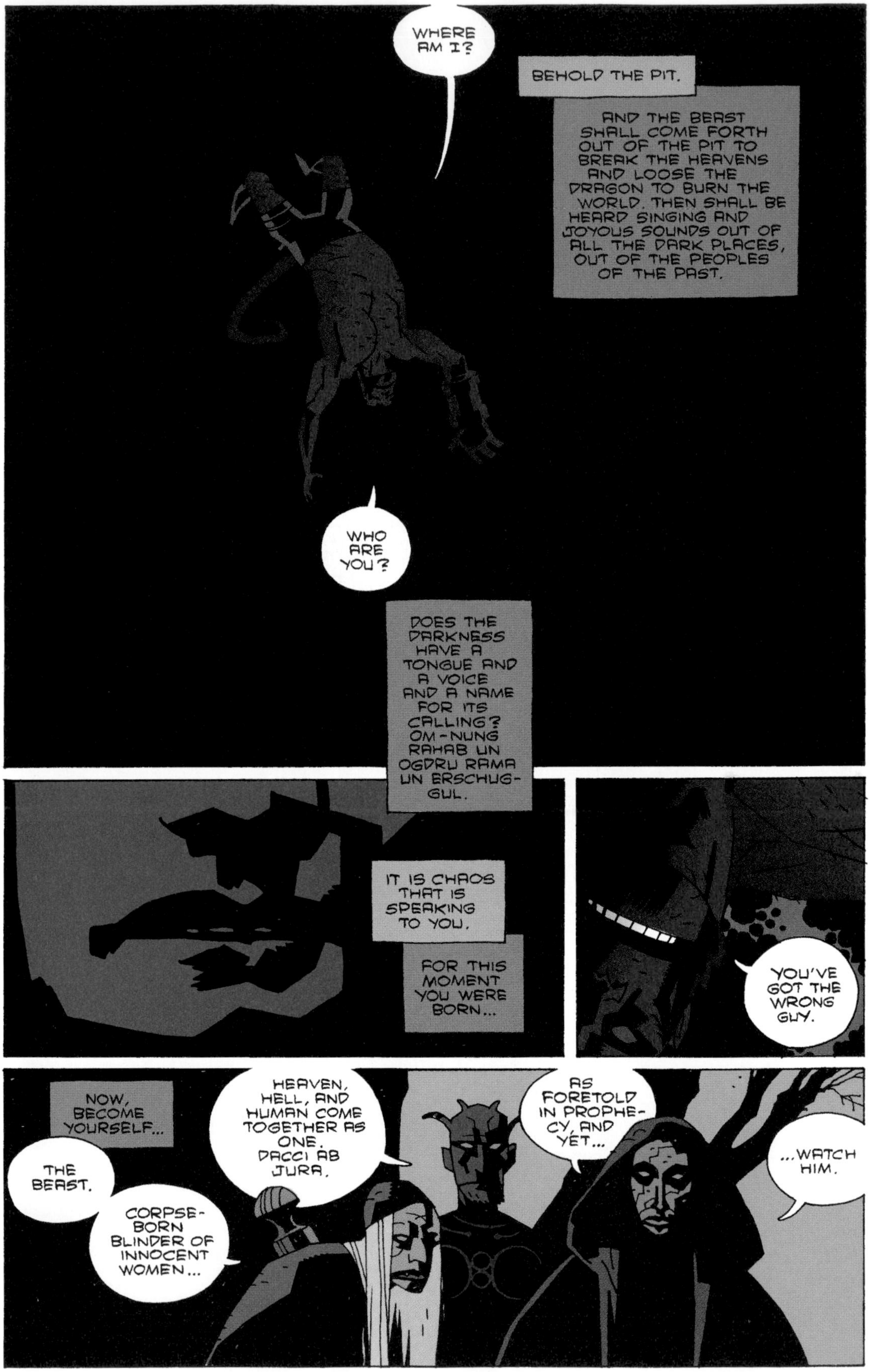
WHERE AM I?
BEHOLD THE PIT.
AND THE BEAST SHALL COME FORTH OUT OF THE PIT TO BREAK THE HEAVENS AND LOOSE THE DRAGON TO BURN THE WORLD. THEN SHALL BE HEARD SINGING AND JOYOUS SOUNDS OUT OF ALL THE DARK PLACES, OUT OF THE PEOPLES OF THE PAST.
WHO ARE YOU?
DOES THE DARKNESS HAVE A TONGUE AND A VOICE AND A NAME FOR ITS CALLING? OM-NUNG RAHAB UN OGDRU RAMA UN ERSCHUG-GUL.
IT IS CHAOS THAT IS SPEAKING TO YOU.
FOR THIS MOMENT YOU WERE BORN...
YOU'VE GOT THE WRONG GUY.
NOW, BECOME YOURSELF...
THE BEAST.
CORPSE-BORN BLINDER OF INNOCENT WOMEN...
HEAVEN, HELL, AND HUMAN COME TOGETHER AS ONE. DACCI AB JURA.
AS FORETOLD IN PROPHE-CY, AND YET...
...WATCH HIM.

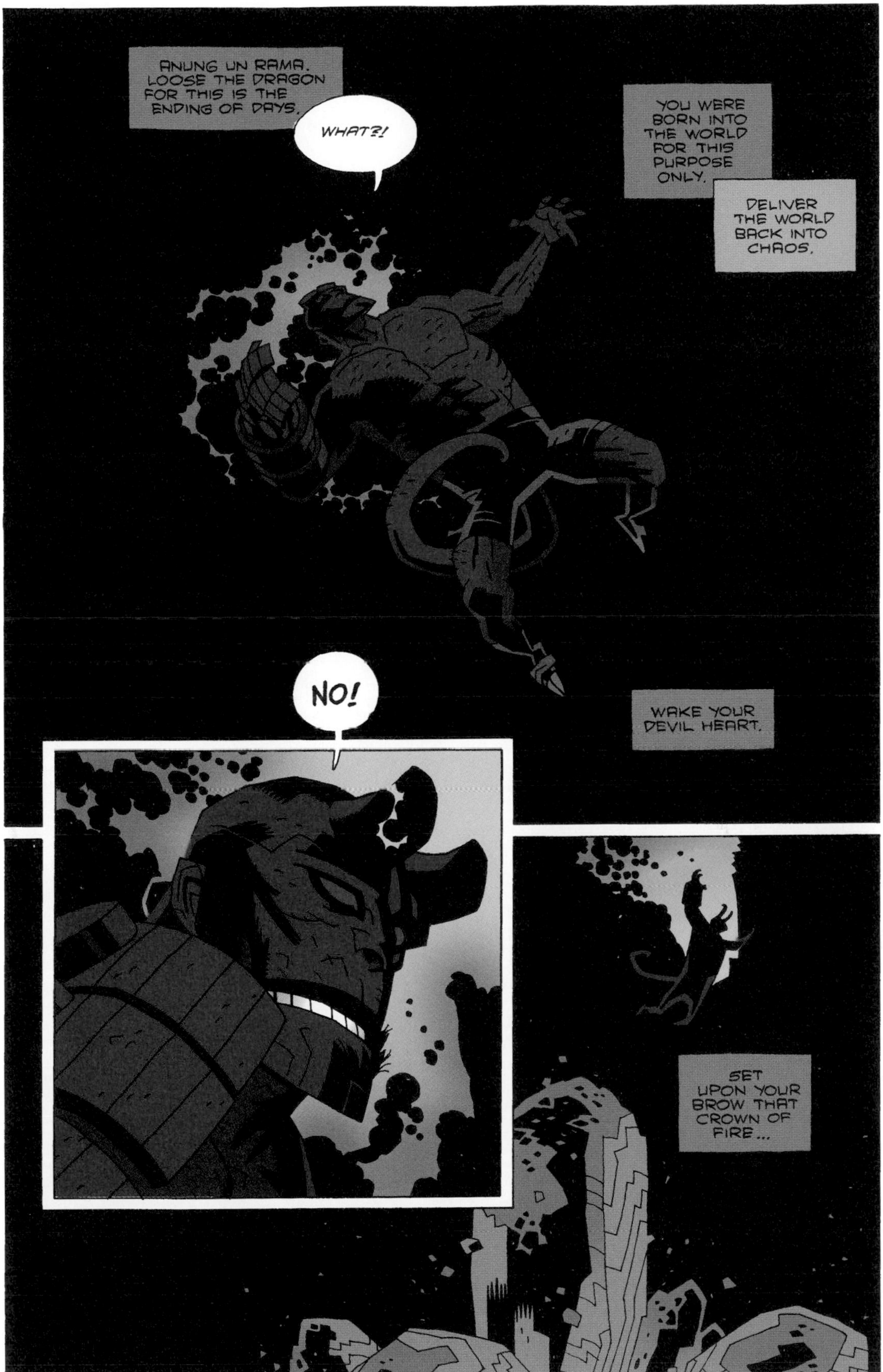
ANUNG UN RAMA. LOOSE THE DRAGON FOR THIS IS THE ENDING OF DAYS.
WHAT?!
YOU WERE BORN INTO THE WORLD FOR THIS PURPOSE ONLY.
DELIVER THE WORLD BACK INTO CHAOS.
NO!
WAKE YOUR DEVIL HEART.
SET UPON YOUR BROW THAT CROWN OF FIRE...

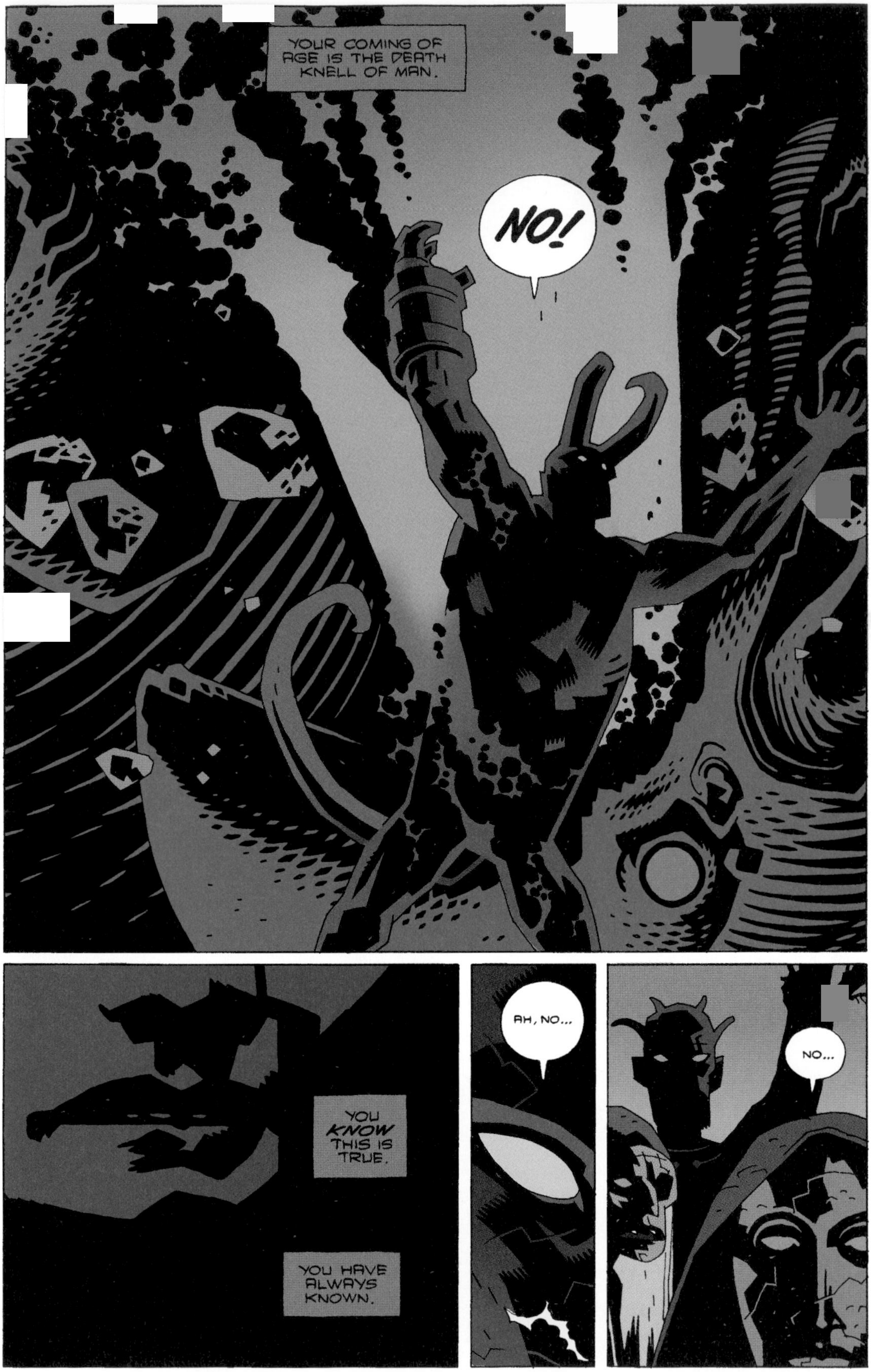
YOUR COMING OF AGE IS THE DEATH KNELL OF MAN.
NO!
YOU KNOW THIS IS TRUE.
YOU HAVE ALWAYS KNOWN.
AH, NO...
NO...

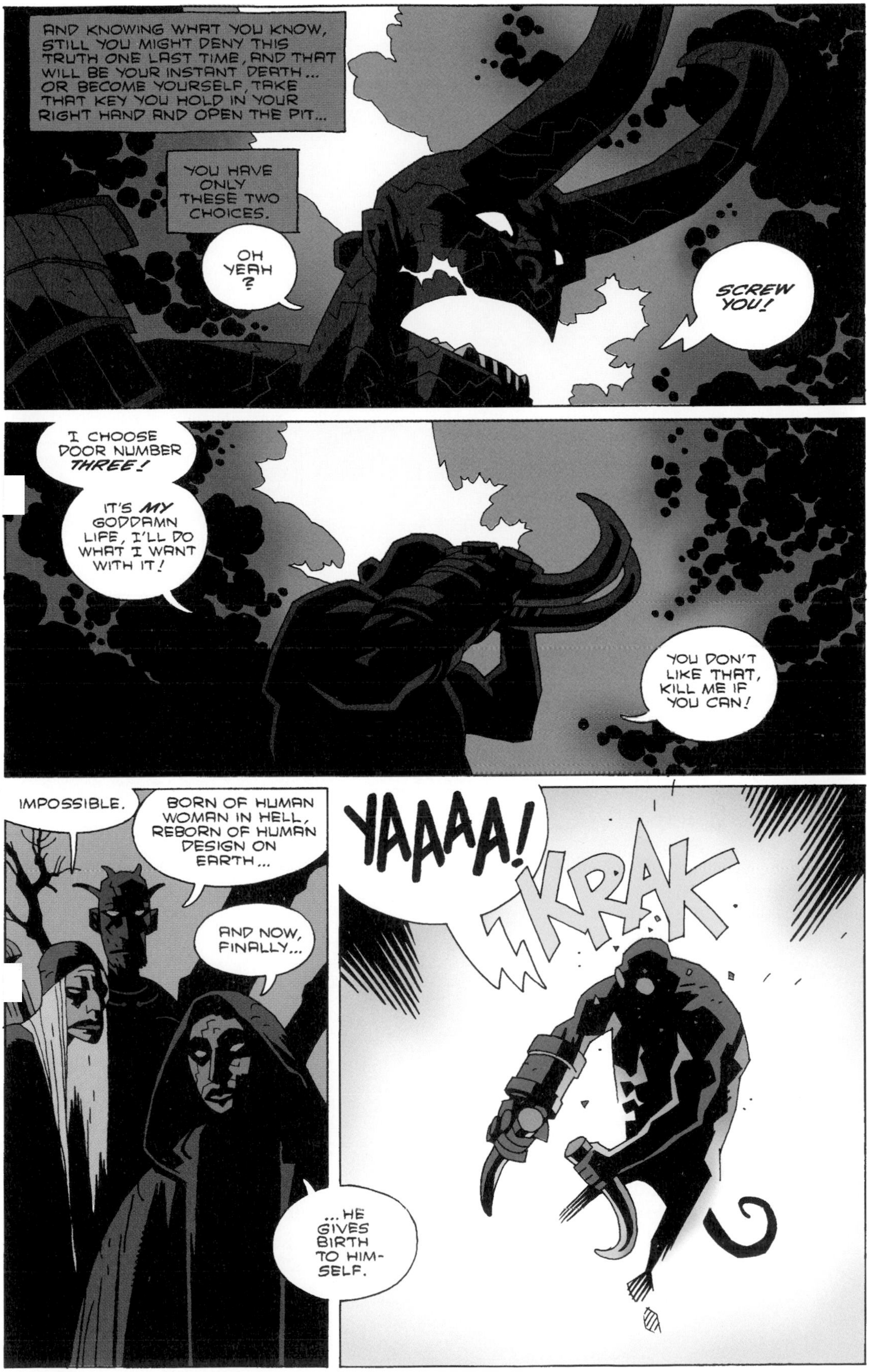
AND KNOWING WHAT YOU KNOW, STILL YOU MIGHT DENY THIS TRUTH ONE LAST TIME, AND THAT WILL BE YOUR INSTANT DEATH... OR BECOME YOURSELF, TAKE THAT KEY YOU HOLD IN YOUR RIGHT HAND AND OPEN THE PIT...
YOU HAVE ONLY THESE TWO CHOICES.
OH YEAH?
SCREW YOU!
I CHOOSE DOOR NUMBER THREE!
IT'S MY GODDAMN LIFE, I'LL DO WHAT I WANT WITH IT!
YOU DON'T LIKE THAT, KILL ME IF YOU CAN!
IMPOSSIBLE.
BORN OF HUMAN WOMAN IN HELL, REBORN OF HUMAN DESIGN ON EARTH...
AND NOW, FINALLY...
...HE GIVES BIRTH TO HIM-SELF.
YAAAA!
KRAK

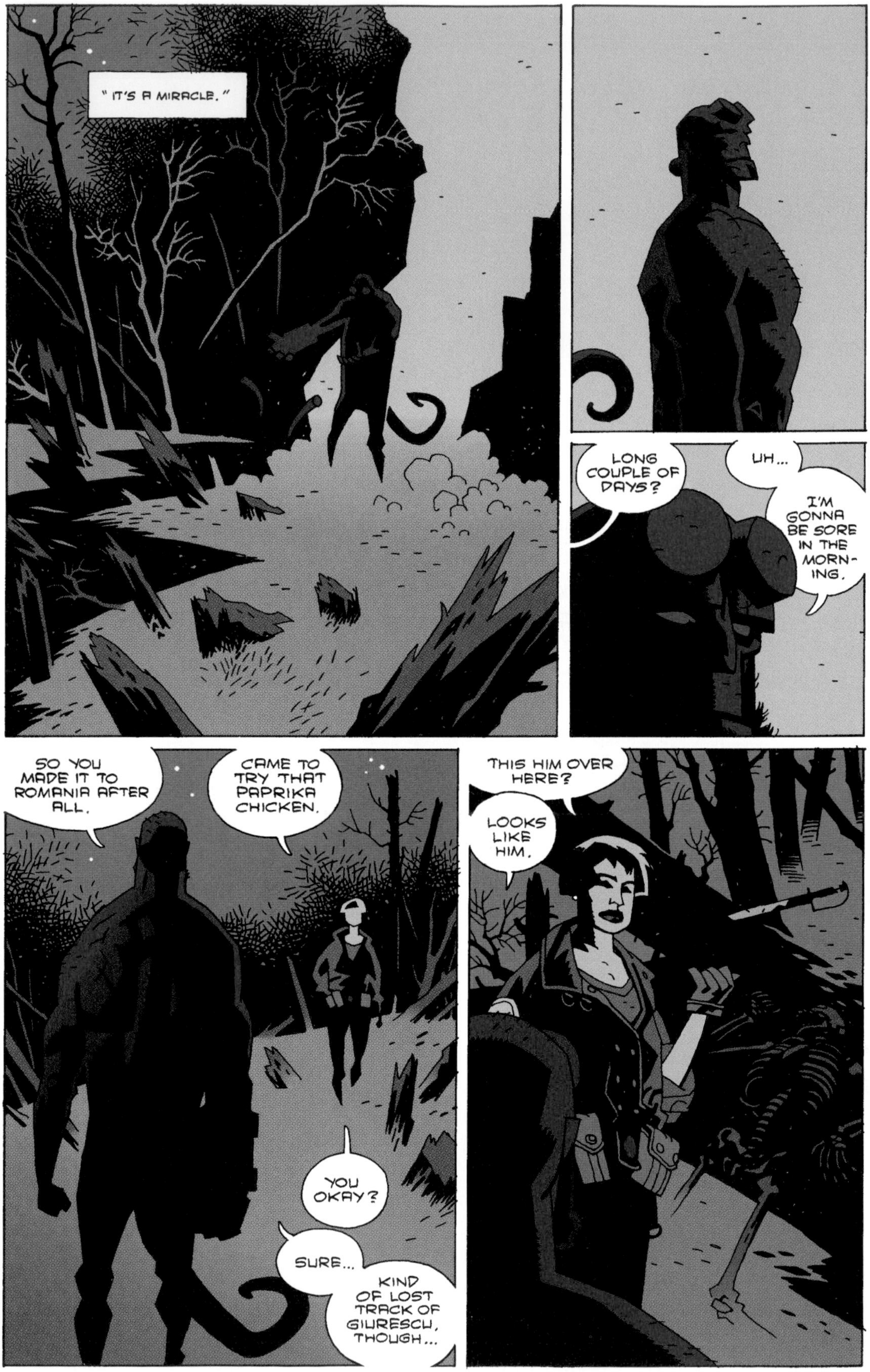
"IT'S A MIRACLE."
LONG COUPLE OF DAYS?
UH...
I'M GONNA BE SORE IN THE MORN-ING.
SO YOU MADE IT TO ROMANIA AFTER ALL.
CAME TO TRY THAT PAPRIKA CHICKEN.
YOU OKAY?
SURE...
KIND OF LOST TRACK OF GIURESCU, THOUGH...
THIS HIM OVER HERE?
LOOKS LIKE HIM.

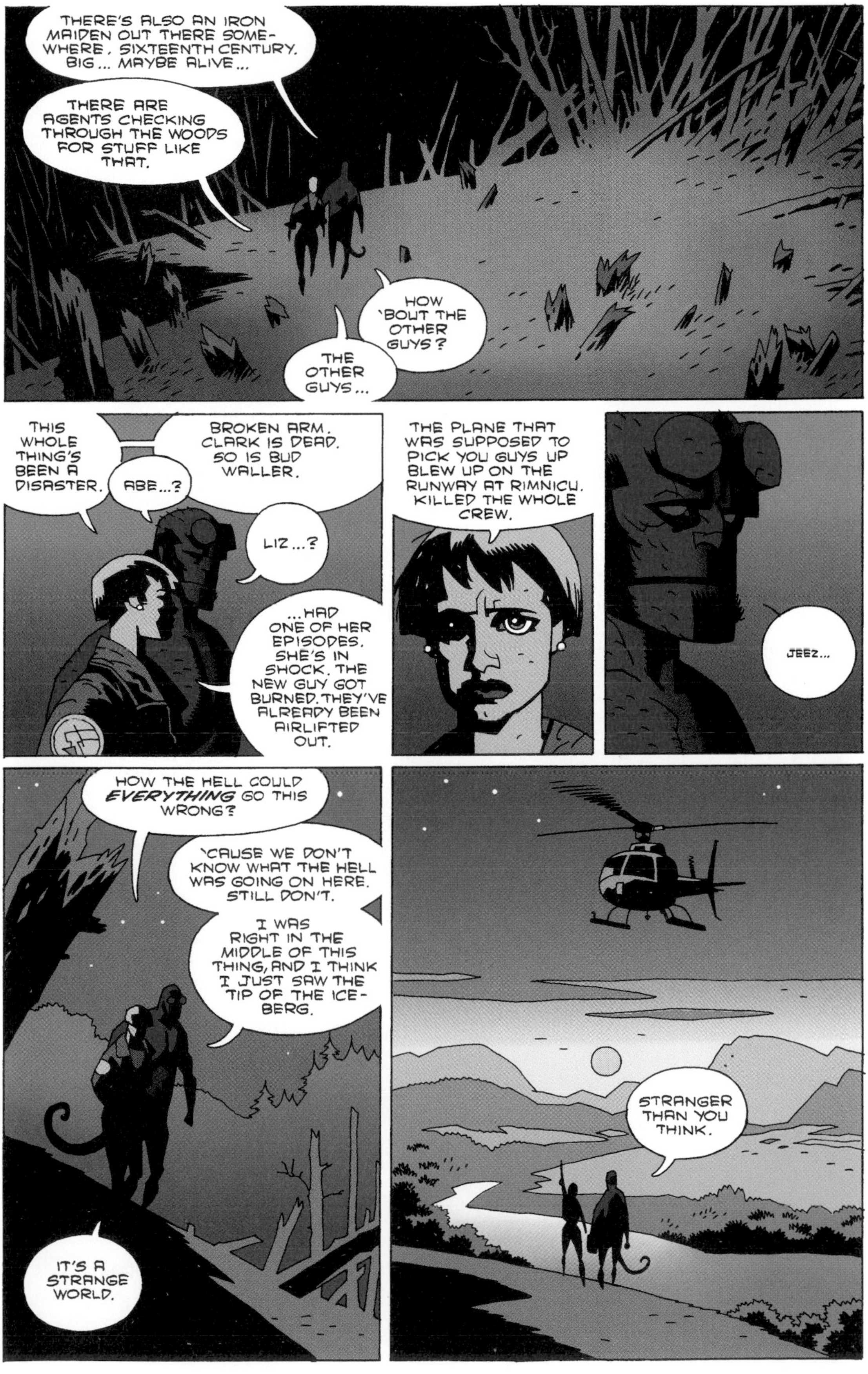
THERE'S ALSO AN IRON MAIDEN OUT THERE SOME-WHERE. SIXTEENTH CENTURY. BIG... MAYBE ALIVE...
THERE ARE AGENTS CHECKING THROUGH THE WOODS FOR STUFF LIKE THAT.
HOW 'BOUT THE OTHER GUYS?
THE OTHER GUYS...
THIS WHOLE THING'S BEEN A DISASTER.
ABE...?
BROKEN ARM. CLARK IS DEAD. SO IS BUD WALLER.
LIZ...?
...HAD ONE OF HER EPISODES. SHE'S IN SHOCK. THE NEW GUY GOT BURNED. THEY'VE ALREADY BEEN AIRLIFTED OUT.
THE PLANE THAT WAS SUPPOSED TO PICK YOU GUYS UP BLEW UP ON THE RUNWAY AT RIMNICU. KILLED THE WHOLE CREW.
JEEZ...
HOW THE HELL COULD *EVERYTHING* GO THIS WRONG?
'CAUSE WE DON'T KNOW WHAT THE HELL WAS GOING ON HERE. STILL DON'T.
I WAS RIGHT IN THE MIDDLE OF THIS THING, AND I THINK I JUST SAW THE TIP OF THE ICE-BERG.
IT'S A STRANGE WORLD.
STRANGER THAN YOU THINK.

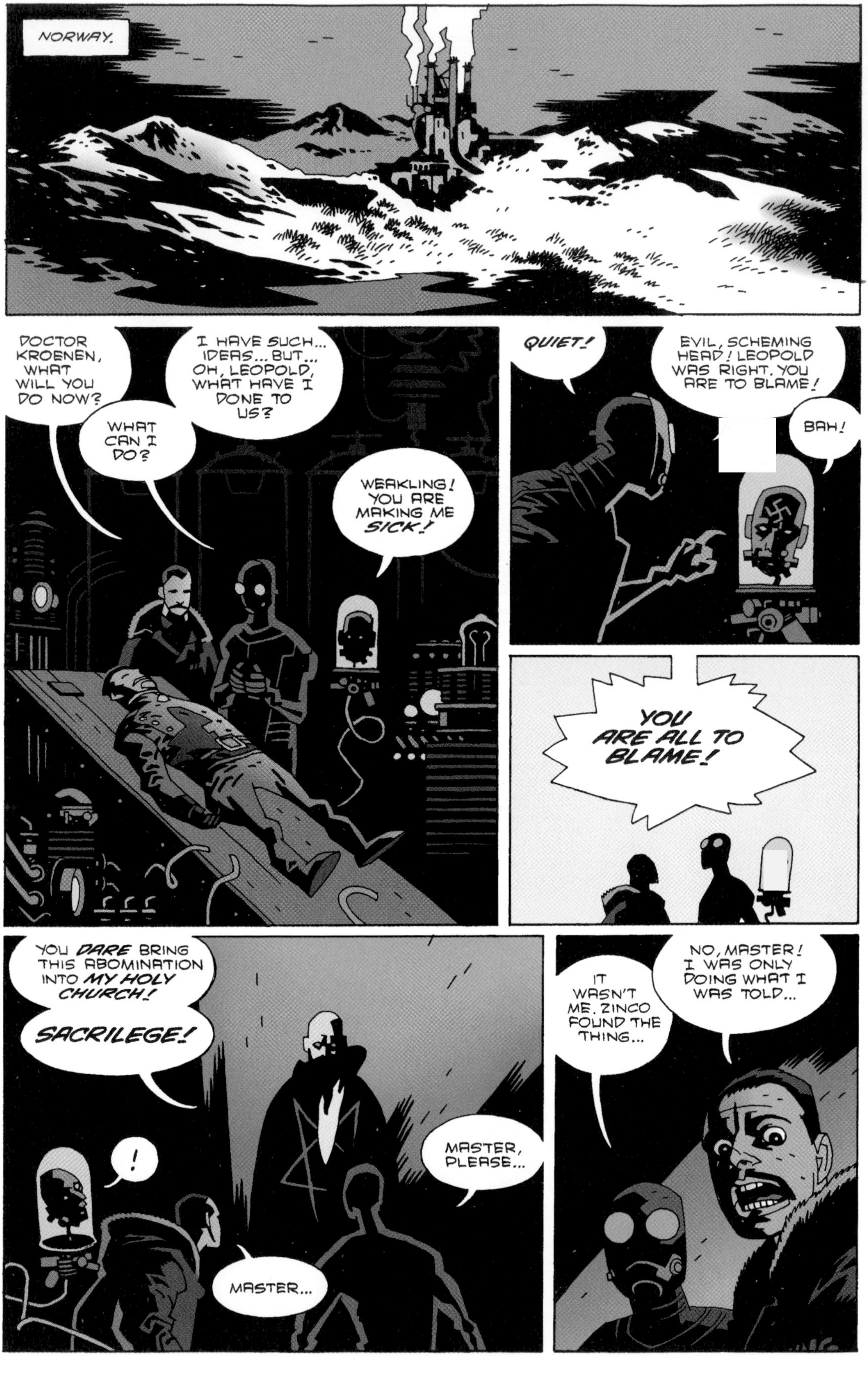
NORWAY.
DOCTOR KROENEN, WHAT WILL YOU DO NOW?
I HAVE SUCH... IDEAS... BUT... OH, LEOPOLD, WHAT HAVE I DONE TO US?
WHAT CAN I DO?
WEAKLING! YOU ARE MAKING ME SICK!
QUIET!
EVIL, SCHEMING HEAD! LEOPOLD WAS RIGHT. YOU ARE TO BLAME!
BAH!
YOU ARE ALL TO BLAME!
YOU DARE BRING THIS ABOMINATION INTO MY HOLY CHURCH!
SACRILEGE!
!
MASTER, PLEASE...
MASTER...
NO, MASTER! I WAS ONLY DOING WHAT I WAS TOLD...
IT WASN'T ME. ZINCO FOUND THE THING...

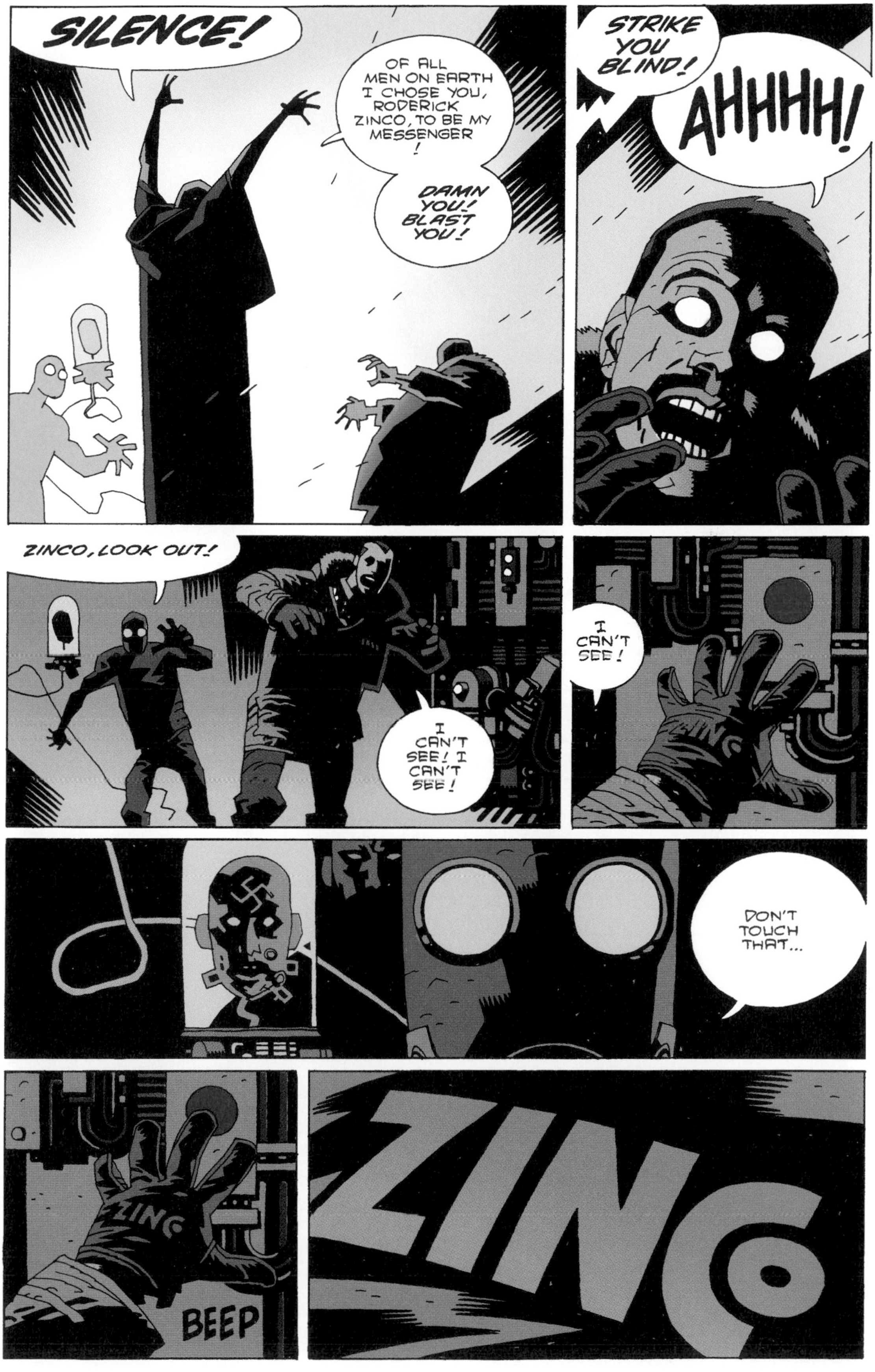
SILENCE!
OF ALL MEN ON EARTH I CHOSE YOU, RODERICK ZINCO, TO BE MY MESSENGER!
DAMN YOU! BLAST YOU!
STRIKE YOU BLIND!
AHHHH!
ZINCO, LOOK OUT!
I CAN'T SEE! I CAN'T SEE!
I CAN'T SEE!
DON'T TOUCH THAT...
ZING
BEEP
ZINCO

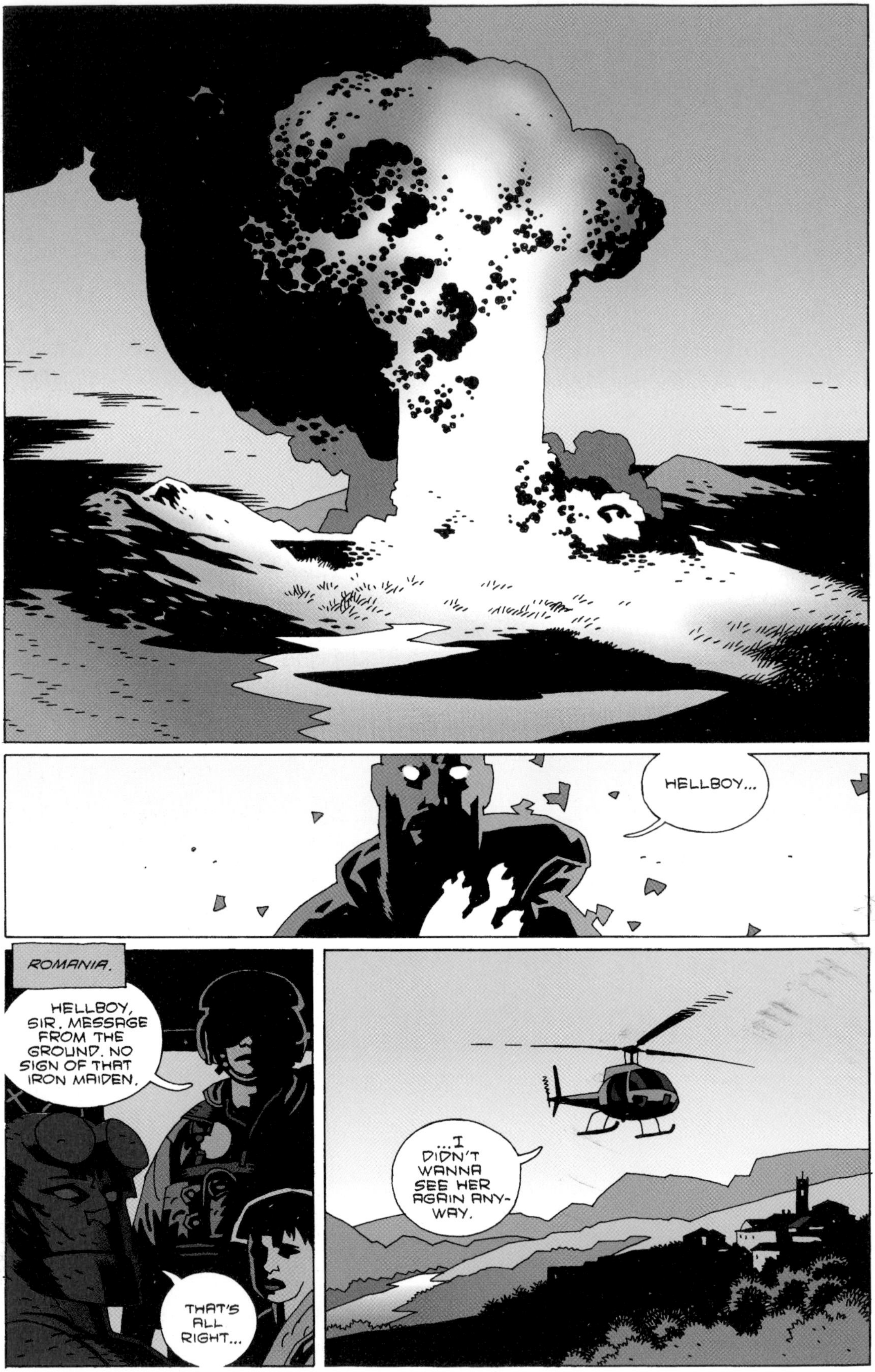
HELLBOY...
ROMANIA.
HELLBOY, SIR. MESSAGE FROM THE GROUND. NO SIGN OF THAT IRON MAIDEN.
THAT'S ALL RIGHT...
...I DIDN'T WANNA SEE HER AGAIN ANY-WAY.

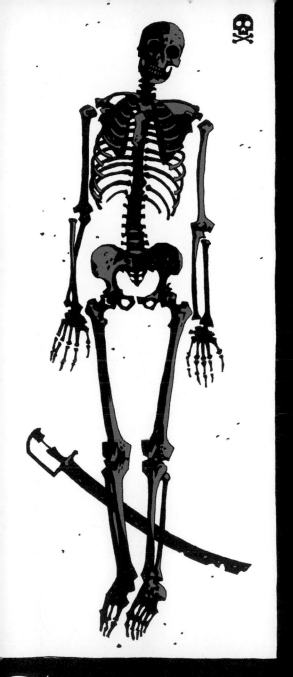

THE SKELETON of Vladimir
Giurescu was to have been moved
to BPRD headquarters in Fairfield,
Connecticut. It was placed in temporary
storage at the Bucharest airport, where it
disappeared. It has never been recovered.

THE HEAD of Father Nicholas Budenz never spoke again, but for weeks continued to be the focus of poltergeist activities, including sudden temperature changes and the levitation of objects. It is currently on loan to the Paulvé Institute in Avignon, France.

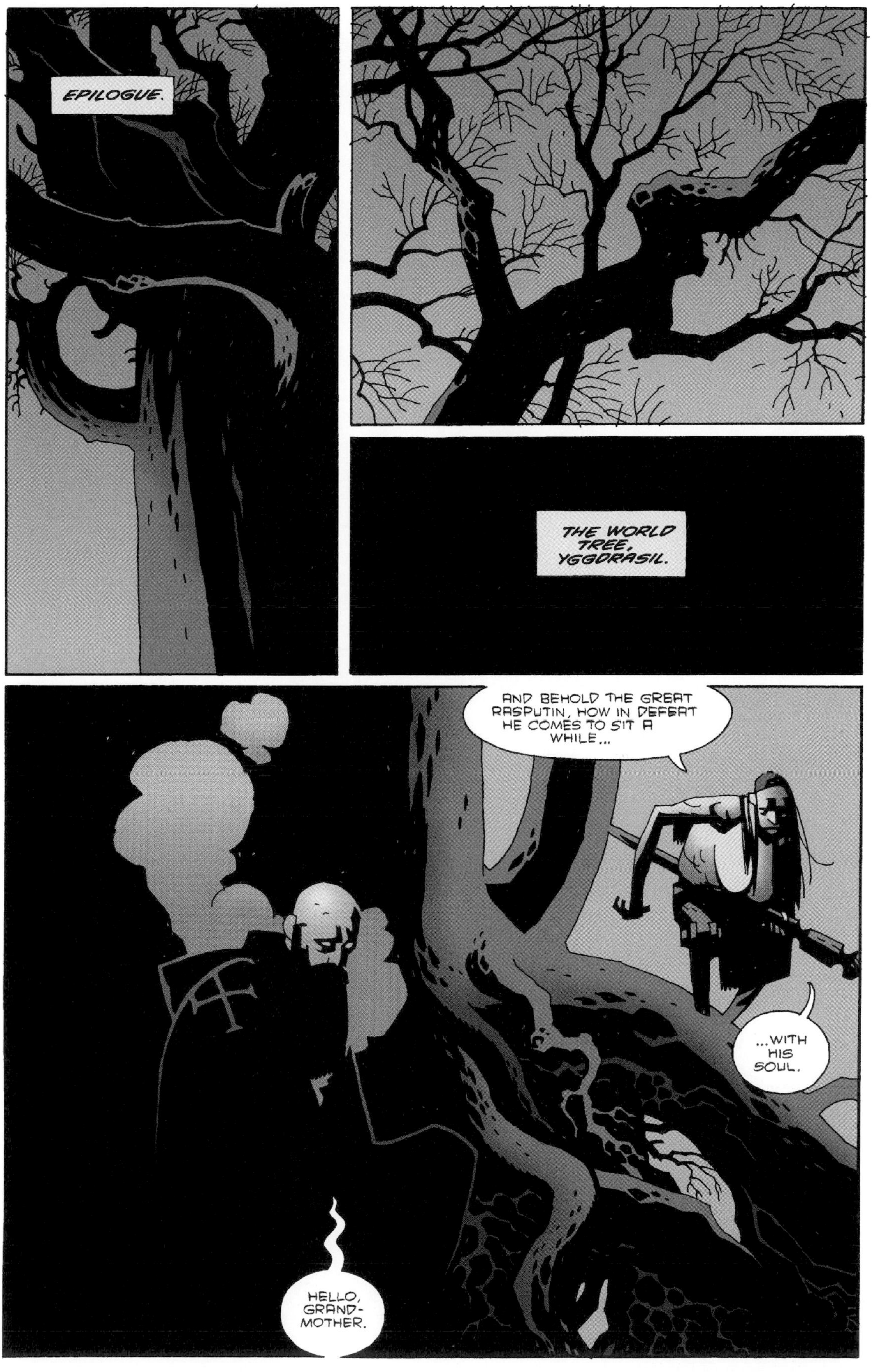
EPILOGUE.
THE WORLD TREE, YGGDRASIL.
AND BEHOLD THE GREAT RASPUTIN, HOW IN DEFEAT HE COMES TO SIT A WHILE...
...WITH HIS SOUL.
HELLO, GRAND-MOTHER.

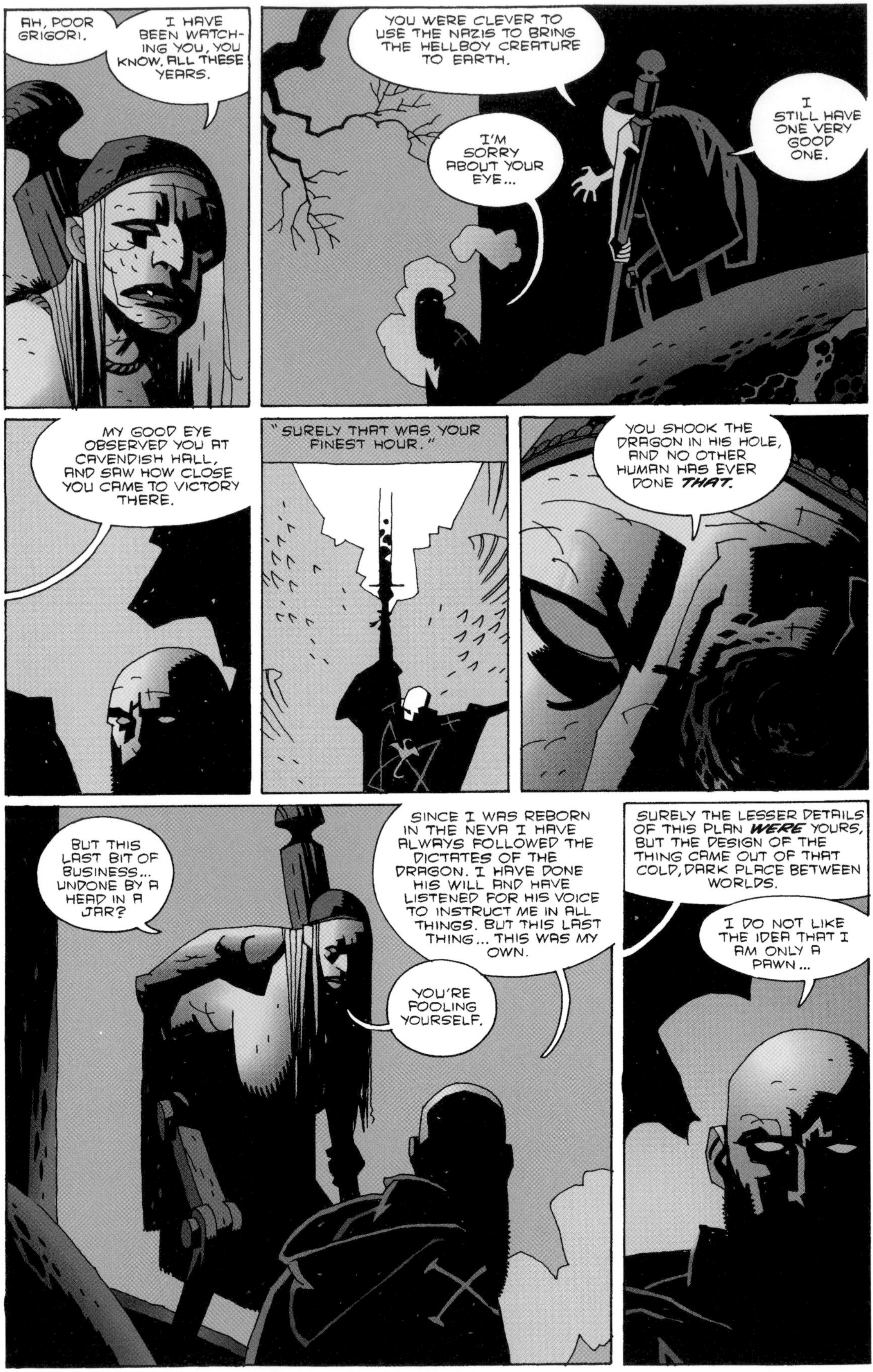
AH, POOR GRIGORI.
I HAVE BEEN WATCHING YOU, YOU KNOW. ALL THESE YEARS.
YOU WERE CLEVER TO USE THE NAZIS TO BRING THE HELLBOY CREATURE TO EARTH.
I'M SORRY ABOUT YOUR EYE...
I STILL HAVE ONE VERY GOOD ONE.
MY GOOD EYE OBSERVED YOU AT CAVENDISH HALL, AND SAW HOW CLOSE YOU CAME TO VICTORY THERE.
"SURELY THAT WAS YOUR FINEST HOUR."
YOU SHOOK THE DRAGON IN HIS HOLE, AND NO OTHER HUMAN HAS EVER DONE ***THAT.***
BUT THIS LAST BIT OF BUSINESS... UNDONE BY A HEAD IN A JAR?
SINCE I WAS REBORN IN THE NEVA I HAVE ALWAYS FOLLOWED THE DICTATES OF THE DRAGON. I HAVE DONE HIS WILL AND HAVE LISTENED FOR HIS VOICE TO INSTRUCT ME IN ALL THINGS. BUT THIS LAST THING... THIS WAS MY OWN.
YOU'RE FOOLING YOURSELF.
SURELY THE LESSER DETAILS OF THIS PLAN ***WERE*** YOURS, BUT THE DESIGN OF THE THING CAME OUT OF THAT COLD, DARK PLACE BETWEEN WORLDS.
I DO NOT LIKE THE IDEA THAT I AM ONLY A PAWN...

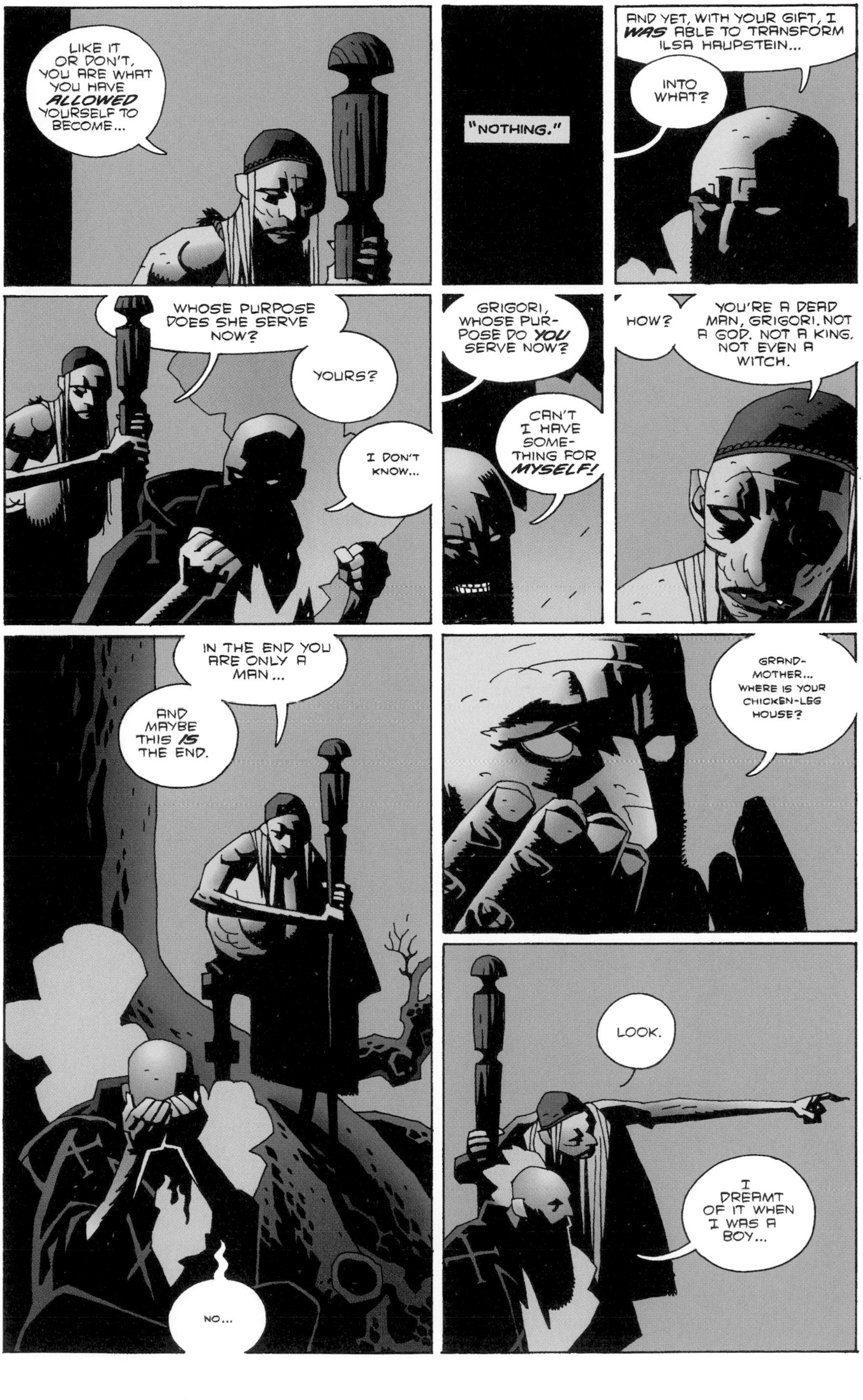
LIKE IT OR DON'T, YOU ARE WHAT YOU HAVE ALLOWED YOURSELF TO BECOME...
"NOTHING."
AND YET, WITH YOUR GIFT, I WAS ABLE TO TRANSFORM ILSA HAUPSTEIN...
INTO WHAT?
WHOSE PURPOSE DOES SHE SERVE NOW?
YOURS?
I DON'T KNOW...
GRIGORI, WHOSE PURPOSE DO YOU SERVE NOW?
CAN'T I HAVE SOMETHING FOR MYSELF!
HOW?
YOU'RE A DEAD MAN, GRIGORI. NOT A GOD. NOT A KING. NOT EVEN A WITCH.
IN THE END YOU ARE ONLY A MAN...
AND MAYBE THIS IS THE END.
NO...
GRANDMOTHER... WHERE IS YOUR CHICKEN-LEG HOUSE?
LOOK.
I DREAMT OF IT WHEN I WAS A BOY...

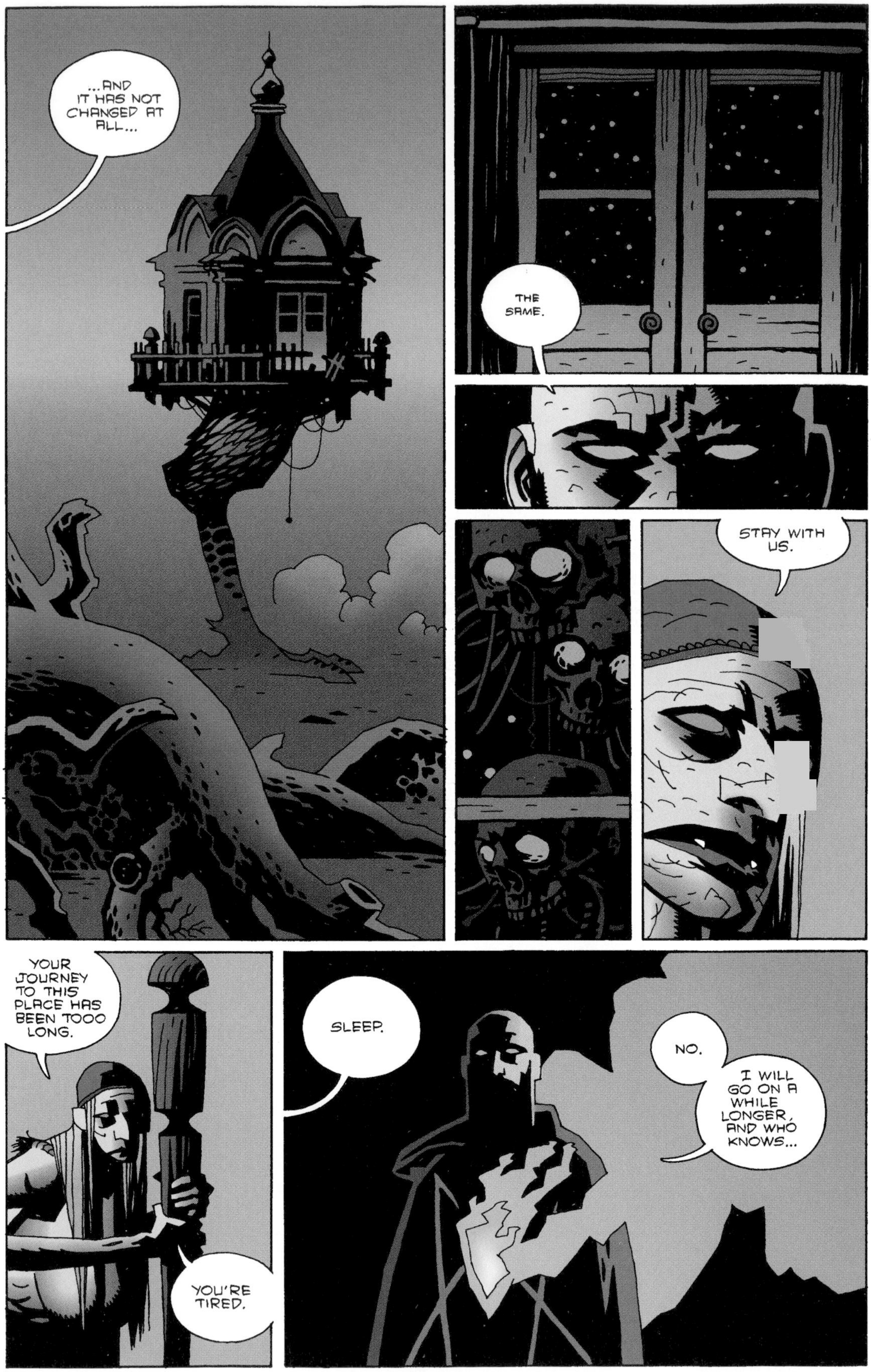
...AND IT HAS NOT CHANGED AT ALL...
THE SAME.
STAY WITH US.
YOUR JOURNEY TO THIS PLACE HAS BEEN TOOO LONG.
YOU'RE TIRED.
SLEEP.
NO.
I WILL GO ON A WHILE LONGER, AND WHO KNOWS...

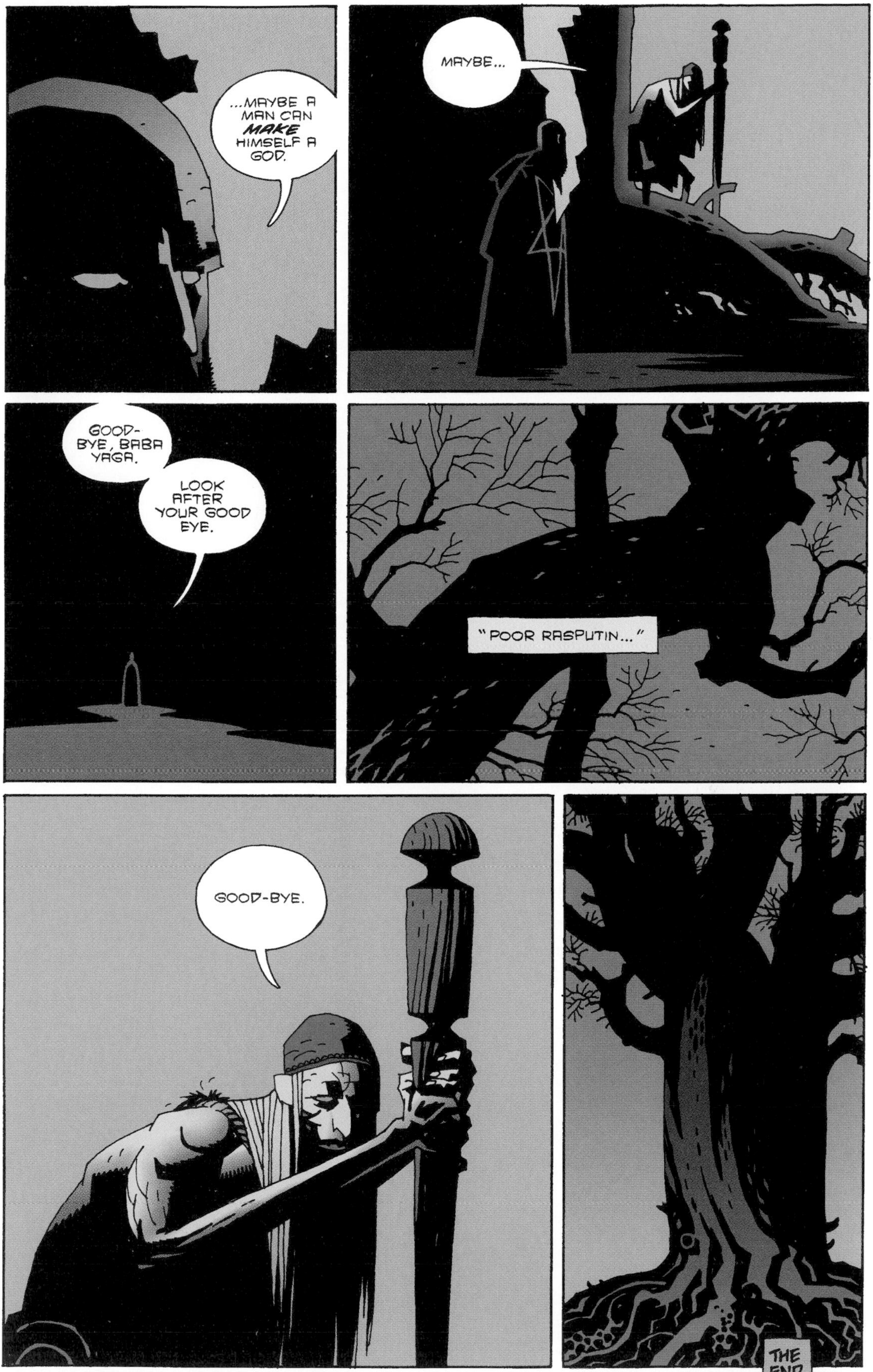
...MAYBE A MAN CAN MAKE HIMSELF A GOD.
MAYBE...
GOOD-BYE, BABA YAGA.
LOOK AFTER YOUR GOOD EYE.
"POOR RASPUTIN..."
GOOD-BYE.
THE END

THE BOOK YOU'RE HOLDING is the most ambitious comics project I've ever attempted as both writer and artist. When I began drawing issue one, the plot was different. The Nazis, Karl and Leopold, had a much smaller role and Herman Von Klempt, the head in a jar, wasn't in the book at all (hard to believe I would have left him out). The biggest difference was the last chapter. In the original version, Hellboy was freed from the stake at the crossroads by the Homunculus from issue three (a bit of a stretch even for me), then had a big fight to the death with Giurescu. It was okay, and probably would have worked just fine, except when I got to issue four, Hecate did all that talking about Hellboy's destiny. Well, that sort of screwed up everything. Suddenly my ending was too small. With the help of my wonderful editor (who is constantly saving me from myself), I replotted the more cosmic ending and, in the process, I think I finally made clear what those things on Hellboy's forehead are. The epilogue is brand new, done specifically for this collection.

I want to thank my wife, Christine, for putting up with me, and Scott Allie, James Sinclair, Pat Brosseau, and Cary Grazzini for making me look better than I am. Thanks to Gary Gianni for letting me run his beautiful MonsterMen story as my backup feature. Thanks to everyone who bought the comics, and a special thanks to everyone who wrote in. You've been great. You seem to want more Hellboy, so now I'm going back to work.

Goodnight.

Mike Mignola

Mike Mignola
Portland, Oregon

HELLBOY ™

GALLERY

featuring
BRUCE TIMM
P. CRAIG RUSSELL
DEREK THOMPSON
DAVE COOPER
JAY STEPHENS
and
OLIVIER VATINE

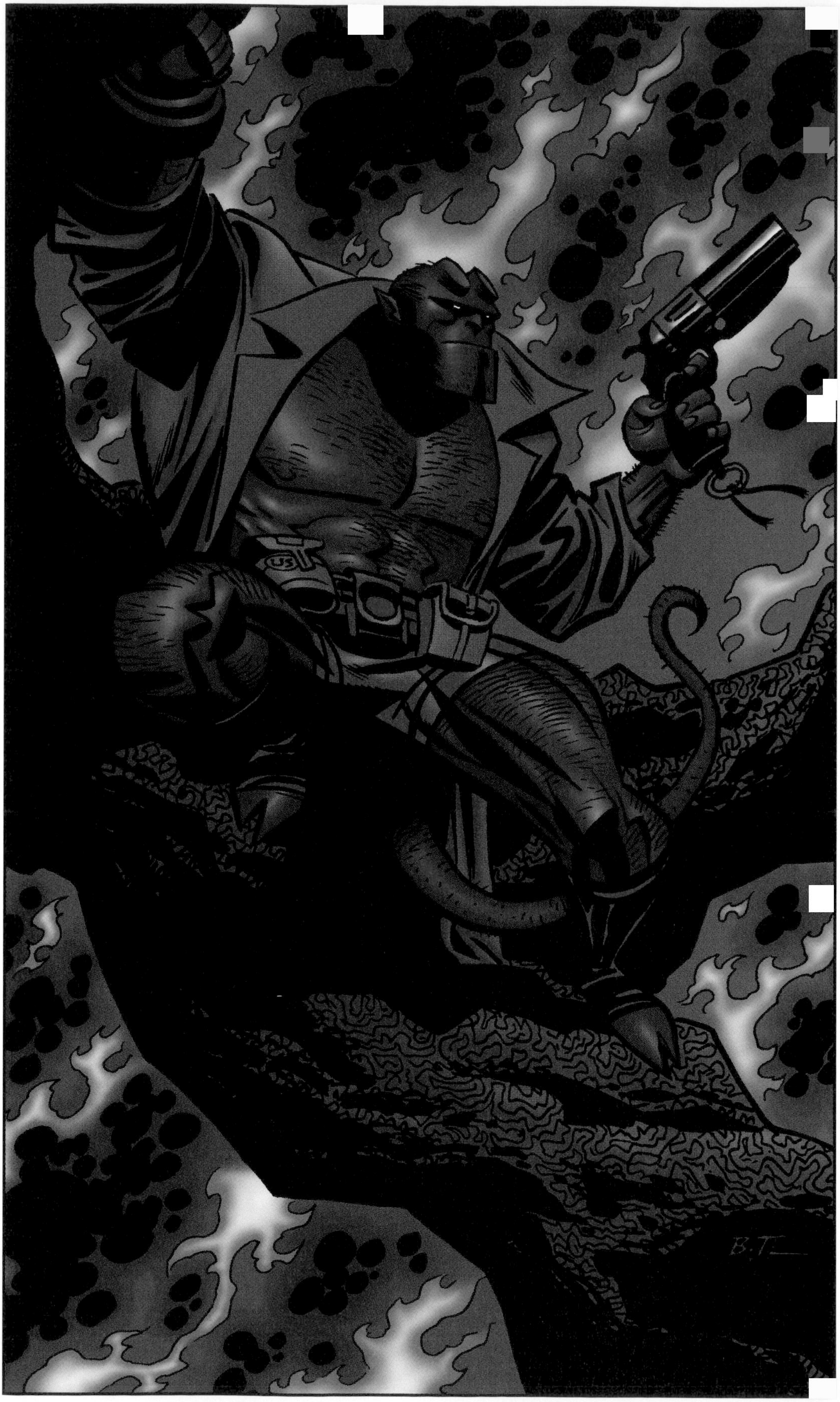
B.T.

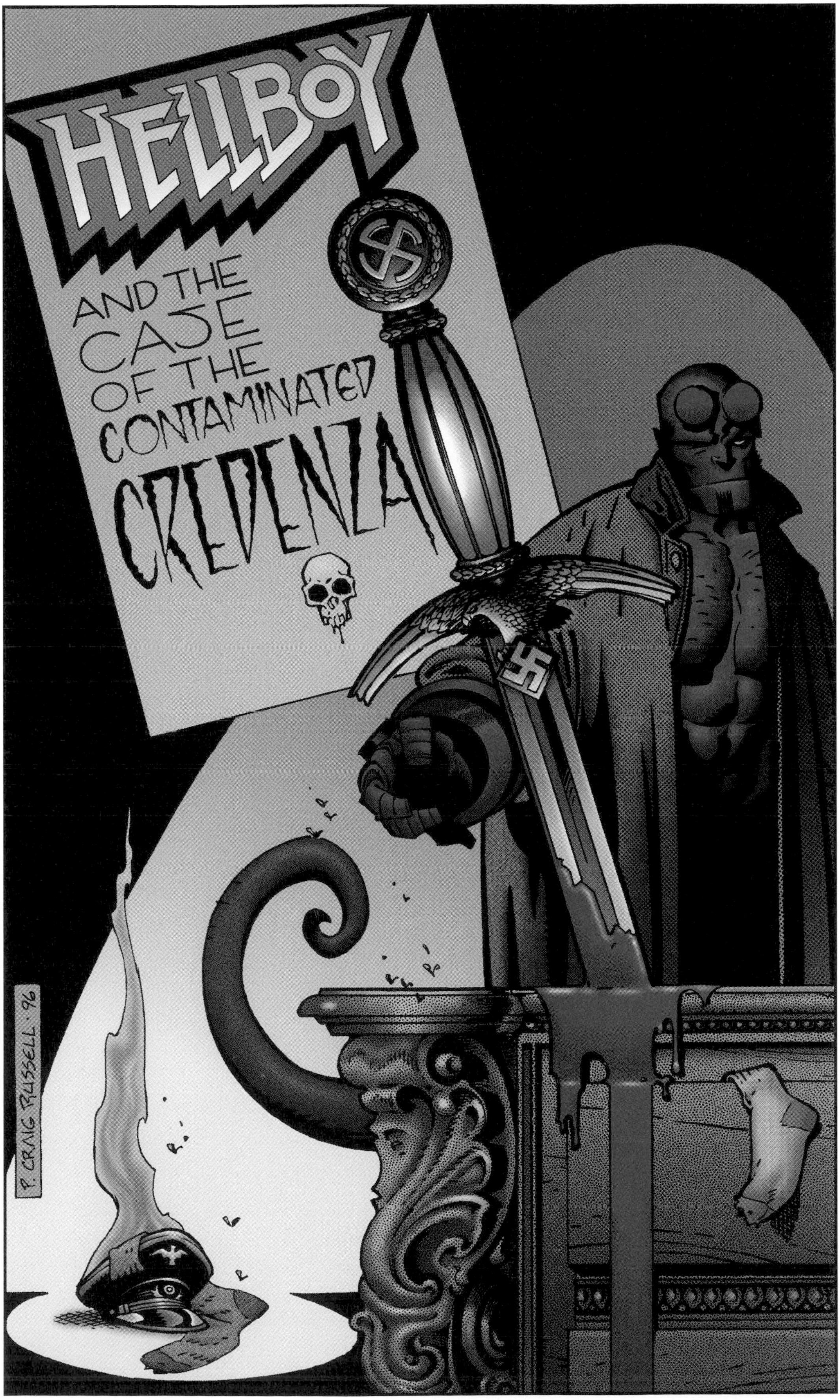
HELLBOY
AND THE CASE OF THE CONTAMINATED CREDENZA
P. CRAIG RUSSELL · 96

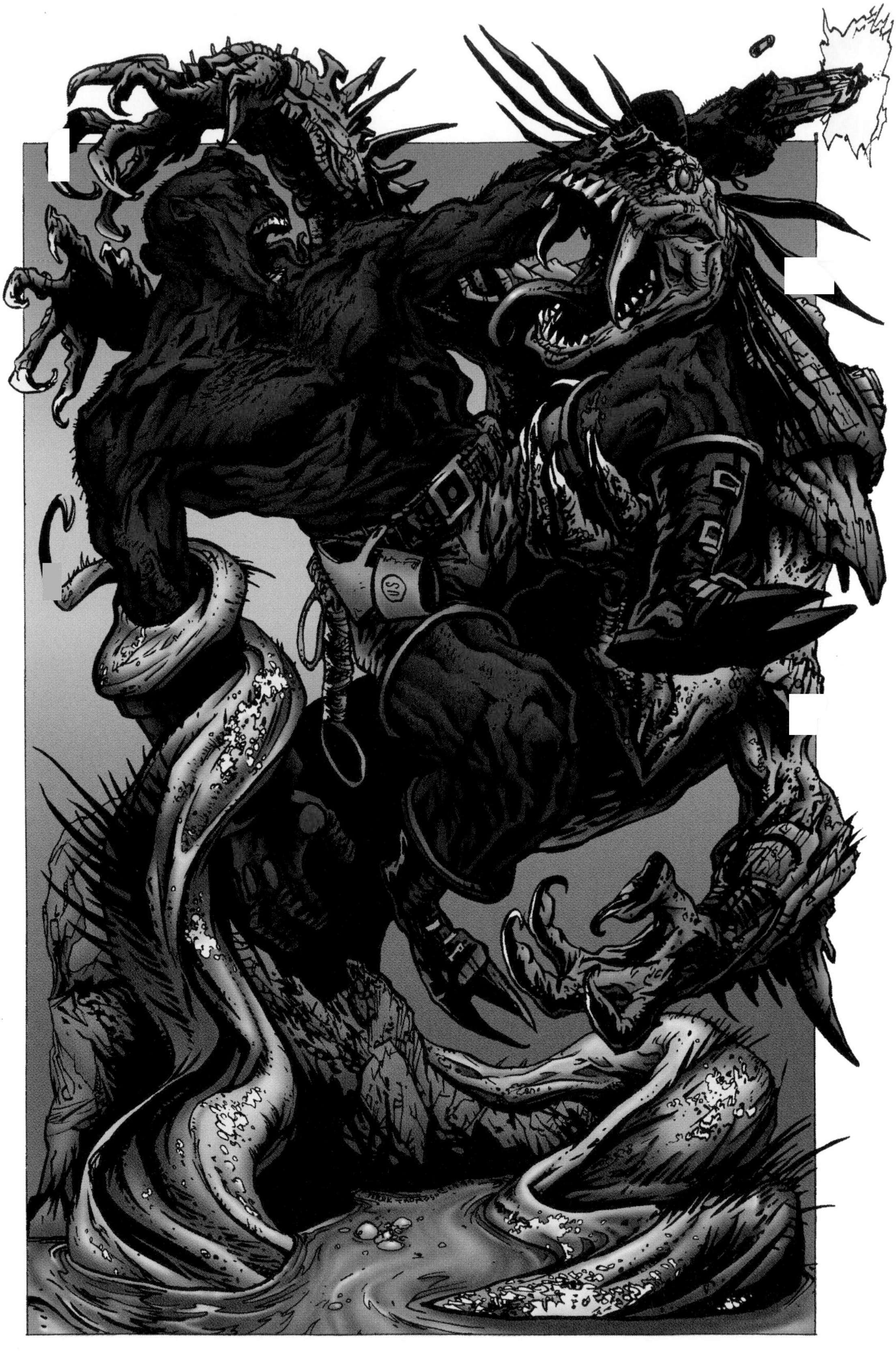

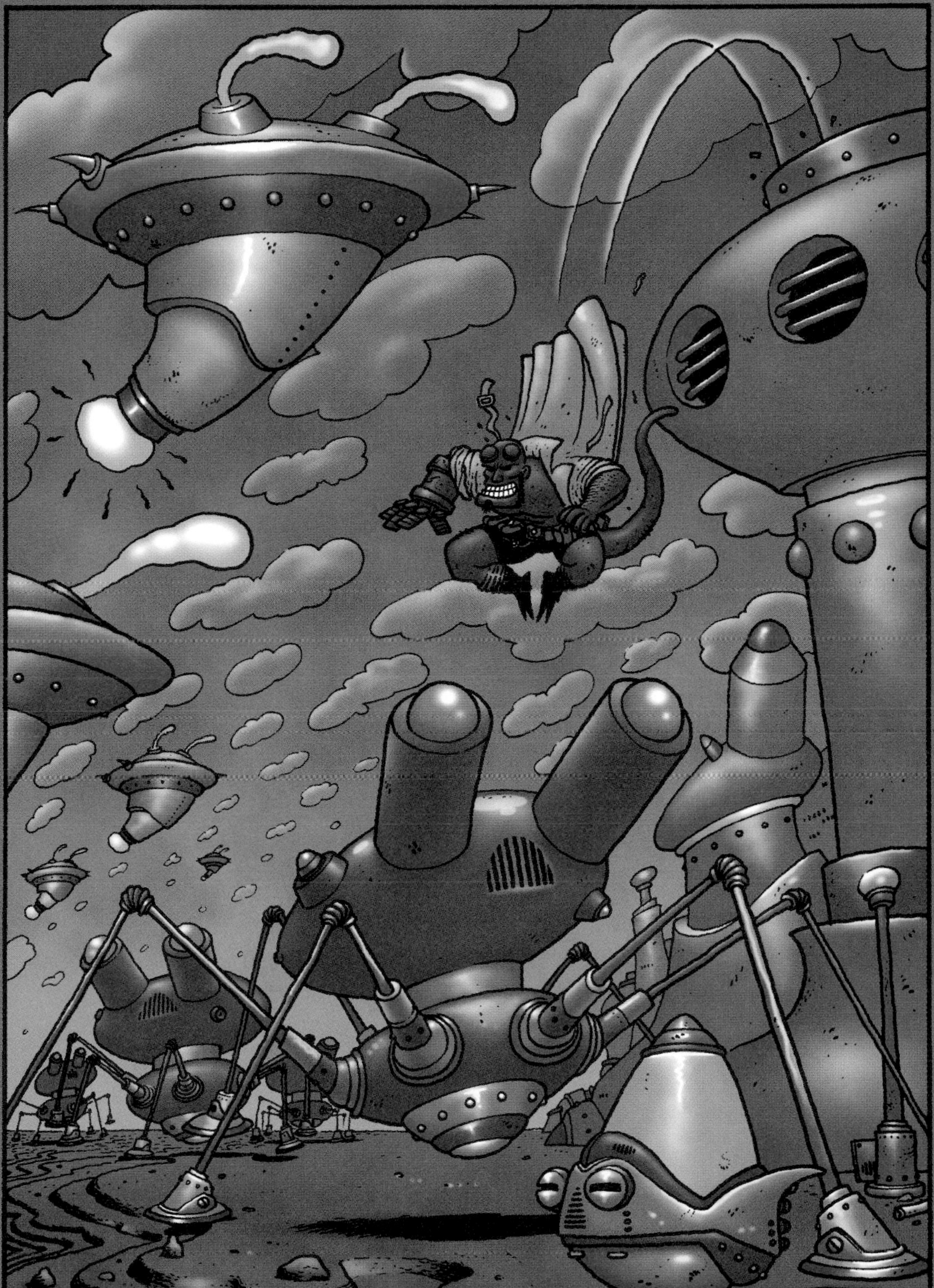
dave
COOPER '96

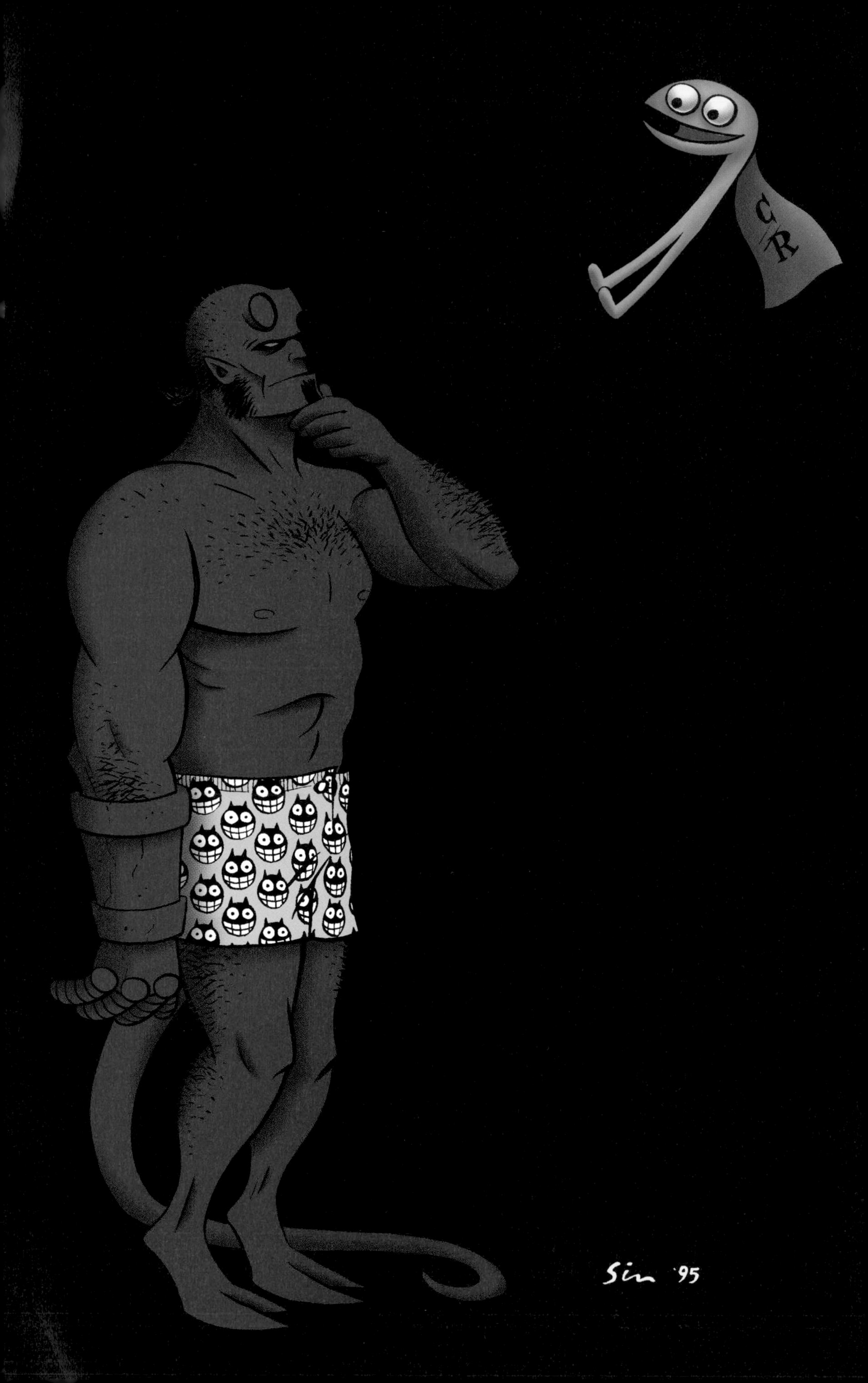
CR
Sin '95

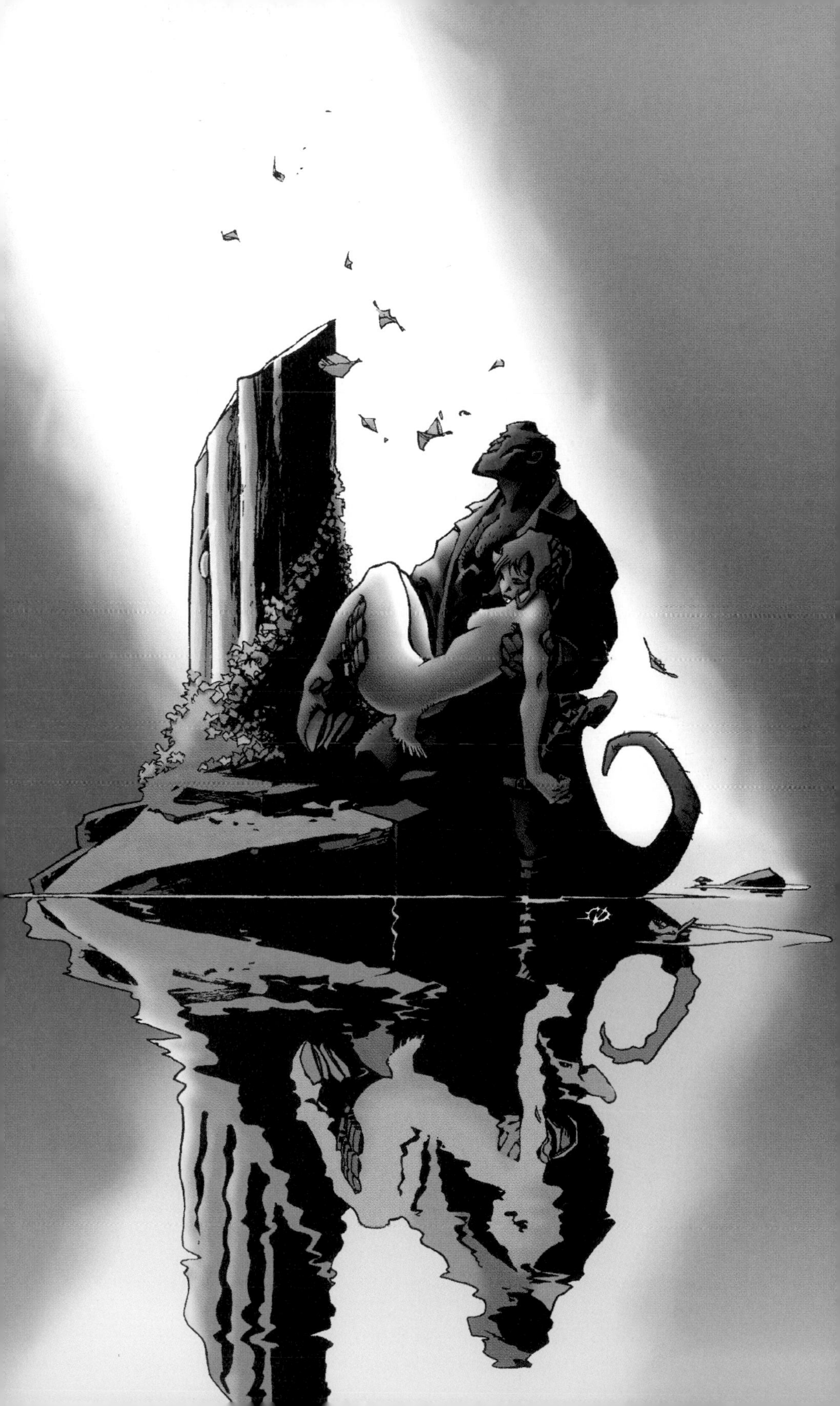

HELLBOY
by Mike Mignola
THE LOST ARMY
200-page B&W paperback
ISBN: 1-56971-185-2 $14.95
SEED OF DESTRUCTION
128-page color paperback
ISBN: 1-56971-038-4 $17.95
WAKE THE DEVIL
144-page color paperback
ISBN: 1-56971-226-3 $17.95
THE WOLVES OF SAINT AUGUST
48-page color paperback
ISBN: 1-56971-094-5 $4.95

ART ADAMS'
CREATURE FEATURES
by Arthur Adams
104-page color paperback
ISBN: 1-56971-214-x $13.95

CONCRETE
by Paul Chadwick
KILLER SMILE
144-page color paperback
ISBN: 1-56971-080-5 $16.95
THINK LIKE A MOUNTAIN
160-page color paperback
ISBN: 1-56971-176-3 $17.95

HARD BOILED
by Frank Miller & Geof Darrow
128-page color paperback
ISBN: 1-878574-58-2 $14.95

JOHN BYRNE'S NEXT MEN
by John Byrne
BOOK FOUR: FAITH
104-page color paperback
ISBN: 1-56971-055-4 $ 14.95
BOOK FIVE: POWER
120-page color paperback
ISBN: 1-56971-061-9 $16.95
BOOK SIX: LIES
112-page color paperback
ISBN: 1-56971-204-2 $16.95

MADMAN COMICS
by Michael Allred
YEARBOOK '95
160-page color paperback
ISBN: 1-56971-091-0 $17.95
VOLUME TWO
160-page color paperback
ISBN: 1-56971-186-0 $17.95

MONKEYMAN & O'BRIEN
by Arthur Adams
136-page color paperback
ISBN: 1-56971-232-8 $16.95

RASCALS IN PARADISE
by Jim Silke
104-page color paperback
ISBN: 1-56971-075-9 $16.95

THE SHADOW
IN THE COILS OF LEVIATHAN
by Joel Goss, M.W. Kaluta, & Gary Gianni
112-page color paperback
ISBN: 1-56971-024-4 $13.95

SIN CITY
by Frank Miller
SIN CITY
208-page B&W paperback
ISBN: 1-878574-59-0 $15.00
208-page B&W hardcover
ISBN: 1-56971-048-1 $25.00
THAT YELLOW BASTARD
240-page B&W hardcover
ISBN: 1-56971-187-9 $25.00

STAR WARS
HEIR TO THE EMPIRE
Baron • Vatine • Blanchard
160-page color paperback
ISBN: 1-56971-202-6 $19.95